THE POETICAL AND DRAMATIC
WORKS OF SIR CHARLES SEDLEY

Portrait of a Lady, said to be

Katherine Sedley, Countess of Dorchester

THE POETICAL AND DRAMATIC WORKS OF SIR CHARLES SEDLEY

Collected and Edited from the Old Editions

WITH A PREFACE ON THE TEXT, EXPLANATORY AND
TEXTUAL NOTES, AN APPENDIX CONTAINING WORKS
OF DOUBTFUL AUTHENTICITY, AND A BIBLIOGRAPHY

By

V. DE SOLA PINTO

VOL. II

AMS PRESS
NEW YORK

Reprinted with the permission of V. De Sola Pinto
From the edition of 1928, London
First AMS EDITION published 1969
Manufactured in the United States of America

Library of Congress Catalogue Card Number: 70-85905

AMS PRESS, INC.
New York, N.Y. 10003

CONTENTS

APPENDIX

WORKS ASCRIBED TO SEDLEY ON DOUBTFUL AUTHORITY

v

Contents

LIST OF ILLUSTRATIONS

Sir Peter Lely pinxit.   Emery Walker phsc.

Barbara Palmer
Duchess of Cleveland

By Gracious permission of His Majesty the King

BELLAMIRA,

OR THE

MISTRESS,

A Comedy :

As it is Acted by Their Majesties Servants.

Written by the Honourable

Sir *C H A R L E S   S E D L E Y* Baronet.

Licensed, *May* 24.   1687.

Rog. L'Estrange.

L O N D O N :

Printed by *D. Mallet,* for *L. C.* and *Timothy Goodwin,* at the
Maiden-Head over against St. *Dunstans* Church
in *Fleet-Street.*   1 6 8 7.

B

EDITOR'S PREFACE

Source and Analogues. The main source of this play, as the author himself tells us in his preface, is "The Eunuch" of Terence, the third of that author's comedies, first acted in Rome in 161 B.C. and translated, according to Terence's own prologue, from a lost comedy of the same name by Menander. Sedley's play is not a translation but a clever rehandling of the story of "The Eunuch" in terms of Restoration life. For a detailed account of how this rehandling is carried out see "Sir Charles Sedley," pp. 266–276. Sedley's chief departures from his original are the substitution of the jovial toper Merryman for the cunning valet Parmeno, the introduction of the character of Thisbe, Merryman's pretty ward, who has no counterpart in Terence's play, a considerable development of the part of Isabella (Terence's Pamphila), and the dexterous use of a number of suggestions from the Falstaff scenes of Shakespeare's "Henry IV." Falstaff's character is divided between Merryman and Dangerfield, the latter receiving his cowardice and braggadocio, the former his conviviality and charm. The names Merryman and Cunningham are apparently borrowed from Thomas Betterton's comedy "The Amorous Widow" (acted c. 1670, published 1706), and the bare hint of the contrast between Thisbe's fat and thin lovers may, as Genest points out, have been provided by James Howard's "All Mistaken" (acted 1667, published 1672), where the same situation is used in a much cruder manner. According to Genest ("Some Account of the English Stage," I. 455), Bellamira is a portrait of Barbara Palmer, Duchess of Cleveland, whom she resembles in her beauty, licentiousness and rapacity. The escape of Cunningham in a boat from her bedchamber narrated in Act I. scene ii. is said by Genest to be founded on a similar adventure of Colonel Churchill (afterwards Duke of Marlborough), who once took his leave from the Duchess in this way.

Topography. We may notice that the scene of fashionable life has shifted westward since the date of "The Mulberry Garden." We hear no more of Coleby's or St. James's Park, but one scene is laid in Knightsbridge and another in Kensington.

Stage History. "Bellamira" was probably staged for the first time at the King's House in Drury Lane on May 12 (O.S.), 1687. It is certain that King James II witnessed a performance on that night (Warrant cited in Allardyce Nicoll's "Restoration Drama," p. 313). No record of the cast has survived. The play was staged by the united company formed out of the old King's and Duke's Companies in 1682.

3

This Company, which acted at the King's House in Drury Lane, was the only theatrical Company in London till 1695. Its chief members were Betterton, Mountford, Underhill, Gillow, Griffin and Anthony Leigh, and among the actresses Mrs. Betterton, Mrs. Barry, Mrs. Mountford, Mrs. Bracegirdle, and Mrs. Leigh. Mrs. Barry took most of the leading female parts (*e.g.* Porcia in the " Soldier's Fortune," Leonora in " Sir Courtly Nice," etc.), and it is highly probable that she " created " the character of Bellamira.

THE PREFACE TO THE READER

I know very well the danger of Writing in [1 such an age where the beſt Wits Chose rather to be lookers on, then expose their ſtock of reputation to Publick censure. Nor did I design any to my self by this Play : It was originally *Mænanders* in the [5 Greek, *Terence*'s in the Latin ; whose great names gave me a Curiosity to try how I cou'd make it run in English : A Friend came to my Chamber as I was upon the firſt Act, he seem'd to approve my design : I told him I found it extream easie to go [10 through with : And that if he cou'd get it Acted under his own or anothers Name, I wou'd finish it for him : But for I know not what reasons he cou'd not do it ; and I was oblidg'd to own it my self, or my friend had loſt his third day. The whole Play [15 runs upon a Rape committed by a Lover under the disguise of an Eunuch, and an indulgent Keeper, govern'd and Jilted by his Imperious Miſtress, which parts were so essential that they cou'd not be omitted, nor well fitted to our Stage without some [20 expressions or Metaphors, which by persons of a ticklish imagination, or over-quick sense that way, seem'd too lascivious for modeſt Ears ; I confess after the Plays I have seen lately Crowded by that fair Sex : the exception did not a little surprise me ; And [25 this suddain change of theirs made me call to mind our English weather, where in the same day a man shall Sweat in Crape, and wish for a Campagn Coat three hours after. I am very unhappy that the Ice that has borne so many Coaches and Carts, shou'd break [30 with my Wheel barrow : I confess to have taken my Idea of Poetry more from the *Latin* than the *French* :

and had rather be accus'd of some Irregularities, than
tire my Reader or Audience with a smooth even ſtream
of insipid words and accidents ; such as one can [35
neither like nor find fault with. But Reader between
what will not please, and what will not pass at this
time ; there is so little left to be said on this or any
other Subjeƈt, that I will keep thee no longer at the
Door. Go in and Judge for thy self, see what [40
the Modeſty of this year takes offence at, and I am
confident thou wilt with me congratulate the happy
change. And yet absolve both the Poet and the
Translator from any unpresidented indecency. [44

PROLOGUE

Is it not strange to see in such an Age
The Pulpit get the better of the Stage?
Not through Rebellion as in former days,
But Zeal for Sermons and neglect for Plays.
Here's as good Ogling yet, and fewer spies.　　　　　5
For Godly Parents watch with whites of Eyes.
Here Gallants do but pay us for your Room,
Bring if you please, your own brisk wit from home.
Proclaim your drunken fray's three benches round ⎫
What Claps y'have met with, and what punks are ⎬　10
　found ⎪
Who are the Bully-rocks: and who gives ground. ⎭
We take all in good part, and never rage:
Tho the shrill Pit be louder than the Stage.
There you must sit demure, without a word: ⎫
Nor Perruque comb'd, nor Pocket tortoise stir'd ⎬　15
Here you may give the Lye, or draw your Sword. ⎭
Be low'd and sensless, huff, dumbfound, and roar;
Till all the Lady's and some gallants scowre.
What free born subject, or true English heart,
Wou'd with such Rights and Priviledges part?　　　20
When our two houses did divide the Town, ⎫
Each Faction zealously maintain'd their own, ⎬
We liv'd on those that came to cry us down. ⎭
Our Emulation did improve your sport:
Now you come hither but to make your Court:　　　25
Or from adjacent Coffee Houses throng
At our fourth Act for a new Dance or Song.
To set all right we yet could make a shift:
Had we a few good Livings in our gift.
Your hearts are ours, and let whoever preach　　　30
The young and fair will practice what we teach.
Our Play old virtuous Rome *the* Eunuch *nam'd*
But modest London *the lewd title damn'd.*
Our Author try'd his own and cou'd not hit:
He now presents you with some Forraign Wit.　　　35

7

DRAMATIS PERSONÆ

Merryman.
Keepwell.
Lionel.
Euſtace.
Cunningham.
Dangerfield.
Smoothly.
Pisquil.

Bellamira.
Isabella.
Thisbe.
Silence.
Betty.

Bullies.
Bayliffs.
Linkboyes.

8

BELLAMIRA, OR THE MISTRESS

ACT I. SCENE I

⟨*Outside Bellamira's House.*⟩

Merriman and *Keepwell.*

Merry. I ever told you, this Woman wou'd be the ruine of you : all muſt go to make her fine, and every New Gown you give, gets you a new Rival.

Keepw. Thou thinkſt all Mony thrown away, that is not spent in a Tavern : thou haſt no taſt of Love, [5 scarce any remains of Luſt, or thou would'ſt never Rail at so Divine a Creature as my *Bellamira.*

Merry. You are resolved to go to her again ; notwithſtanding the damn'd trick she serv'd you with the Sea Captain and your noble resolution to the [10 contrary ? I'll see her hang'd firſt ! No, tho she beg it a thousand times, and with a thousand tears, I'll n'e'r go near her !

Keepw. Did I say such bug-words ?

Merry. Yes, and a great deal more. [15

Keepw. 'Twas when I was in my Altitudes, what ? Rebell againſt my Lawful Sovereign *Bellamira* ! I'll go to her tho, and shew her I am not such a Cully as she takes me for.

Merry. Have a care what you do. If you [20 once begin and don't go through with her, you settle her Empire for ever ; and when she finds her own ſtrength, that you are not able to leave her, she will use it like a Tyrant : And tho you be the injur'd party, after six kind words and a false tear or two, you [25 muſt make your peace with a Present of *China* or a *French Petticoat.*

Keep. These are sad Truths; but when my *Bell.* frowns I had rather be in a Sea-Fight for the time, I'll say that for her, tho 'tis soon over. I gave her [30 but a dozen pair of *Marshal* Gloves, and she was in the purest Humour all day! We took the Air in the afternoon, Sup't and went to Bed together.

Merry. That was a gawdy day indeed, but I fear you'l give so long, till you have nothing left. [35

Keepw. I had rather give a little Mony, than Lye, Flatter and Forswear my self as the Gallants of the Town do: I love to go to Sleep with a good Conscience.

Merry. And rise with ne'r a Penny in your [40 Pocket; if she lov'd you she would not be so expensive.

Keepw. 'Tis all to please me. Before I knew her she wore a Gown six months; and had but one poor Point of her own making.

Merry. Matters are well mended with her [45 indeed since that time.

Keepw. I had the most to do to make her accept of an Imbroider'd Toylet.

Merry. How so?

Keepw. She said 'twas Mony thrown away. [50

Merry. And wou'd have it in Guineas, I warrant.

Keepw. Thou art a Witch, she cares not a Farthing for Fine Cloaths; and but for fear the Women of the Town shou'd get me from her wou'd not dress her self in a Month. [55

Merry. You are too indulgent a Keeper: the poor Sinners of the Town complain of you; you raise the Market upon 'em.

Keepw. Why what wou'd a man do?

Merry. Let one Nail drive out another: [60 Take me a fresh Wench, a Bottle of Wine or two, and go hear some Scandal at the Rose—— But here she comes, who with one Look will confound all our Devices.

Enter Bellamira.

Bella. Oh, my dear *Keepwell*! I am afraid [65
thou art Jealous of me, because I did not let thee in
sooner; the news of it put me into such Fits, all our
Maids were too few to hold me.

Keep. The news of what?

Bella. Of a Duel I was told thou hadſt [70
fought: there was no body to run to the Door; but
thou saw'ſt there was no man with me.

Keep. I saw no man indeed, but am much miſtaken
if I did not hear one leap out of your low Window
into a Boat. [75

Bella. This Summer one or other is leaping into
the River all night long.

Keep. Oh, that you lov'd like me; or I like you!

Bell. Why my dear *Keepwell*?

Keep. Why, then you'd never use me thus, [80
or if you did, it wou'd not thus afflict me: my heart
is as full of Jealousie as an Egg full of meat.

Bell. I swear by all thats good there is no man
on Earth so welcome to these Arms, as thy dear self.

Keepw. Why did not you let me in sooner [85
hen?

Bell. I was juſt rising out of a Bath, and I will
be seen naked by no man Living.

Merry. Kind Soul! firſt she was in Fits for fear
you were hurt; but now she was coming out [90
of a Bath, and cou'd not in modeſty let you in.

Keepw. She fell into Fits juſt as she came out
of her Bath.

Bell. I have alwaies your good word: But I had
rather you shou'd say any thing of me, than kill [95
my dear *Keepwell* with Drinking. But now I'll tell
you the business I came about: Can your Drunken
Friend keep a Secret?

Merry. If it be a Truth; but it prove a Lye, a
Flam, a Wheadle, 'twill out: I shall tell it the [100
next man I meet.

Bell. My Father was a Merchant, and Breaking here in Town, my Mother went to *Jamaica*, and took me with her.

Merry. This may be kept secret. [105

Bell. There a Person of Quality fell in Love with her, and amongſt other Presents, gave her the fineſt Girl I ever saw, ſtoln out of *England* by some Kidnappers.

Keep. What are they ? [110

Bell. Rogues that make a Trade of Stealing Children and Selling them.

Merry. Was she a Gentlewoman ?

Bell. She said so, and she seem'd so.

Keep. Not so pretty as thou art I warrant [115 her.

Bell. Her Father and Mother were Dead; her Brothers name she told us ; my Mother bred her as if she had been her own Child, so that moſt people thought us Siſters ; I came back with a Friend, [120 the only Person I had then a Concern with, who gave me all I have.

Merry. These are two Whiskers !

Bell. Why so ?

Merry. Because you were never true to one [125 Man : nor did he give you all you have ; my Friend here having presented you with two thousand Pound at leaſt.

Bell. Will you let me go on with my Story ? My Mother left this pretty Creature *Isabella* [130 almoſt grown a Woman, to an Uncle of mine, for some Mony that she ow'd him, and cou'd not otherwise pay : He thinking she might yeild a good Price, carries her over into *Spain*, and there Sells her to one *Dangerfield*, who buys her and puts her to wait [135 on his Siſter : he is now in *England*, and offers her me.

Merry. Did he know that she was formerly your Companion ?

Bell. Not in the leaſt ; but since hearing of my

concern with you, he seeks all the excuses he   [140
can, not to perform his Promise; and says that he
knows as soon as I have her he shall be slighted, and
you received; for he has heard how dearly I Love
thee.

Keepw.   All the Town knows there is no   [145
Love loſt.   Is this all?

Bell.   No, I have a small requeſt to thee my Dear.

Merry.   Now for a Coach, new Bed, or the Payment
of an old Debt.

Bell.   You are miſtaken Sir; cou'd I help it   [150
I wou'd not put my dear *Keepwell* to the Charge of
one of your Drunken Clubs in a Year.

Merry.   You spend it him in Coach-hire, Puppy-
water and Paint, every day of your Life.

Bell.   Peace, thou moving Dropsie, that   [155
wadleſt with Fat, worse than a Goose with Egg.

Merry.   No man that had to do with you, e're
loſt his Shape; Fluxing and Sweating are great
Preservatives.

Keep.   This is rudeness and not Wit; come   [160
thou art my beſt Companion and she my deareſt
Miſtress.   As our modern Poet has it;
"If not in Friendship, live at leaſt in Peace.⟨"⟩
What is it thou woud'ſt Command?

Bell.   Command! only a trifling Suit I   [165
have.

Keep.   It muſt be a ſtrange one if I refuse it; Is
it in my power?

Bell.   It is.

Keep.   Then speak and be sure to obtain it,   [170
as if thou ask'dſt it of thy self.   I have not given thee
any thing all this day.

Bell.   'Tis no Mony matter: there are many
Reasons why I wou'd have this *Isabella* from *Danger-
field*: Firſt because we were bred together like   [175
Siſters, and of all the World I love her next thy dear
self; and if I cou'd reſtore her to her Friends, who I hear

are very considerable, I doubt not of a good Reward:
so that I shall never need trouble thee for any thing
more. [180

Merry. This is a good Wheadle.

Keep. But how will you get her? You say
Dangerfield repents him of his promise.

Bell. 'Tis but thy going into the Country for a
day or two, and I shall easily perswade that [185
swaggering Fool out of her. You don't answer me.

Keep. What shou'd I answer thee, thou worst of
Women?

Merry. She wou'd only lie with this roaring
Rascal a Night or two, while you are in the [190
Countrie: can you have the heart to deny her?

Keep. If I deny her, she'l be outragious; and if
I do not, I shall have Elks horns at my return. I
understand you⟨:⟩ *Isabella* and you were bred up
like Sisters, you wou'd restore her to her [195
Friends, and so *Dangerfield* must be received, and I
banish'd; and why? but that you love him better
than ever you did me, and are affraid this Young
Wench should get the Lusty Stallion from you.

Bell. She loves me so, she wou'd not be my [200
Rival, tho' in thee, young, kind, and handsome as
thou art.

Keep. Is this Souldier then the only Man that
made a considerable Present? When has my Bounty
fail'd? Did not you ask the other Day a *Black-* [205
amoor, and then an *Eunuch*, out of a meer Humour
because Princes use 'em, and straight I pawn'd a
Ring to buy 'em for you? I should not urge my
Bounty, did I not find that you forget it. There was
a Settlement drawing too. [210

Bell. Nay, rather than you shall take it ill, I will
Renounce this *Isabella*, the dear Companion of my
Youth, for ever, and all the World beside.

Keep. Did not you say you cou'd renounce this
Isabella, and all the World for me? [215

Merry. Yes, rather than lose your Settlement.

Bell. I did; and will, my Dear! I can go into a *Cloyster*, since I have lost my power with you, I care not for the rest, I'll to a *Monastery*, and there I'll Pray for you.   [220

Keep. I scorn to be out-done in Kindness: I will go into the Country for a day or two, and let *Dangerfield* do his worst. Go into a *Monastery*! I had rather hold the Door my self.

Merry. When she's a *Nun* I'll be a *Fryer*: [225 They all say as much.

Keep. But, if she shou'd, where shou'd I have such another Dear Pretty, Sweet Rogue?

Merry. There are hundreds as fine Women to be had, by the day, by the week, or how you will. [230

Keep. 'Tis not the first time she has threatened to go into a Monastery, upon discontents between us: I was forced to give her a New Bed, the last Summer, and Plate for her Chamber, or I had lost her.

Bell. 'Tis but two days, and I am thine for [235 ever.

Keep. Hang two days among Friends.

Bell. 'Tis I shall be the greatest Sufferer, who must endure the Man I loath, and part with him I love. Besides, this *Dangerfield* is such a [240 troublesome quarrelsome Fellow, I shou'd never have one Minutes quiet, if you were in Town together, for fear of some mischief or other.

Keep. Nay, there wou'd be Bloud-shed every hour, that's certain; I never cou'd endure a [245 Rival in my Life.

Bell. I know thou art both brave and jealous, that makes me so affraid for thee: If he shou'd Kill thee, poor Dear, he has nothing to lose, and wou'd easily get his Pardon; but should'st thou Kill [250 him, all the world can't save thee, thou hast been such a Whig. Besides, I am too honest a Woman to have any interest at Court.

Keep. It shall never come to that, I'le away into the Country, and as it happens have a little [255 business there; I shall come up so vigorous, and so Loving; wee'l have a Sack-Posset, and go to Bed together, tho' it be at Noon-day: But see, my Friend, the Blackamore and Eunuch be deliver'd to *Bellamira* in my absence. [260

Merry. ⟨(*Aside*)⟩ I will carry them my self, and try what Mettle *Bellamira* is made of in his absence: she is the prettieſt Wench in the Town, and his Present will make me welcome.

Keep. For two long Days and tedious [265 Nights, Farewel.

Bell. I fear my *Keepwell*, thou think'ſt me one of those little Creatures of the Town; but I have told thee nothing but the Truth: nor is there Man on Earth I wou'd prefer to thee. All I do, is [270 meerly in compassion to pretty *Isabella*, in hope to reſtore her to her Brother, whom by some Tokens she gave me, I think I have found, and am this Night to Treat with.

Keep. Farewel, my deareſt *Bellamira*, I am [275 gone.

Bell. Well, now I see thou doſt deserve my Love.

⟨SCENE II. *A Street.*⟩

Enter Cuningham *and* Euſtace.

Cun. Yonder's *Merryman*, Fat, Smooth, and looks Young ſtill; a very *Bacchus* Incarnate.

Merry. I swallow more Wine, than Pills or Dyet-drink, sit up till Three, and drink my three Bottles.

Cun. I met the pretty'ſt Creature in New [5 *Spring-Garden*! her Gloves right Marshal, her Petti-coat of the New Rich Indian Stuffs, her Fan Colambor: Angel-water was the worſt Sent about her. I am sure she was of Quality.

Merry. And I warrant, you think she came   [10
to meet you there?

Cun. Not so: She came to take her Fortune
among the Young Fellows of the Town, and Chance
threw her upon me; I have found she lies in the
Mall.   [15

Merry. There are Whores of all sorts: but if she
had lain in an Alley, you might have more hope of her.

Cun. Have not you the beſt Wine and Tobacco,
where you come?

Merry. Yes, that I have.   [20

Cun. Why then shou'd you not think, a Man
that makes it his business, as I do, may have the fineſt
Women?

Merry. I pay 'em well, and get cuſtom to Taverns
where I go; a Wench may ſtarve that has had   [25
to do with you; no Man will venture upon her, who
has any Reverence for his Nose: Nor have you
anything to give 'em but the Pox.

Cun. You can do as little to a Woman as I can
give: And for your soundness, if Palsie, Gout,   [30
and Dropsie may be called so, your drunken impotence
is the reason of it.

Euſt. Will this Quarrel never be at end? *Cuning-
ham* is the Darling of the Ladies, and *Merriman* the
delight of all good Fellows. Whats become of   [35
our Old Friend *Keepwel*?

Merry. We have loſt him: He was once an honeſt
well humor'd Fellow, tho' he had never much Wit,
but since his Acquaintance with *Bellamira*.

Euſt. What, she that was so well known at   [40
Jamaica?

Merry. That's true, but he won't believe it: She
has perswaded him 'twas an Elder Siſter: she is
handsomer, and he more in Love with her than ever.
You know how miserable he was.   [45

Euſt. He always grudg'd his Club, if it came to
above half a Crown.

Merry. How plain he went ?

Euſt. He bought all his Cloaths of a Whole sale Man. [50

Merry. Now there's no Taylor curious enough for him.

Cun. 'Tis a great change, but I cannot blame him ; she is a delicate Creature, and I was one of the first that Debauch'd her. [55

Euſt. I thought you wou'd not have confess'd so much Age.

Cun. I mean I was one of the firſt had her, after she came over : she Lov'd me dearly, poor Rogue, but I was not able to maintain her. [60

Merry. One man may as well satisfie, as maintain her ; she is the moſt expensive Jade I ever knew ; she has run *Keepwell* a thousand Pound in Debt within this Twelve-month : I have been at a woful parting between them. [65

Cun. He has not turn'd her off I hope ? For I go and Sup there sometimes, upon the old account. She is one of my Piz Allez.

Merry. No ; she has turn'd him off for two days : he has left an Eunuch in Town, which I am to [70 present her for him anon.

Cun. I'le tell you a Secret ; I had like to have been surprized there by *Keepwell* himself e'ne now ; we were juſt got to Bed together.

Euſt. And how got you off ? [75

Cun. She made him Knock half an hour at the Door, whil'ſt I leapt out of one of her lower Windows into a Boat that waited for me⟨.⟩ But *Merriman*, you muſt say nothing upon honour, now you are truſted. [80

Merry. Not I, I have told him of thy lying with her and Forty others, an hundred times, and he will never believe me ; he is the moſt incorrigible Cully, I begin to be of her side.

Cun. I will drink a Bottle more with thee at [85

Night for that: A Man of honour shou'd always take the Ladies parts.

Euſt. What made you run away? I thought you had been allowed to visit.

Cun. I am so, but not in my Shirt and Night- [90 Gown, as I was with her. She was juſt out of a Bath, the Sweeteſt, Whiteſt, Plumpeſt, Kindeſt Rogue.

Euſt. 'Twas a Damn'd disappointment.

Cun. Not quite, I took my leave of her like a Gentleman. [95

Merry. I wonder *Keepwell* continues sound, coming after thee in this manner.

Cun. There was a Plague in Sixty Six, but what is that to *London* now? there was a Fire too: but it is since new Built, and more beautiful than [100 ever; are not you Sober now, tho' you were Drunk laſt Night?

Merry. Not quite.

Cun. A Dish of Coffee or two will make you so, and do you think there's no Redemption in [105 other Cafes? When they were firſt acquainted, I Writ all his Billet doux for him, for *Keepwell* you know has nothing but the Purse and Dotage of a good Lover; he wou'd give me now and then five Guineas for a Song for her, which I let her know [110 was mine; when I saw her next, we Laught at the poor Fool together.

Merry. I'le say that for him, he is fitted with a Friend and a Miſtress.

Cun. You know he is but a dull silly Fellow. [115

Merry. And therefore you may very honeſtly pretend Friendship, borrow his Money and lye with his Miſtress.

Cun. A Pious Citizen that goes to Church twice a day, will play the Knave in a Bargain; a [120 Lawyer take your Fee, and for a good Sum of Mony, be absent when your Cause is try'd; a Parson Marry you to a great Fortune without a Licence; We are all Rogues in our way, and I confess Woman is my weak side; And yonder goes an odd Fellow, [125 with a very pretty Wench: what a Toss she has with her head, and a jett with her breech?

Merry. 'Slight, 'tis *Smoothly, Dangerfield*'s man, carrying that pretty Creature to *Bellamira*, for a Present from his Master. [130

|*Cun.* She has as good a Face as *Bellamira* herself.

Eustace's *Man brings him a Note.*

|*Eust.* *Smallwit, Wildman,* and *Lyonel,* have sent their excuses, and cannot Dine.

Merry. Let's give the House something, and Dine there to Morrow: I am invited to a Venison [135 Party, and a dozen bottles among Four.

Cun. I have some Ladies to Entertain at *Knights-bridge;* and hate a nasty Tavern.

Eust. Since you are all provided for, I'le shift, for my self. [*Exeunt.* [140

⟨SCENE III. *A Room in Bellamira's House.*⟩

Enter Bellamira and Thisbe.

Bell. He's gon, and we are free as Mountain Air.

This. You have absolute Dominion over him; but to make him accessary to his own disgrace, was such a Masterpiece!

Bell. Now will he entertain a better opinion of [5 me than ever: he'le think I do nothing without his consent, since I once ask'd him it, and in so nice a Point.

This. What said *Merryman,* my sweet Guardian?

Bell. All he cou'd, you must take him off [10 for me.

This. I am but his second Inclination; a Drawer in a good Tavern has more Interest in him, than I.

I. iii. 14.

Bell. But *Keepwell* is the Loyaleſt Cully! nothing
will make him Mutiny. [15

This. Sure you think he can read in no Book but
his own, or you durſt never use him so.

Bell. There are few of those Clerks now-adays:
this is a Learned Age. When saw you *Cuningham*?

This. He comes sometimes and professes his [20
Love and Soundness to me.

Bell. Believe him in neither, they say he's a false
Fellow.

This. I heard he was formerly a great Servant of
yours. [25

Bell. What a Lying World this is! I never saw
him in my Life.

This. That's ſtrange and live about this Town.

Bell. Is he handsome? Black? or Fair?

This. Between both. [30

Bell. Has he much Wit?

This. As if you did not know!

Bell. I swear, not I.

This. Jilting Devil! I'd not know him so well
for a Thousand Pound but 'tis the Trick of moſt [35
of 'em; tho they own Twenty, they will forswear
some one.

Bell. Oh, that I had thy Youth, and Beauty!

This. You have enough of both, considering your
Judgment and Experience. [40

Bell. We Women are easilieſt deceived, when we
are moſt worth it: Cunning and Wrinkles come
together.

This. You have no reason to complain; all the
young Fellows that come out of *France*, pay [45
Tribute to you, as certainly as to the Groom-Porter:
I wonder *Keepwell* is never told of it.

Bell. He has been told it a hundred times: Two
or three Stories that the Authors have not been able
to make out, have don me great Service; and [50
so confirm'd my Empire.

This. But you are in continual fear.

Bell. I have broke him of all his Censorious Acquaintance.

This. That was a great Point gain'd; but [55 how ?

Bell. I tell him such a one will Cheat him, another will bring him into Quarrels, a third speaks ill of him behind his Back, a fourth is abnoxious to the great ones, and will hinder his Preferment: So [60 that I have scarce left him one Friend that will tell him a true word.

This. You are a great Politician.

Bell. There goes more to our Trade, than a good Face: I have known many of these unthinking [65 Butterflyes, Debauch'd, Pox'd, and in Goal, the same Summer: Let's up into my Chamber; I muſt set my self out for *Dangerfield*⟨,⟩ he'l be here anon.

This. Will you use the Paint was sent in by the French Woman this Morning ? [70

Bell. By all means: Lying and Painting are sure Baits to Catch a Fool with.

This. What sort of Fellow is that *Dangerfield* ?

Bell. A *Beau Garcon* of Fifty, with a Blew Chin, ſtiff Beard, and so forth.——Loves the Old [75 Fashion'd Greasy way of giving Treats, will Dance Country Dances till he Sweat like a Running Footman; tires himself firſt, and then makes Love.

This. They say he has been Hansome.

Bell. 'Twas so long ago every Body has [80 forgot it, but himself: He is a pretender to Wit; but his is worse than none: as a Country Scraper is worse than no Musick at all.

This. And yet this Fellow for a little Mony.

Bell. No, for a great deal of Mony. I will [85 make the Presents he gives me, thy Baits to Catch others with: fine Cloaths and rich Furniture, are great Provocatives to those that don't pay for 'em, which are the Men for our Turn.

This.   Like the Gentlemen that live in Town,   [90
you have your pleasure in one place, and receive your
Rent from an other: 'tis the way to have your Tene-
ment thrown into your Hands.

Bell.   *Keepwell* has taken a Lease for Life, and laid
out so much in Improvements, that I am secure   [95
of him; and for the rest, they shall pay me as they
are Able.

This.   My Guardian and I have now and then a
small Quarrel, about my keeping you so much Com-
pany.   [100

Bell.   What, *Merryman*? I thought he had made
Love to you.

This.   He dos sometimes.

Bell.   He has then forfeited his Charter and ought
to Talk no more like a Guardian.   [105

This.   Perhaps he dos not like it as a Lover.

Bell.   Does he not see that we Govern the Town?
have Power and Plenty follow us? we Visit, Dance,
Play at Cards, go to Hide-Park, St. *James's,* and
Sup together, and are a World among our   [110
Selves.

This.   But like the Inhabitants of the other World,
you neither Marry, nor are given in Marrige; and
he wou'd have me fit for a Husband.

Bell.   Get Mony enough and you can never   [115
want a Husband.   A Husband is a good Bit to Close
ones Stomach with, when Love's Feast is over.   Who
wou'd begin a Meal with Cheese?   Come into my
Chamber, and I will instruct thee farther in these
Mysteries.   [120

ACT II. SCENE I

⟨ *Outside Bellamira's House.* ⟩

Keepwell, and *Merryman.*

Merry. What, not gon yet? hovering like a Ghost, about your Treasure?

Keep. I stay'd to see how my Presents took: you have deliver'd 'em, I hope, what says my *Bellamira*?

Merry. The Meat's hardly out of my Mouth, [5 and I am for no Exercise upon a full Stomach: 'tis too far to walk yet.

Keep. Take a Coach.

Merry. That's as bad as the Rack, to a Man of my Intemperate, and Voracious Appetite: I am [10 so full I should spill Terse at every jolt. We drank Gallons a piece.

Keep. You are Drunk then.

Merry. No, Sober enough to be your Worship's Pimp, and diliver your Humane Gelding to [15 *Bellamira.*

Keep. But will you go about it Instantly, and make hast?

Merry. Survey my Bulk: it was not built for hast; 'Tis the slow product of Tuns of Claret, Chines [20 of Beef, Ven'son-Pastyes, and so-forth.

Keep. Now you are in this humor, you will talk some Wit to her and spoil all.

Merry. I'le be there, before you are half a Mile out of Town, and say the sweetest things of you! [25

Keep. Thou think'st I cannot leave my *Bellamira,* now it comes to the Point.

Merry. I am somwhat doubtful.

Keep. Yes if it were for three days, now I am resolv'd.
[30

Merry. What, a whole three days! Thou hast a Heart of Iron.

Keep. Cou'd you be Sober so long ?

Merry. Yes to save the Nation, or so.

Keep. Nothing less serve the turn ?   [35

Merry. Yes or to oblige Mrs. *Thisbe*, my Charge.

Keep. Thou haſt always Wine and Women in
thy Head together : a sure sign thou are but an
indifferent Tilter——Well, I am in haſt, be sure you go,
and omit nothing that may endear my small   [40
Present to her.   [*Exit.*

Merry. He's gon ; but here comes our Rival's
Servant, with that Beautyful young Creature, again :
It seems *Bellamira* was not at home. I'le ſtep aside
and observe her.   [45

Enter Smoothly, *and* Isabella.

Smooth. There is as much difference between
Man and Man, as between Man and Beaſt : This
Fool my Maſter gives away this pretty young Creature,
to a ſtale Wench, I am but a Servant, and muſt
obey ; but were I to chuse,   [50

Isa. Peace, Impudence ; were I to chuse, I'de
chuse a Halter before either of you.

Smooth. I was not always thus a Servant, as you
see me, I am a Gentleman, and once had an Eſtate,
but now 'tis gon, muſt live on others, as others   [55
did on me.

Isa. Perhaps so.

Smooth. I now am fain to Lye, and Flatter for my
Bread, shift for my Cloaths, and humor every Idle
Coxcomb to get a Piece or two : Does my   [60
Patron lose ? Fortune favours Fools : Does he Win ?
sweet is his hand, and happy are his Servants. Is he
Dwarfish ? his Strength is the more compa{c}t : Is he
Tall ? such the firſt Monarch's were, when Kingdoms
went by Choice : Is he Ugly, and Witty which   [65
muſt ever be ? such *Ovid* was, whom *Julia* so priz'd :
Is he Hansom ? such was *Adonis*, whom fair *Venus*
Lov'd.

Isa. And were you never Cudgel'd, for this nauseous Flattery? [70

Smooth. There are a sort of Men who think themselves the firſt in all kinds, and are the laſt; these I get acquainted with: nor do I attempt to please'em with my Wit, but win their hearts an easier way, by Applauding theirs. If any of 'em tell an old [75 Tale, that I have Read in Print, ſtraight I never heard any thing so well, and liſten to it as if it were my Fathers laſt Will and Teſtament. Does he offer at a Jeſt? I dye with Laughing, before his Mouth opens. Does he walk Home, without taking [80 Cold? he is hardy and fit to be a General.

Isa. You are a fine Rogue all this while! And what else?

Smooth. In short, I say as they say, deny what they deny, like what they like, and if they [85 dispraise it again, I am ready to do so too; and find my account very well in it; while those Fops, that are fond of shewing their own Wit, are hated by all my Cuſtomers; who are the onely Men there's any thing to be gotten by. [90

Merry. This is a notable Fellow; and if he finds Men Fools, is enough to make 'em Mad.

Isa. Were I a Man, I had rather dye than sell my words, and proſtitute my Voice to every Fool.

Smooth. Don't Lawyers, Physitians, and [95 Courtiers, when they take Mony for a good Turn, sell their words? There was a blunt Comrade of mine of your mind; but I found him the other day all in Rags, not a Peny in his Pocket, nor a Friend to help him: I have nothing, and yet want [100 nothing; ſtrong and able; other Mens Meat, and Drink, and Wives serve my Turn.

Isa. Leave your Prating, and move forward.

Smooth. Sure you are some disguis'd Princess, you take upon you so. [105

Isa. What I am I know not, and am only sure I am miserable.

Smooth. What's here ⟨—⟩ my Rivals Friend
Merryman, before *Bellamira*'s Door? I knew him
when I was laſt in Town. Your moſt Humble [110
Servant Worthy Sir.

Merry. Yours, honeſt *Smoothly*.

Smooth. Will you not go in?

Merry. I have no business at present.

Smooth. You may be welcome, for your [115
Friend *Keepwell*'s sake. Do you see nothing here you
wou'd not see?

Merry. Nothing but thy self.

Smooth. You keep your old blunt way; but, look
you what here is! Look you what here is! [120
What will not *Bellamira* do for such a Bribe?

Merry. Every Dog has his day.

Smooth. Let me not keep you here, you were
going some where else.

Merry. Not I. [125

Smooth. Pray then, will you Introduce me to
Madam *Bellamira*?

Merry. You need not fear admittance, with such
a Present.

Smooth. But perhaps you ſtand here, to see [130
that no man brings any Message from *Dangerfield*.

Merry. You are pleasant! but if I did I'de Cudgel
you farther off.

Smooth. He is Angry, and the Fat Fool is Stout:
I'le not provoke him. [135

Exeunt Smooth, and *Isabella.*

Merry. Yonder's *Lionel*, *Keepwell's* younger
Brother, he comes in haſt, and seem's to have some-
thing in his Head.

Enter Lionel.

Lionel. I am undone! ruin'd! I have loſt the
sight of this Pretty Creature, and shall never [140
find her more! which way shall I go? whom shall
I enquire of? what shall I do, to have a Glimps of
her? I have only this comfort; where e're she is,

she is too Beautiful to be long Conceal'd. From henceforth, I blot all former Faces out of my [145 heart: I am tir'd with these daily Beauties of the Town, whom we see Painted and Patch'd in the Afternoon in the Play house, in the Evening at the Park, and at Night in the Drawing room; so that we have half enjoy'd 'em before we speak to 'em⟨.⟩ [150

Merry. Loſt! Undone! Beautiful! I am sure I heard these words plain: he is in Love, and after the manner of that sort of Madmen is talking to himself, of his Miſtress; If he be we shall have fine work; there are Ten *Keepwells* in that *Lionel*: [155 he'l commit Rapes, Burglaries, Fire houses, or any thing, but he'l have her; and for Mony, he'l throw it away like Dirt. I pity his poor Father; but he Grudg'd his Mony for honeſt Terse, and so he's right enough serv'd. [160

Lion. Eternal Palsies on that *Cuningham*'s Hands, may he never be able to put his Dice into the Box; but when he does may he throw out for ever. May he Win of Beggars and lose to Bullies, and dote on Whores as Rotten as himself. But I was mad [165 to mind him: how I envy yon' *Merryman*, whose sluggish Blood moves in an even ſtream, and never knows these Storms!

Merry. What's the matter? you look as if you were Drunk. [170

Lion. I am worse; I am mad; I am any thing; I am in Love.

Merry. How *Keepwell* will Laugh at you! But with whom?

Lion. Not with a ſtale Wench, like him; [175 nor any of the little Tinsel, short Liv'd Beauties of the Town, squeez'd into shape by Taylors, and ſtarv'd into it by their Mothers.

Merry. How then?

Lion. A new turn of a Face, unknown till [180 now to Nature's self, in all her Numberless Varieties.

Merry. 'Tis wond'erous; you are Mau'ld; *Cupid* has shot you with a Blunderbus.

Lion. What Eyes! Teeth, white——

Merry. As a new Tobacco-pipe⟨.⟩ [185

Lion. Peace Prophane Wretch, thou art not fit to mingle in these Misteries. Her own Complexion; her Body solid and full of Juice; the Noblest Fabrick of unstinted Nature!

Merry. Her Age? [190

Lion. Seventeen.

Merry. I have drunk excellent *Hockamore* of that Age.

Lion. Damn thy dull *Hockamore* and thy base Jaded Pallat, that affects it; Cou'd I but get [195 this Divine Creature into my hands, by Fraud, Force, Price, Prayer, any way so that I enjoy her, I care not.

Merry. Who is she? she may be a Person of Quality, and you may bring an old house upon your head⟨.⟩ [200

Lion. 'Tis but a Duel or two that way; and if her Relations be Numerous, we'l Fight Six to Six, and make an end on't.

Merry. What Country Woman is she?

Lion. I know not. [205

Merry. Where does she live?

Lion. I can't tell⟨.⟩

Merry. We are upon a very cold Scent: where did you see her?

Lion. In the Street; with a Servant behind [210 her.

Merry. How come you to lose her?

Lion. That's it I was Cursing at, as I met you: Nor do I think there is a Man whom all the Stars conspire against like me. What Crime have I [215 committed, to be thus Plagu'd?

Merry. The Stars are Pretty Twinkling Rogues, that light us home, when we are Drunk sometimes, but neither care for you, nor me, nor any man.

Lyon.   You know *Cuningham*?   [220

Merry.   Intimately: a good honeſt Fellow; a little too much a Servant to the Ladies, given to Gaming.

Lion.   Pox of his Chara&ter!

Merry.   The Pox is part of his Chara&ter [225 indeed, but I had forgot that.

Lyon.   Will you not let me go on with my Story? This Fellow meets me in the nick of time, while I was following this Divine Creature, pulls me aside, and tels me I muſt be his Second; I go with [230 him, we Fight, Disarm our Men, but when I came back the Bird was flown: nor cou'd I learn any News of her.

Merry.   That's very unlucky.

Lion.   'Twas a Disaſter never to be re- [235 cover'd, a Total over-throw to all my happiness: I had not seen him neither these six Months.

Merry.   Why did you not refuse him?

Lion.   He's a Malicious Fellow, and wou'd have told the whole Town of it, if I had; it was [240 Impossible. I loſt her in this Street.

Merry.   Are you sure of that? I'le be Sober a Twelve Month, if this be not the very young Woman *Dangerfield* presented this Afternoon, to *Bellamira*, your Brothers Miſtress.   [245

Lion.   There was a Man follow'd her.

Merry.   The very same: and that was his Servant *Smoothly.*

Lion.   You know her then?

Merry.   Not I; but I know whither she [250 went⟨.⟩

Lion.   Doſt know where she is, my Dear *Merryman*?

Merry.   Don't I tell you she was presented to *Bellamira* by *Dangerfield*, your Brother's Rival? [255

Lion.   A Mighty Prince this *Dangerfield*, that is able to make such a Present: My Brother will have a hard time on't.

Merry. You wou'd say so indeed, if you saw his
Present. [260

Lion. What is it?

Merry. An Eunuch.

Lion. What, that Illfavour'd Fellow he bought
yesterday, that looks like an old Woman or a Ginney
Ape? [265

Merry. The same.

Lion. He that carries him will be kick'd out of
Doors with his Present.

Merry. I hope not so; for I have promis'd to
diliver him. [270

Lion. I did not know *Bellamira* was our Neighbour.

Merr. She is lately come hither.

Lion. Is she very handsome?

Merr. She is well.

Lion. Not comparable to mine. [275

Merr. That's your fancy: Of Children Mistresses,
and Religions our own are still the best.

Lion. But is there no way to come at her? Thou
usest to be good at a dead lift: I'le Fire the house
and then at least I shall see her again. [280

Merr. Violent waies are to be us'd at last: I'le
see what I can do for you.

Lion. Oh happy Eunuch! that art to live in
the same house with this Divine Creature.

Merr. Why so? the nearer he is to a fine [285
Woman, the more sensible must he be of his loss.

Lion. But he'l see continually his fair fellow
Servant, sit by sometimes and talk with her, eat with
her, and if nothing else, sleep near, and hear her
breath. [290

Merr. What if I should make you this happy
man?

Lion. It is Impossible: but speak; men past
recovery are pleas'd to talk of Remedies.

Merr. I am intrusted to present this [295
Eunuch to *Bellamira*: what if you put on his Cloaths,
and went with me in his room?

Lion. I'd gladly change Conditions, Fortunes, and every thing but one with him.

Merr. I will present you instead of him; [300 and you shall injoy those rare Felicities you reckon'd but up now, you shall sit by her, dress and undress her, touch, play with, and sleep near her; your age and Face will easily pass you for an *Eunuch*, and somwhat mend your Brother's ill-favour'd [305 Present.

Lion. You say right: I never knew a better design; let's about it instantly, undress me, dress me, and bring me to her immediately.

Merr. You are too hot: I was but in jest [310 all this while.

Lion. Cut my Throat, Stab me, if thou wilt not go on with this design.

Merr. Let me think a little: Is not this Plot too fine spun to hold? you must be gelt indeed, or [315 'twill never pass; you will betray yourrself.

Lion. Never fear it, my Face is not so much as known among 'em, the Plot is admirable, and cannot fail, what shou'd I do there, if I were gelt?

Merr. You might look upon, touch, and [320 sleep near your fair Fellow-Servant.

Lion. That won't do: I must and will enjoy her; thou'lt hear of me in *Bedlam* else.

Merr. I shall have all the blame: besides, 'tis a dishonest action. [325

Lion. To save a Friend's life, is an honest action: nor can it be any wrong, to Cozen those that Cozen all the World.

Merr. I'le serve you for once; but if any mischief comes on't, thank your self. [330

Lion. I'le dye, and never accuse thee.

Merr. You are strangely smitten at the first sight!

Lion. No. I saw her once when I was last in *Spain*, kneel'd by her at Mass, and talk'd of Love to her; but could not learn her Name or Quality: [335 next day, she said she was to come for *England*. I might have been dreſt, and there by this time, let⟨'⟩s away.   *Exeunt.*

⟨SCENE II.   *A Room in Bellamira's House.*⟩

Enter Bellamira, ⟨*and*⟩ Isabella.

Bell.   My deareſt *Isabella*! now I have gotten thee here, I cou'd hug thee to pieces.

Isa.   I am your Slave, your Servant, and all my Hopes the Creatures of your Goodness.

Bell.   How did thy Youth and Beauty scape   [5 the roaring *Dangerfield*?

Isa.   He plac'd me with his Siſter in the house, and she took care of me; but if at any time he offer'd to be rude, I held a Dagger to my Breaſt, and vow'd to kill my self.   [10

Bell.   How chance he did not take it from thee?

Isa.   He did, and then I vow'd I'de ſtarve my self to Death: he laugh'd at me a while; but when he saw me pale, and weak, fully resolv'd to perish, he gave it me again: and so I escap'd.   [15

Bell.   My *Isabella,* tell me truly, wert thou ne'r in Love?

Isa.   What mean you, Madam?

Bell.   Did'ſt thou never find a Man more Charming than the reſt, whose every word reach'd through   [20 thy Ears, thy Heart, whom thou cou'd'ſt sit and gaze upon all day, and sigh, and wish for all night?

Isa.   I have so many defeⒸts already, why will you press me to own a weakness, perhaps you will despise me for?   [25

Bell.   No, I my self have been in Love, and have had alwaies some one Friend to whom I wou'd gladly sacrifice what I got from others.

Isa.   If that be to be in Love, I never was.

Bell.   That's our way, who know the Per-   [30

juries and Villanies of Men; How they all begin
alike, with Vows, Oaths, and Proteſtations; and end
alike with Slights and Scorns and Falshood: some
difference there may be for a while, but no great
matter.   [35

Isa.   And are they all of this deceitful make?

Bell.   All that ever I met with; What is it a false
hearted Man won't swear to such a pretty young
Creature as thou art?

Isa.   And will they Lye too, when they have   [40
Sworn?

Bell.   Moſt certainly: but we that have experience,
mind words no more than they themselv's do, and
only regard their Presents.   Say a kind thing! every
pitiful Fellow can do that: give me a Man that   [45
will do a kind thing.

Enter Thisbe.

This.   Are you upon that subjeét? I have a couple
of Servants, one is as much too Lean, as the other is
too Fat; I wou'd not lose one of 'em for the World,
they are Admirable in Consort, Grumbling Base,   [50
and Squeaking Treble.

Bell.   What, *Merryman* your Guardian and *Cuning-
ham*?

This.   The same; Men of Wit both: one a plain
subſtantial Drunkard, I am sure to hear of him   [55
when he gets a Bottle in his Head, for then he ever
thinks of Women; as Cowards do of Quarrelling,
and moſt commonly I am she.

Bell.   How does the other behave himself?

This.   He's seldom in a condition to drink   [60
Wine; but he will sit a whole Afternoon at Cards,
and say the softeſt things!

Bell.   And the sharpeſt behind your back.

This.   'Tis all one for that, 'tis like I am even
with him at the Years End.   [65

Bell.   But prety *Isabella* will not make her Con-
fession to us.

Isa. 'Tis not worth your hearing. When I was Sold to *Dangerfield* by your wicked Uncle, in *Spain* I saw a man. [70

Bell. That's my dear Girl! Come up with it.

Isa. Of the Divinest Form these Eyes had e'er beheld.

This. Ne'r be asham'd: Love, like the Small Pox, since it must be, is best had while we are [75 young.

Isa. He Kneel'd by me one day at Mass, and look'd and said, and sigh'd, the kindest things! He seem'd surpris'd with me, as I was Charm'd with him. [80

Bell. Damn'd wheadling Rogue! And all this at first sight I warrant.

Isa. We never met, but then: next day I came for *England*: but sure I never shall be won to love another. [85

Bell. Pretty Innocence! this is a Nation of such men thou talk'st of; every Street affords a dozen of 'em. Come, thou shalt Love, and Love, and Love again, never fear it.

This. We'l shew her the Park, the Play- [90 house, and the Drawing-Room.

Bell. She needs no Paint, for Complexion, but 'twill not be amiss to use Juniper Water, for good Humor, she is so melancholy, and looks as if she would not be acquainted. [95

This. It is fit men make the advance.

Bell. Some are such Jades, they must be Spur'd up, with a quick Eye, or wanton Glance.

Enter Silence *and* Betty.

Silence. Madam the Picture drawer staies for you: he saies you need not sit above half an hour. [100

This. This is some new Intrigue: Who is this Picture for?

Bell. It was begun for *Keepwell*, but I have promised it to *Dangerfield*. I hate the boistrous Fool,

he may have that, but never the Original, tho [105
he shall pay for every Inch on't.

Ex. all but Silence *and* Betty.

Betty. We are Servants and muſt be diligent in
our Calling. I am sorry we are like to be troubl'd
with this puling *Isabella*, there's more ado with her,
then with my Miſtress herself: she is so proud [110
and Melancholly, one can't get a word from her in
a day.

Sil. Who can blame her? she is well Born of a
good Family in *Devonshire*; her Father and Mother
dy'd when she was a Child, she has no friend [115
left but her Brother, and him she knows not where
to find yet, and if she shou'd, 'tis doubtful after being
so long loſt, whether he wou'd own her now.

Betty. As the World goes 'tis like he may be
willing to save her Portion. [120

Sil. She has nothing at present to depend upon,
but the Friendship of *Bellamira*: and if she be
vertuous, as I believe she is, what a trouble muſt that
be to her! Go and see if she wants any thing.

Betty. Let's both go, I hate a ſtrange Face. [125
Sil. Especially if it be better than your own.

Exeunt.

ACT III. SCENE I

⟨*Outside Bellamira's House.*⟩

Dangerfield, *and* Smoothly.

Dang. I fear poor *Bellamira* will lay it to Heart,
I have not seen her yet: how does she like my Present?

Smooth. She is Ravish'd with it: yet seems to
Prise the Giver Incomparably beyond the Gift.

Dang. I'le say that for *Dangerfield*, and a [5

Figue for him, he makes his Presents with the beſt
Grace of any Man in *England*, they are always well
received.

Smooth. I have observ'd it ever. A Beating is
better taken from you then any Man living.   [10

Dang. I thank 'em for that; who dares do other-
wise ?

        Enter Merryman *and* Lionel.

Merry. Hold your Countenance, for yonder's
Dangerfield.

Lion. Never doubt me : Tho I could laugh   [15
heartily, at this Martial Dress, and Furious Meen.

Dang. What ever was bravely perform'd in the
Army. I ſtill had the Honour on't; the General
wou'd have it so : to others he was not so Favourable.

Smooth. He that has your Wit, will make a   [20
small Service go a great way; and often Reap in
safety, the Fruit of other Mens dangers⟨.⟩

Dang. Right: Not but I venture my Body as
bravely as the meaneſt Soldier, when the General will
let me, but, to say the Truth he seldom will, he   [25
loves me so Intirely,

Smooth. You charge as if you were Shot-free.

Dang. 'Tis my Comfort, that he that Shoots one
Bullet into me, may chance to drive another out.
The General wares me next his Heart, and often   [30
Truſts the Army to my single Conduct.

Smooth. It shews he is well Skil'd in Men.

Dang. And if at any time he's Tir'd with Im-
pertinence of Suitors ; the Noise and tumults Incident
to his great Charge; he ſteals away with a   [35
Friend or two to me, there he unfolds his Wrinkled-
Brows and Steeps his Cares in Wine within my Tent.

Smooth. The General, it seems, underſtands his
Pleasure, and knows good Company.

Dang. No Man better. The Officers began   [40
to Envy me, and Mutter some od things ; speak out

the Boldest of 'em dare not. How does this Feather become me ?

Smooth. Most Victoriously; You look like the Black *Prince* when he had just Plum'd the Prince [45 of *Denmark.*

Dang. Thou art a pretty Historian, I have been told I am like him : but I'le tell thee, a certain young Captain, Bolder then the rest, seeing me Gay and Frolick, lashing every Body with my Wit, as [50 thou know'st my way is ; Sneer'd me in the Face, and ask'd me, if I wou'd never have Sown my wild Oats ? I told him I cou'd never Sow 'em in a better time, than when there was such a Goose as he by to pick 'em up. [55

Smooth. Ha, ha, ha ! You put the Goose upon him finely there ; but what said he ?

Dang. Nothing : the whole Company Laugh'd on my side ; and he sneak'd away like a Dog, with a Bottle at his Tail. [60

Smooth. I'le say that for you, You are the best at Repartees !

Merry. This is the most Flattering Knave, and *Dangerfield* the greatest Coxcomb, I ever saw.

Lion. He Swallows any thing : they are well [65 met.

Dang. Did'st never hear how I serv'd the Collonel, at *Bartholomew-Fair* ?

Smooth. (He has told it me Fifty times ; but I must prepare to Laugh at it again.) Never Sir ; [70 I long to hear it.

Dang. I had a pretty Wench with me ; he star'd her in the Face somewhat Rudely : at last I told him, I wonder'd he that was but a Hare himself, shou'd have a mind to a 'Cony ! [75

Merry. That's one of the vilest Quibbles, I ever heard.

Lion. Let's hear how that Rogue will Flatter him for it.

Smooth. Ha, ha, ha! You had as good   [80
have call'd him Coward: a Hare is the fearfulleſt of
all Beaſts. Ha, ha, ha! I cou'd dye with Laughing,
methinks I see him poor Fool!

Dang. I meant it so; but he durſt not under-
ſtand me. From that time forward I kept the   [85
whole Town in Awe with my Wit⟨.⟩

Smooth. I wou'd not come under your Lash, for
a Thousand Pounds.

Dang. No, no, thou art an honeſt Fellow, and a
great Judge of Wit and Parts. Thou shalt hear   [90
me Sing a Song that I made upon a Spanish Princess.

°SONG

When firſt I made Love to my Cloris,
Cannon Oaths I brought down
To Batter the Town,
And I fi⟨r'⟩d her with Amorous Stories.   95

Billets Doux like small Shot did ply her,
And sometimes a Song
Went whizzing along,
But ſtill I was never the nigher.

At laſt she sent Word by a Trumpet,   100
If I lik'd that Life
She wou'd be my Wife,
But never be any Man's Strumpet.

I told her that Mars *wou'd not Marry,*
And Swore by my Scars,   105
Single Combats, and Wars,
I'de rather Dig Stones in a Quarry.

But is *Bellamira* satisfi'd I have no concern for
Isabella?

Smooth. Have a care of that: on the Con-   [110
trary do all you can to make her Jealous. T'will
keep her in Awe: and when she Names *Keepwel,* be

sure you to Answer her with *Isabella*: If she com-
mend his Dancing, be sure to praise her Singing;
if she speak of his Shape, Extol her Face: give [115
her as good as she brings; 'twill make her Mad.

Dang. Ay, if she Lov'd me.

Smooth. How can she Chuse? Your Person,
your Parts, and your Reputation, are able to Charm
any Woman Living: they all Love Soldiers; [120
and while she expects, and Loves what you give, she
Loves you, and will fear that the Stream of your
Bounty shou'd turn another way.

Dang. Thou say'st right; I wonder I shou'd not
think of it my self. [125

Smooth. If you had thought at all, you wou'd
certainly; and of a Thousand better Devices than
my poor Brains can furnish you with.

Enter Bellamira, *and* Silence.

Bell. I think I heard the Thundring Voice of my
brave Man of Warr, welcome, my *Hero*, my [130
Hercules! what wou'd thy Enemies give that I cou'd
hold thee thus for ever?

Dang. It wou'd save 'em Ten Thousand Mens
Lives, besides Castles, Towns, and their Dependances:
but, my Life, my Joy, how dost thou like my [135
Present? Is't not a fine Girl? I cou'd have had what
Mony I wou'd of my General abroad, or here; but,
I thought that below a Man of Honour: We had
like to have Quarrel'd about her.

Merr. This is a Bragging Coward, as sure [140
as a Painted Whore has an ill Complexion of her
own: How bravely he begins with his own Honour,
his Courage and his General!

Lion. And how he magnifies his own Present!
which, to say truth, another cou'd not praise too [145
much.

Merr. I have a small Present from your banish'd
Servant *Keepwell*; but you are going out.

Bell. Not yet; but anon I muſt.

Dan. What, do we ſtay? I am in a [150 Feaver; I have not had Woman these two days.

Merry. I will but deliver what was committed to my Charge for her, and then leave the Feaver you complain of, to her Cure.

Dan. Some rare business, I warrant, we [155 know the depth of *Keepwel's* Purse.

Merry. You shall see that, this Girl here is of *Ethiopia*, of the Royal Bloud there. I'le out lye him, if possible.

Dang. I bought a better for five Guineas, [160 and gave her this Morning to my Landladi's Daughter.

Smooth. She looks like a Warden Roaſted in the Embers, or the outside of a Gammon of Bacon.

Merry. Come forward, here's an Eunuch; a rare Jewel, how like you him? [165

Bell. He has a very good Face! How long have you been an Eunuch?

Lion. I never remember my self otherwise.

Merry. What saies *Dangerfield*, and *Smoothly*, ha, what fault do you find? They are silent, [170 that's praise enough for an Enemy. Try him in *Italian*, *French*, *Spanish*, Musick, Danceing.

Dan. If I had this Eunuch alone, he shou'd find I were none.

Bell. Go in *Pisquil*, and look to your Charge. [175

Merry. And yet, Madam, my Friend that sends these Gifts, do's not ask that you shou'd live for him alone. Nor does he tell of his Fights, Battles, Storms, Sieges: nor does he boaſt ⟨o⟩f his Scars as some do; but, when it shall be no trouble to you and [180 when you please, think it enough if he then be Receiv'd.

Dang. You are very officious for your Friend Sir.

Merry. I shall take a time to tell you, what you are, Sir. [185

Smooth. Officious for your Friend! Ha, ha, ha! You had as good have call'd him Pimp.

Dang. What dost Laugh at?

Smooth. At what you said to him even now.

Merry. Thou that ca⟨n⟩st stoop to Flatter [190 him thus, woud'st Eat Fire in a Fair for thy living, or Rake thy Meat off from a Dunghil⟨.⟩

Bell. Let's not go together.　　　[*Exit Merryman.*

Dang. I long to play my lower Tire of Guns at thee.　　　　　　　　　　　　　　　　　　[195

Bell. Go before to the Walk you know of by *Kensington*, and I'le meet you there.

Dang. I'll fly thither, as I were to beat up an Enemy's Quarters.　　　[*Ex. Dang.* and *Smooth.*

Bell. If *Eustace* comes hither; when I am [200 away, desire him to stay: If not, to come again: If he cannot, bring him to me; you know where I Sup: Be sure you take care of *Isabella*, and let none come to her but the Eunuch.　　　　　　　[*Ex. Omnes.*

　　　⟨SCENE II.　*A Room in Bellamira's House.*⟩

　　　　　Enter Lionel, *and* Isabella.

Isa. Why dost gaze and follow me thus, as if thou wert my Shadow?

⟨*Lion.*⟩　I am the Shadow of a Man indeed.

Isa. Leave me; and when I want thy Attendance, I will send for thee.　　　　　　　　　　　　[5

⟨*Lion.*⟩　*Bellamira* charg'd me, not to stir from you, 'twou'd ill become me to disobey her first Commands.

Isa. Thou art my Gaoler then?

⟨*Lion.*⟩　Not so; I am your faithful Servant, [10 and hope my Attendance, as it is to me a Pleasure, is to you no Burthen.

Isa. Wert thou ne'r in *Spain*?

⟨*Lion.*⟩ Why do you ask?

Isa. I know not, only a Foolish Curiosity I [15
had: but 'is Impossible. Joy seeks out Crouds, and
Numbers; but Griefs, like mine affect Retirement.

⟨*Lion.*⟩ You do Indulge your Melancholy too
much; If I may be so Bold, it ſtrik's an Air of Sadness
through the House. [20

Isa. I wou'd not have my Griefs Infectious: Go
play among your Fellows.

⟨*Lion.*⟩ I have no power to ſtir.

Isa. How so?

⟨*Lion.*⟩ I fear you'l do your self some [25
mischief, when I am gon: I dare not truſt the Tempeſt
on your Brow.

Isa. It is a harmless Storm, and will fall suddenly
in Tears. The more I look upon this Youth, the
more I think on him I lov'd in *Spain*: Those [30
Eyes, that Face, and that bewitching shape! Pray
leave me.

⟨*Lion.*⟩ If I have offended, be gracious; and
chide me; but do not thruſt me from your presence.

Isa. Alas! I find no fault with thee at all; [35
'Tis Fate and my unhappy Stars, that I repine at.

Enter Betty.

Betty. Madam, the Bath that was Commanded,
is prepar'd.

Isa. There I may ſteep my Limbs, but not my
Grief asswage. [*Exeunt.* [40

Enter Euſtace.

Euſt. The more I think of *Bellamira*'s sending
after me in this manner, the more I am to seek what
she means. When I went firſt to her, she enter-
tain'd me with a deal of Discourse, far fetch'd, nothing
to the purpose: At laſt she ask'd me, how long [45
my Father and Mother had been Dead? I told her,
a great while; then if I had not a Seat in *Devonshire*,

near the Sea? which I have. May be she has a mind to it, and thinks to get it of me. At laſt, if I had not loſt a young Siſter? who she was with, [50 and what she had about her when she was loſt? What she ask'd all these Queſtions for, I cannot guess; unless she wou'd put her self upon me for that Siſter, but if she be alive, she cannot be above seventeen; and *Bellamira* is as old as my [55 self. Now she shall speak her mind plainly, or trouble me no more. Is your Miſtress within⟨?⟩

Enter Silence.

Sil. No; but she desires to speak with you to Morrow, about the old business.

Euſt. Come hither, let me talk with you a [60 little about the old business.

Sil. I'le come no nearer; I know your Tricks well enough.

Euſt. Will Ten Guineas do you any harm?

Sil. Nor Twenty neither; but what shall [65 I tell my Miſtress? Will you come?

Euſt. I go into the Country to Morrow.

Sil. Pray come: She say's you'l repent it, if you do not⟨.⟩

Euſt. I can't possibly. [70

Sil. Will you ſtay here at our house, till she comes in?

Euſt. Yes if you'l ſtay with me.

Sil. Not I. You do so touse and tumble one, and keep one so hot. [75

Euſt. Thou art a pretty Maid, and may'ſt be a Miſtress thy self. I have seen worse Faces in Glass Coaches.

Sil. And better in *Bridewell*. I think I might serve for a Month or two; but what then? [80

Euſt. Nay, if you be so cautious, you'l never have a house in the Mall.

Sil. Nor Dye in a Ditch, like *Jane Shore*.

Euſt. Pattens, Worſted Stockins, and course Smocks, go with thee for a Fool.   [85

Sil. Will you go to my Miſtress where she sups anon, and I'le bring you to her?

Euſt. But come hither, prethee come, you are as skittish, as if you were that same all over. She is as Nimble as a Squirrel, there's no catching her.   [90

(She runs from him.

⟨SCENE III.   *A Room in Thisbe's House.*⟩

Enter Cuningham, Thisbe, *and her Maid.*

This.   Come, now we are alone, sing me the laſt New Song.

SONG

Thyrsis *unjuſtly you Complain,*
   And tax my tender heart
With want of pity for your pain,   5
   Or Sense of your desert.

By secret and Myſterious Springs,
   Alas! our Passions move;
We Women are Fantaſtick things,
   That like before we love.   10

You may be handsome, and have Wit,
   Be secret and well-bred,
The Person Love muſt to us fit,
   He only can succeed.

Some Dye, yet never are believ'd;   15
   Others we truſt too soon,
Helping our selves to be deceiv'd,
   And proud to be undone.

Cun.   Your humble Servant Madam: I left some

Friends of yours at the *Rose* ; *Merryman* begun [20
your health in a Bumper. I had much ado to get
away ; but your Commands——

This. No body here sent for you ; and of all Men
living, I leaſt expeéted you.

Cun. When I received this pretty Billet [25
Doux, my Heart went pit-a-pat ; and knew 'twas
your's before I open'd it.

This. 'Tis a false Heart, believe it not another
time.

Cun. If it be false, it was you⟨r⟩ Beauty [30
firſt made it so.

This. Lightly come, lightly go ; and if I lose it,
to another.

Cun. No Madam, you Conquer like the King of
France. Your Subjeéts for ever after are at reſt. [35

This. You said as much to the Flame-colour'd
Petticoat in New *Spring Garden.*

Cun. She has Spies upon me ; 'tis a good sign !
There was a Lady I muſt confess much of your hight,
your shape and meen ; at firſt I thought it was [40
your self, and therefore I accoſted her : And when
I was entred into discourse, she ply'd me so faſt with
the Intrigues of the Town, I cou'd not handsomly
get off.

This. I am not jealous of her : You need [45
not take all this pains to clear your self. Was she
of Quality ?

Cun. Yes, sure : She knew me, and desired my
Proteétion againſt some Bullies that were there.
Your Note here speaks of Company that were [50
to meet at Cards ; but 'tis more obliging in you to
be thus alone.

This. Thou incorrigible piece of Vanity ! I
neither sent for thee to Cards, nor any thing else.
Let's see this Note : 'Tis a Scriv'ner's hand. [55

[*Reads it.*

Cun. I have heard yours commended, and am
apt to hope——

This. The moſt that ever I knew any man.

Cun. Those pretty Lips shou'd be correſted, for their pouting, and press'd with Kisses into [60 their former Figure.

This. You shou'd be correſted, and made know your diſtance.

Cun. I am sorry to find you in so ill a humour, but I'le swear, that time at *Spring Garden*, we [65 scarce spoke of any thing but your self: She as 'tis the manner of fine Women one of another, maliciously enough, but I, with all the tenderness and transport imaginable. I see *Merryman* coming; I will take some fitter time for an Ecclaircissement. [70
[*Exit.*

This. This Fellow has Vanity enough to extraſt Love out of an affront, and wou'd Kiss the pretty Foot that shou'd Kick him down Stairs: He thinks all this is meer jealousie.

Enter Merryman.

Merry. These are those that can come, come [75 without being sent for.

This. Or they shou'd not come at all for me.

Merr. We have drunk every Letter of your Name twice over; and spelt it with a double *E* at laſt.

This. 'Twas done like a discret Guardian: [80 You are drunk then.

Merr. No; half a score Glasses do but whet Wit and sharpen Appetite: A Bottle is the Spring-Tide of Love, and dull Sobriety the Loweſt Ebb.

This. I love to see things at the worſt, that [85 I may know what to truſt to.

Merr. You wou'd not be seen so your self: Don't you Ladies Dress, Patch and Curl, and Paint too, if there be occasion before you come abroad?

This. That's to please our selv's, and in [90 competition to one another.

Merr. And that competition is about us filthy Fellows⟨.⟩ Was not *Cunningham* here?

This. He's juſt gone.

Merr. I sent him to you: We had a mind [95
to drink a Bottle by our selv's, and cou'd not get rid
of him, till I contriv'd a Letter in your Name for
him. He shew'd it us like a vain Fool, immediatly.

This. He'le tell the whole Town: Pray undeceive
him when you see him next; for all I cou'd say [100
cou'd not do it.

Merr. Have you any *Mirabilis*?

This. I shou'd not see you so often if I had
not.

Merr. We good Fellows have our Qualms, like
Breeding Women. [105

This. And your great Bellies too, moſt of you:
Which you go to lay at *Epsome,* and *Tunbridge* Waters.

Merr. When we are Marry'd I'le turn over a
New Leaf.

This. Hold, 'tis not come to that yet; you [110
are the envy of your Club: Four Hundred
Pounds a Year and neither Wife nor Child, and
spend it all in Drink.

Merr. I am very conjugally given: I love of late
to drink hand to hand with an old Friend; have [115
left off supping, and go to Bed at Ten.

This. These are signs of a Body far spent in the
Service.

Merr. I will leave off drinking, Eat much, and
get Children innumerable. [120

This. Not till you have been Flux'd: You are
an old sinner, and I dare not venture upon you.

Merr. I am as sound as a Bell, Fat, Plump, and
Juicy, and have drunk my Gallon a day these seven
Years. [125

This. However, 'twill mend your shape.

Merr. I have been told, I am as true a shap'd
Drunkard as heart can wish; Great Belly, double
Chin, thick Legs: You wou'd not have a Pad look
like a Racer? [130

This. No; but I wou'd have you thought to get your Children, if I Marry you.

Merr. I'le Cut any Man's Throat that says the contrary.

This. But they will whisper and make [135 Libels: Your great Belly will be a continual jeſt upon mine.

Mer. I will Drink Raking Rhenish, Eat Butter'd Wheat, Sweat in the Bagnio, and do any reasonable thing, to render my Person Gracious. [140

This. Every Jocky will do as much, to win a Tankard; but I muſt have no Morning Draughts, no Qualms that keep off Dinner till three a Clock, no Tun-belly'd Rogues, that fright Chair-men from the house, no Noisie Fools to diſturb the whole [145 Street with Loyal Catches, and senseless Huzzah's.

Merr. I have some Provisoes to offer too, in order to our future Peace and Quiet: I will have none of your Gaming Ladies to keep you up at Cards till I am ready to go out in the Morning, so that [150 we have scarce time for the great end of Matrimony. No meetings at the China-houses; where under pretence of Rafling for a piece of Plate, or so, you get acquainted with all the Young Fellows in Town; three such accidental meetings go to visit, and [155 three visits to something that shall be Nameless. No *Epsome* nor *Tunbridge* Waters, where Ladies and Gentlemen walk and prate up acquaintance, as faſt as if it were in a Tavern.

This. You muſt either get me with Child [160 the firſt Year, or give me leave to use the Lawful Means: I hope I may visit *Bellamira*.

Merr. She is not so handsome as she was, and begins to look something procurish; she is more dangerous than any Man; one Setter deſtroys [165 more Patridge than ten Hawks, when you take me for better for worse, you muſt forsake her and all her Works.

This.   When you take me for Rich or for Poor, you shall either leave your Drink or your   [170 Jealousie.   I will not be troubled with an *Italian* and a *Dutch* Man, bound up in one Greasie Volume.

Merr.   'Tis a mad Age, a Man is Laught at for being a Cuckold, and wonder'd at if he take any Care to prevent it; well, I will leave all to thy   [175 discretion; and as thou haſt been careful of thy own Credit hitherto, hope thou wilt be as tender of mine when I am thy Husband.

This.   That's all you have to truſt too: Now to shew you I will not be out-done in Generosity,   [180 you shall Dine in the City, and get Drunk among your old Companions sometimes; but I will have no Women brought into the Company, on any pretence whatever.

Merr.   My Land-lady, an Oyſter-Wench, or so.

This.   Not if she be under Fifty; you may   [185 be drunk at home: I will Dine with you, to keep off Beer Glasses while you Eat.

Merr.   Content: I have a beaſtly Bumper at my Meals; we will have two Beds, for I will not come home drunk and get Girls, without I knew   [190 where to get Portions for 'um; in this Age they sowre and grow ſtale upon their Parents hands. *Lucrece*'s will scarce off, but to Forraigners.

Enter a Servant.

Serv.   A young Gentleman in the Street hard by, says he muſt speak with you immediately.   [195

This.   'Tis One of your drunken Companions; you had beſt go to him, we shall have him come hither else.

Merr.   I wou'd Kick the beſt Friend in Chriſtendom down Stairs, shou'd he offer it.   Adieu for   [200 a while.   [*Exeunt.*

⟨SCENE IV.   *Outside Thisbe's House.*⟩

Enter Bellamira *in Man's Cloaths, to her* Merryman.

Mer.   What's you business with me Sir?

Bell.   If you will walk a little farther into the Square, I'le satisfie you, Sir. [*They walk a little farther.*] Now we are alone, the time and place convenient, I muſt tell you; you abus'd a person   [5 of Quality laſt Night, forc'd open her Lodgings, beat her Servants, broke her Windows, and call'd her all the Names imaginable.

Merr.   That may very well be; I went home drunk, and scour'd outragiously: But what of   [10 that?

Bell.   I am her Brother.

Merr.   And come to swagger in her behalf?

Bell.   I am come for satisfaction.

Merr.   Her Name, Sir?   [15

Bell.   *Emilia.*

Merr.   Her Lodging?

Bell.   The Flower de Luce.

Merr.   I always took it to be a Baudy-house⟨.⟩

Bell.   It seems so; but I come to convince   [20 you to the contrary.

Merr.   Sir, I believe you: And if you will bring me to wait on her, I will ask her Pardon: I am as much asham'd of a rudness offer'd to a Person of Quality, when I am sober, as any Man living.   [25

Bell.   I thought what a Fellow I shou'd find.

Merr.   My little Bully, will nothing serve you but Battle, Murder and sudden Death?

Bell.   I came to fight Sir; not to hear you prate.

Merr.   Then pluck out, that I may Tap thee   [30 presently.

They go to Fight, Bellamira *pulls up her Peruke.*

Bell. Hold, hold *Merryman*; doſt thou not know me yet ?

Merr. *Bellamira* in disguise !

Bell. The same. [35

Merr. Why this to me ? Faith you shall never find me backward to Man or Woman.

Bell. No, thou art a brave Fellow, I have occasion for such a one, and (now I have try'd you, and see you dare fight) all's well⟨.⟩ [40

Merr. Am I to be your Ladyships Second ?

Bell. An easier Business.

Merr. As how ?

Bell. I have appointed *Dangerfield* to wait for me in the Walk neer *Kensington*, which I so much [45 delight in : Thus disguised I intend to Rob him, and have chosen thee for my Fellow-Adventurer. When we have frighted the roaring Fool sufficiently, we'l find some way to give him his Mony again.

Merr. We may be hang'd together very [50 lovingly in earneſt, tho' we Rob in jeſt.

Bell. If he shou'd discover, which he never will, I can prevail with him not to Prosecute ; Besides, the Lying Fool will swear for his Credit, we were at leaſt a dozen ; my Heart is set upon this [55 Frolick ; don't deny me.

Merr. 'Tis admirable ! 'twill be the beſt News for my friend *Keepwell*.

Bell. He shall know it in due time⟨,⟩ I hate this *Dangerfield*, and now I have gotten *Isabella* out [60 of his hands, I care not if he were hang'd.

Merr. And shall we Cudgel his Buff Coat sufficiently ?

Bell. 'Till it be as gentle as a Sheepskin.

Merr. Thou art a brave Wench, I Faith, I [65 will drink thy Health hereafter by the Name of the *Pretty Padder*. I will borrow a Vizor of some overgrown Baud, and about it inſtantly. But shall we Sup together in Town afterwards ?

Bell.   Sure you'l not wrong Friend *Keepwell*   [70
so much ?

Merr. Not for a World, if I thought you wou'd
not; but, he is at a diſtance, the Temptation present,
and not to be resiſted by frail Man.

Bell.   You were always an Enemy of mine;   [75
and yet I know not how, I ever lik'd your blunt way;
and cou'd not hate you heartily for it.

Merr.   If you will make a Convert of me, this is
the time.

Bell.   You shall then promise me drunk or   [80
sober, to speak well of me to *Keepwell*.

Mer.   That's too hard, but, if I speak any ill of
you, drunk: I will promise to deny it again when I
am sober.

Bell.   You shall never more tell him I will   [85
undo him, nor read him any discreet Lectures about
my extravagance in Cloaths, Furniture, Equipage,
Hours, or Company.

Merr.   I never did sow dissention but with intent
you shou'd make your benefit of it; for I am   [90
told after every little Quarrel, he buys his peace with
a Coach and Horses, a Country House, Pearl Neck-
lace, or some such trifle.

Bell.   He does so; yet, but frequent Disputes
may end in a Breach, and there are many fine   [95
Women that lie upon the Catch, to get him from me.

Merr.   Fear him not, next to you he loves Money,
and will never begin such another Expence in a new
place. You have more Plate, than ten Chriſt'nings,
more China, than many a Shop, more good   [100
Cloaths than the Play-house.

Bell.   You had like to have undone me for all
that, with your Stories; but he told me all when I
had him alone.

Merr.   I don't doubt it; I see advice is   [105
thrown away upon him, and I will trouble him with no
more; but be thy Servant to all intents and purposes.

[*Kisses her.*] Now the Peace is agreed on, we'll Sign and Seal anon.

Bell. You'l tell him one time or other when [110 you are drunk together.

Merr. He'll not believe me if I shou'd. Well I am a Rogue to betray my Friend thus; but, who wou'd not be taken off with such a Bribe? Besides, in matter of Women, we are all in the State [115 of Nature, every man's hand againſt every man. Whatever we pretend. [*Exeunt.*

<SCENE V. *A Street.*>

Enter Euſtace.

Euſt. I wonder what's become of *Lionel*; he has not appear'd this day or two. I will go to *Bellamira*'s and know where she Sups that I may meet her, and know the end of her affair with me. Who's this walks this way? He is transported, and talks to himself. [5

Enter Lionel.

Lion. If a man car'd to be alone he shou'd be troubled with forty Coxcombs, and ten times as many impertinent Queſtions: But now I am ready to burſt with Joy, and Secrets, I can meet no Friend to vent myself to. [10

Euſt. This is *Lionel*, for all his disguise, I know him. How now, *Lionel*? What's the meaning of this habit? I never saw a man so overjoy'd: are you in your Wits?

Lion. Oh, my Friend! There is not a man [15 on Earth, to whom I would so gladly impart my secret Joy, or inward Grief as to thy self.

Euſt. 'Tis the happiness of friendship that the one is improv'd, the other lessen'd, by our doing so: But what means all this? [20

Lion. I am impatient till you know; this is the happiest day of all my Life: And I cou'd be contented to die this Minute, least some succeeding Misfortunes shou'd defile this sincere Joy. You know *Bellamira*, my Brothers Mistress.   [25

Eust. I have seen her twice or thrice.

Lion. There was this day a young Maid given her by *Dangerfield* my Brothers Rival, the finest Creature that ever my Eyes beheld; not above seventeen, a man flying for his Life wou'd stop   [30 to gaze upon her.

Eust. I am not of your opinion, but what of her?

Lion. Seeing her in the Street, I fell in Love with her. By good fortune, we had an Eunuch, which my Brother had promis'd to *Bellamira*:   [35 Nor was he yet deliver'd; *Merriman*, who undertook to carry him advis'd me, seeing me dying for this young Woman.

Eust. What did he advise you?

Lion. To change Cloaths with this Eunuch,   [40 and be presented to *Bellamira*, in his stead.

Eust. What, for an Eunuch.

Lion. I have a pretty Voice, Smooth Chin.

Eust. What cou'd you propose to your self?

Lion. To see her, and be alone sometimes   [45 with the Divine Creature: Do you count all that nothing? In short, I was presented to *Bellamira*, and received with great Joy, and without the least Suspicion, she left me at home, and recommended this beautiful Creature to my sole care.   [50

Eust. 'Tis impossible.

Lion. She did it.

Eust. Most discreetly.

Lion. Most fortunately. I'le tell thee more, she commanded no Body shou'd come near her, but   [55 my self; and that I shou'd not stirr from her, in the farthest part of the house. I Blush'd, look'd down, and modestly said it shou'd be done.

Euſt.　Oh Rogue ! thy Discourse has Fingers in it.

Lion.　*Bellamira* goes out to Supper, her　[60
Servants follow her, except some of the meaneſt sort :
Presently they prepare a Bath for the fair Stranger ;
this beautiful Creature is call'd to go into the Bath.

Euſt.　What before you ?

Lion.　Yes, before an Eunuch sure.　She　[65
goes in, returns, the Servants put her to Bed : I ask
if they have any service for me : *Pisquil,* says one,
(for so I was call'd) Take this Fan, and cool my
Miſtress with it, as she lies.

Euſt.　Oh, that I cou'd have seen thee with　[70
those gloating Eyes, Fanning a Naked Woman ! an
Asinego as thou art.

Lion.　Presently all the Maids run, some one way,
some another, as Servants do when their Maſters
are abroad ; in the mean time this beautiful　[75
Creature falls asleep : I look about me, to see if all
were faſt, I Bar the Door,

Euſt.　What then ?

Lion.　What then, my *Euſtace* ? Can you ask and
know me ? Shou'd I have slipt so fair, so wish'd,　[80
so unexpeſted an Opportunity, I muſt have been that
Eunuch that I seem'd.

Euſt.　You ravish'd her then⟨ ?⟩

Lion.　What else ? I took her by Storm, having
no leisure for a Siege : I found her the same　[85
Woman I fell in Love with in *Spain.*

Euſt.　She we so often talk'd of ?

Lion.　The same : and which is more, she re-
membred me again : Never was Man so Happy !
never was Accident so Fortunate !　　　　　　　[90

Euſt.　Did she not Cry out ?

Lion.　There was no Body within hearing.

Euſt.　'Twas somthing a harsh way.

Lion.　No Woman ever heartily fell out with a
Man about that Business, I'le try to soften her　[95
in my own Person !

Euſt. Won't you change your Cloaths?

Lion. How shall I change 'em? Or whither shall I go? I dare not go home, for fear of my Brother: Then again, if my Father shou'd be come out [100 of the Country!

Euſt. Come to my house, out of the Street however.

Lion. Agreed. [*Exeunt.*

ACT IV. SCENE I

⟨*A Walk in Kensington.*⟩

Dangerfield, *and* Smoothly.

Dan. 'Tis ſtrange *Bellamira* appears not, we have been here a great while.

Smooth. I wonder she mak's no more haſt to her own happiness! the *Spanish* Ladies wou'd not have serv'd you so. [5

Dan. Nay, I'le speak a bold word; *French*, *Spanish*, or *Italian*; I was ever the delight of Ladies, I was the Terror of Men.

Smooth. Perhaps she has been overturn'd, broke a Wheel, or some such Accident: may be her [10 sneaking Lover's return'd.

Dan. Who *Keepwell*? that fearful Hind, that ran out of Town at the News of my Arrival, leaſt I shou'd Kick him to Jelly?

Smooth. 'Tis almoſt Night, what if we shou'd [15 be Robb'd here?

Dan. What if the Skie shou'd fall? or a Flock of Sheep root a marching Army? If all these Hedges were lin'd with Musqueteers I wou'd not yield.

Smooth. ⟨[*Aside*⟩ If a Hog shou'd ſtart out [20 and ruſtle, he wou'd run away. A Volley of Shot is

Musick to your great Heart; but what shall poor I do?

Dan. This Fellow is as Cowardly as I am Rash, and Advent'rous, Creep behind me, and be as [25 safe as in a Brazen Tower, I'le shew thee how I kill'd *Don Alonzo* in *Spain*.

Smooth. I dare not ſtand: You'l run such a Fellow as I through with a Scabbard on.

Dan. On my Honour, as I love danger, I [30 will not hurt thee. He ran furiously upon me.

Smooth. And did you look so terribly, as you do now?

Dan. Worse if possible.

Smooth. He was a brave Man then. [35

Dan. The braveſt Fellow I ever had to do with: He had Kill'd Nine Men in Duel, made two and twenty Campagns, been in eight Sea-Fights and thirteen pitch'd Battles.

Enter Merryman *and* Bellamira.

Merr. Here he is Fencing with his Man. [40

Smooth. Thieves, Thieves! Murder! Look to your self.

Bell. Your Mony.

Merr. Deliver Sirrah.

Dan. Take it you Scoundrels, and thank [45 Heav'n I am not in an angry Mood.

Merr. Will a good Cudgle put you into it?

[*Lays him on.*

Dan. No: *Venus, Venus,* rules the day, I am all Peace and Love: My Vigour is design'd to other purposes than Fighting with Rascally Fellows. [50

Merr. We muſt have this Pearl out of your Ear.

Dan. 'Twas given me for my service at the Siege of *Dunkirk*, as a Mark of Honour.

Bell. Make haſt, we shall be forcd to Crop you else. [55

Merr. Let's remove 'em a little farther, and tie 'em Back to Back, and leave 'em.

Dan. I'le have satisfaction for this Affront, you Rascals, I scorn the slow pac'd Revenge of Law, 'tis Blood I'le have.   [60

Merr. That you may not forget, I will give you this farther Remembrance.

Bell. Come away with the Rascals.

Dan. Well, Stripling well, no more to be said.

                                          [*Exeunt.*

⟨SCENE II.   *A Street.*⟩

⟨Enter⟩ *Thisbe* in the *Bailiffs* Hands.

1. *Bay.* I'le stay no longer sending up and down : Can you pay the Mony ?

This. In a short time I can.

2. *Bay.* Have you any Friend that will be bound with you ?   [5

This. I have ; but I am so unfortunate, they are not within.

1. *Bay.* Come, come, away to Prison.

This. If you have the Hearts of Men, take Pitty on my Youth.   This is all the Mony I owe in [10 the World, and I shall suddenly discharge it ; but if you disgrace me thus, I am undone for ever.

1. *Bay.* We are Officers, and must obey our Warrant.   Come along.

Enter Cuningham *and* Eustace.

Cun. What's here *Thisbe* in the hands of [15 Bailiffs ! I will Kill two Birds with one Stone at once, I will shew my Courage, and my Love in rescuing my Mistress.   Let's never suffer these Rascals to carry her off.

Eust. I will not Fight against the Law : A [20

Bailiff and a Hangman are as necessary as a Lord Chief Juſtice, in a Government.

Cun. I will draw and be Knock'd down, in her Quarrel by my self then.

Euſt. Hold, hold: I will draw my Purse [25 and rescue her a surer way.

This. Is there no way for my deliverance?

Cun. I'le Bail her.

1. *Bay.* We muſt have City Security; no *Covent Garden* Bully?   [30

Euſt. What's the Sum?

1. *Bay.* Two Hundred Pound. What do we ſtand talking with her? away.

This. Oh I am Miserable!

Cun. Hold, you shall have your choice of [35 six Play Debts: Sir *Thomas Whiskin* ows me three hundred pound; will you take that for your Mony? or *Harry Hothead* shall be your Pay-maſter.

1. *Bay.* Nothing but our Mony down, or good Security.   [40

Euſt. Why, Then here's your Mony down you Rascals.

2. *Bay.* Now you say something. Much good may do you: She is very pretty, and as cheap as Neck-Beef.   [45

This. This Redemption as I never can deserve, so I cannot too much acknowledge your surprising Generosity to a Stranger, known to you by nothing but diſtress.

Euſt. Preserve your thanks till you find to [50 whom they are due, I am but the Inſtrument of your deliverance, and was employ'd by a Servant of yours, who cou'd not come himself, for some reasons you shall know hereafter.

This. May I not know his Name? that I [55 may return him his Mony at leaſt.

Euſt. He charg'd me to the contrary.

Cun. I cou'd almoſt forswear Play, since my ill

Fortune has put me out of condition of doing this
small Service, but I was ready with my Sword.   [60

This.   'Tis much better as it is.

Cun.   I did not throw one Main in two hours, I
lost three sets at|Back-Gammon, and a Tout at Trick-
track, all ready Mony; the rude Fellows have frighted
the Roses from your Cheeks.   [65

This.   This Rogue my Taylor that Arrested me,
came but three days ago to know if I had any service
to command him: There must be something farther
in't.

Cun.   Perhaps some envious Woman set him   [70
on: there is as much malice among the Beauties as
among Wits: Will you give me leave to wait on you
home! there are rude Fellows abroad, and you may
meet with some Affront.

Eust.   Madam we will secure you from that.   [75

This.   Your Servant.   [*Exeunt.*

⟨SCENE III.   *A Room in Bellamira's House.*⟩

Enter Keepwell *and* Silence.

Keep.   How does my dearest *Bellamira*?   Does
she not think I have mortified my self enough.

Sil.   You may guess: She is gone out with
Dangerfield.

Keep.   I know it too well.   [5

Sil.   Oh this Villain, Viper, Satyr! where shall I
find him? or how torment him when I have found
him? we are all undone, Abus'd Cheated!

Keep.   My heart misgives me strangely, and I
have scarce Courage to ask what's the matter.   [10
Here have been Scourers, breakers of Windows:

Sil.   As soon as he had his will of her, to run away,
and leave us thus! but if I light of him, I'le tear his
Goatish Eyes out.

Keep. Here has been some disorder in my   [15
abscence : who is't you threaten thus ? whom do
you speak of ?

Sil. As if you did not know, and be hang'd with
your pretious Gifts.

Keep. They are such your Mistress wou'd   [20
never let me rest till she had 'em : if she don't like
'em, now, she may thank her self. But what's the
matter ?

Sil. The Eunuch you gave us made brave work!

Keep. Oh, is that all ? not work for a Mid-   [25
wife, I am sure.

Sil. It may be in time. He has Ravish'd the
young maid *Dangerfield* gave my Mistress.

Keep. 'Tis impossible : he is as innocent as the
Child Unborn.   [30

Sil. What he is I cann't tell ; but by his works,
he's no more an Eunuch than your self : the young
Maid is all in Tears : We cannot get a Word from
her : Pray Heaven she does herself no mischief.
She casts down her Eyes, and sighs as if her   [35
heart wou'd break ; The Rascal's no where to be
found ; 'tis well if he have not robb'd us at parting
too.

Keep. I am strangely amaz'd ! he knows no place
in Town, no person, and has no where to go, but   [40
to my House.

Sil. Let's see if he be there. Our Maids have
sworn every one to have a Limb of him.

Keep. I have heard these Eunuchs have been
very amorous ; but never heard of such a Prank ;   [45
besides this was taken in an *Algerine*, an Eunuch after
the *Turkish* manner.

Sil. He look'd so demurely, I thought Butter
wou'd not have melted in his Mouth, I hope you will
make sure work with him before you send him   [50
again. But see *Isabella* herself.

Enter Isabella.

Keep. I'll speak to her, and know the truth.

Sil. You had better step aside and observe her : you'l put her out of Countenance.

Isa. Torn from my Parents and my Country   55
    young ;
Then in a Foreign Land expos'd to Sale.
After some few removes when but a Child,
I to the hands of *Bellamira* fell,
Then to rude *Dangerfield* by Fortunes spite   60
Strangely betray'd ; and now again restor'd
I know not how, nor why, nor on what score.
Misfortune sure like mine ⟨there⟩ never was.
In every Change and State I still preserv'd
My Honor boldly by Contempt of Life,   65
Vow'd the same hour should rob me of 'em both :
The Resolution was so new, it check'd his Lust.
But what do's it avail to keep from Thieves
That Wealth we must anon to Pyrats lose ?
No sooner here, but like an Eunuch,   70
A bold Lover com's and rifles me of all ;
Vow'd to return, Marry and take me hence ;
But Men are False, Women believing Fools :
Yet this is he that Lov'd me when in *Spain*,
And my poor heart first kindled at his Fire   75
Till he returns I will not Cherish Life,
Nor sleep nor nourishment shall prop this Frame :
My Husband he will be or Murtherer.   [*Exit.*

Keep. Poor Lady ! she has dissolv'd my Eyes.
Her Passion's great ; but I'll go home and kill   [80
Pisquil : thou shalt go and see the Execution.

Sil. We'l flay the Lustful Swine.   [*Exeunt.*

⟨SCENE IV.   *Knightsbridge.*⟩

Enter Bellamira, Dangerfield, *and* Smoothly.

Bell.   My dear man of War! bouncing Bully! did'ſt thou not begin to dispair of me?

Dan.   When we were ty'd back to back and thrown into that Ditch, I began to think we muſt have lain in the Field all Night, as I have done,   [5 for my part, half my life time.

Bell.   You have not been robb'd I hope?

Dan.   Yes, faith the Rogues surpriz'd us e're we cou'd get our Swords out.

Bell.   Not of much?   [10

Dan.   Of a hundred Pieces, and some Medals, given me by Forraign Princes and States, for my good Service in the Wars.

Bell.   I am the unhappieſt woman in the World! and all this ſtaying for me! how many were the   [15 Rogues?

Dan.   Half a Foot Company.

Smoo.   Such as we us'd to Muſter in *Flanders*.

Bell.   How many is that ⟨in⟩ *English*?

Dan.   A dozen Arm'd with Sword and Piſtol. [20

Smoo.   There were more of 'em not far off if need had been.

Dan.   The Captain of 'em was such another fat fellow as *Merryman* : I shall know him again if I see him ; and if I do, I make one entire bruise of   [25 him.   He laid on me moſt unmercifully.

Bell.   Who unbound you?

Dan.   An honeſt Country fellow, who came by, by accident.

Bell.   I have been overthrown too by a   [30 Gentlemans Coachman, who threw us in the dirt; and I was forc'd to go home to shift.

Dan.   Know you the Livery?   I will have satis-

faction, or make him turn away his sawcy Servant:
I am rusty, for want of Fighting.   [35

Bell. If I did I wou'd ⟨not⟩ tell you, you are so apt
to thrust your self into Quarrels; 'tis a sad thing to
love a brave man, a Woman is ever in one fright or
other : if they have the discretion not to be Principals,
they must be Seconds in every idle business.   [40

Dan. I never fail'd but once, of disarming my
man.

Smoo. And then you had the Misfortune to run
him clean through the heart.

Dan. I fled into *France* upon it.   [45

Bell. What if I help you to your Money and
Jewels again ?

Dan. I'll give you Fifty Pounds. Can you guess
who robb'd us ?

Bell. No, but I'll take you at your word. [50
Stop here at *Knightsbridge*, there is a Justice, swear
your loss before him since you were robb'd between
Sun and Sun, and the Country is oblig'd to make it
good.

Smoo. Here's Fifty pounds well gotten.   [55
This is a Witty Wench, I am half in Love with her
my self.

Dan. I had rather lose it all, then swear before
one of those Children of the Gown.

Bell. Nay you shall do it : 'twill soon be [60
over, and then we'll Sup in Town.

Smoo. Now must I forswear my self, or lose my
Place : Let me see, that I may not be out : The
Robbers were Twelve, the Mony lost, a Hundred
Pieces, besides Medals and Rings to the value [65
of as much more.   [*Exeunt.*

⟨SCENE V. *A Room in Keepwell's House.*⟩

Enter Keepwell, Pisquil, Silence, Betty.

Keep. Come out you Rogue, you Rascal: will nothing go down with you, but, Maiden-heads?

Pisq. I beseech you, Sir.

Keep. How came you hither again? What's the meaning of these Cloaths? speak; if we [5 had ſtay'd never so little longer he had been gone, he was preparing for his journey, I see.

Betty. Where is he? That I may ſtick my Bodkin in him.

Keep. Don't you see him? [10

Betty. No if I did, I'd teach him to come with his edg'd Tooles amongſt poor harmless Maids.

Sil. It might have been some of our Cases; and I pitty *Isabella* with all my heart: But are you sure you have him faſt? [15

Keep. Why there he is, juſt before you.

Sil. What that poor Wretch? That swallow face was never within our doors. There's a Ravisher indeed!

Bett. Cou'd you think this was he that we [20 complain'd of?

Keep. I never had any other.

Sil. This fellow is no more to our *Pisquil*, than a Calf is to a Lion.

Bett. He you sent us had a sweet Face, [25 delicate Shape, quick Eye, and a promising Countenance.

Keep. Fine Feathers make fine Birds: You see him now in plain Cloaths, at his worſt.

Sil. There's more in't then so: Ours was [30 young, handsome in his prime; this is a Wither'd, Worn-out, Weather-beaten, Weasil-fac'd Fellow.

Keep. I shall begin to think I don't know my

right hand from my left, if this be true. Come hither
Sirrah, *Pisquil*, did not I give Fifty pound for   [35
you?

Pisq. You did, Sir.

Bett. Now let me ask him a queſtion: Do you
know our house.

Pisq. No, nor you neither.   [40

Sil. Merryman brought us a young fellow of
Nineteen that wou'd have known us all over and over,
if he had ſtay'd.

Keep. How come you by these Cloaths? Why
don't you answer me, you Rascal?   [45

Pisq. One Mr. *Lionel* came.

Keep. What, my Brother?

Pisq. He said so.

Keep. When?

Pisq. To day.   [50

Keep. With whom?

Pisq. With *Merryman* only.

Keep. Did you know he was my Brother?

Pisq. Mr. *Merryman* told me so: he gave me
these Cloaths and took away mine; then they   [55
went both together.

Keep. I am undone, *Bellamira* will never endure
this affront, nor ever be perswaded but I was privy
to it.

Sil. It may coſt you a Weeks Banishment or   [60
so; but what think you, am I sober? am I in my
right Wits? No, I ly'd! I was a Fool! the Eunuch
was as Innocent as a Lamb. Poor *Isabella*! Is not
she undone, ruin'd for ever.

Keep. No, he shall marry her and make her   [65
an honeſt woman, will not that satisfie?

Pisq. Alas Sir I have nothing to satisfie a woman
with neither by night nor by day, I am a poor despic-
able Eunuch. If I Marry your Worship muſt get
my Children and keep 'em too.   [70

Sil. My Miſtress will never like that.

Keep. The Wench he Ravish'd is but a Servant Maid, or at moſt one that has no friends, I'll give 'em a Farm of twenty pound a year, and make up all that way: [75

Pisq. I beseech you Sir Drown or Hang me out of the way, but name not Marriage to a wretch in my condition.

Keep. Sirrah I'le have it so. *Will nothing down with you but forbidden fruit? you have no ſtomach* [80 *to a Woman in a lawful way and behang'd.*

Pisq. I am your true, your very Eunuch *Pisquil!* what pranks have been play'd in my name I know not; let any of these Maids examine me, alas! I am under no circumſtances of Wedlock.   [85

Betty. Out upon him filthy Creature. I wou'd not touch him for a World.

Sil. I had rather handle a dead Corps; three such Fellows were enough to breed a Plague.

Bett. I'll take my Corporal Oath this is not [90 he that was at our House.

Sil. I never saw two men in my life more unlike than this odious Fellow and our *Pisquil.*

Keep. I am resolv'd he shall Marry her though it coſt me Forty pound a year; *Bellamira's* [95 House muſt not be thus affronted.

Sil. Sir you miſtake, *Isabella* is a Gentlewoman sits at Table with my Miſtress, and wou'd not Marry such a fellow for all you are worth.

Keep. What shall we do then?   [100

Sil. Let's find out the true Ravisher, if he refuse to marry her, take the Law of him and Hang him.

Keep. Come hither *Pisquil* : Did *Lionel* put on thy Cloaths and leave thee his?

Pisq. By all that's good he did.   [105

Keep. And put on thine?

Pisq. Yes in the Room.

Bett. He came to us indeed in a ſtrange fashion'd habit.

Keep. This *Lionel* is the moſt wicked, Im-   [110
pudent, and I the moſt unhappy of mankind! I
have sent a Stone-horse among Mares.

Sil. Now don't you think my Miſtress has been
finely serv'd by you and your lewd Brother?

Keep. I am undone if all this comes to   [115
Bellamira's Ear: she talk'd of a great Summ she
hop'd to get by reſtoring this young Woman to her
Friends: I am afraid 'tis I muſt pay it now; No
man will own her, having been thus abus'd. Sirrah
deny all again inſtantly.   [120

Pisq. Let me alone, Sir I'll set all right.

Keep. I'll get the truth out of thee, or I'll beat
thee in a Mortar. When was my Brother here?

Pisq. Four days ago.

Keep. Never since?   [125

Pisq. No indeed Sir,

Keep. See what a Lying Rogue this is now! I
have had him but two days, and he saies my Brother
chang'd his Cloaths with him four dayes ago.

Bett. He said quite otherwise but now, and   [130
that it was this day.

Keep. Damn him Rogue, he faulters in his
Evidence, and I wou'd not hang a Dog upon his
Testimony; are not you a fine Rascal to lay this
villany upon my Innocent Brother?   [135

Pisq. I do confess; pray Sir pardon me, I was
afraid.

Keep. Get you out of my sight you lying Rogue.

Sil. He is a Lying Rogue now I dare swear.

Betty. He dares not ſtand to his firſt ſtory: [140
Keepwell has threatned him.

Sil. This is all *Merryman*'s contrivance; but if I
be not even with him, may I dye a Maid. Well
Dangerfield and my Miſtress were at high words
after Supper: She gave me her Gold and Jewels   [145
to carry home; a sure sign she'l not ſtay long behind.

Betty. I'll go Home.

Keep. I'll go to *Merryman* and learn the bottom of this business, that I may know what to say to my offended *Bellamira.* [150

⟨SCENE VI. *A Room in Merryman's House.*⟩

Enter Merryman *and* Bellamira.

Merry. I will turn Turk but I will avoid Wine hereafter, that Æternal Foe to better sport, Can my dear *Bellamira* forgive her poor entertainment.

Bell. Why not, as well as you do a weak Brother who can drink but his Bottle. You may sit up [5 till morning tho he leave you at Nine, the Application is easie.

Merr. I will leave my Mornings draught of Mum and Wormwood, and Breakfaſt hereafter upon new laid Eggs, Amber-greece and Gravy. [10

Bell. Trouble not your self, I will Breakfaſt before I come to you, and Sup heartily before I go to bed.

Merr. This Paunch of mine shall down, I will no longer suffer my Virile virtue to be Eclips'd [15 by this Globe of Earth, Bisket my Meat, Fennel Water and Vinegar shall be my Drink this twelve Months.

Bell. Your Pennance is too severe, meerly for a sin of Omission, I like you the better for it: [20 Your honeſt nature wou'd not suffer you to wrong your friend too much, when it came to the point.

Merr. My honeſt over-grown body wou'd not keep pace with lewd Will; for which I am resolv'd to mortifie it, no more Bumpers, no Dinners [25 that laſt till Midnight, no City Feaſt, no Huzzahs.

Bell. You are in Love elsewhere, and keep your self for pretty Miſtress *Thisbe.*

Merr. I never saw Play, but I was willing to throw away what I had about me. [30

Bell. Well I muſt leave you, *Keepwell* I fear is in Town.

Merr. That word leave you, alwaies puts me into a Cold Sweat, and if a man were Cock'd and Prim'd, is enough to make a man miss Fire. Can't [35 you ſtay one Minute?

Bell. To what purpose, I have been here a great while, sure 'tis late, your Company ſtay for you, the Bottles are upon the Table by this time.

Merr. Wou'd you had never talk'd of going, [40 I am the worſt at paying Mony upon a Pinch, can't you ſtay one quarter of an hour?

Bell. I have appointed business with *Euſtace* and muſt be gone.

Enter a Servant.

Serv. Sir, *Keepwell* is coming up Stairs, I [45 told him you were asleep, he muſt needs speak with you.

Merr. Step in there, I'll send him away presently.

Enter Keepwell, *he gets a glimpse of* Bellamira.

Keep. *Merryman* with a Wench, nay then we are all Mortal. [50

Merr. 'Tis only a Wine Cooper's Daughter that has brought me some taſt of *Pontack* out of her Father's Cellar.

Keep. ⟨[*Sings*]⟩ *Her Breaſts of Delight, are two Bottles of White, and her Eyes are two Cups of* [55 *Canary.* I hope we shall have no more Lessons of Thrift, no pious Exhortations, no Lectures againſt Love: Why she has as good Cloaths as my *Bellamira.*

Merr. But I don't Pay for 'em as you do.

Keep. Prithee let me see her, I have truſted [60 thee with my *Bell.* a hundred times.

Merr. You won't like her and then I shall be laughed at, besides this is the firſt time, she is a young modeſt Sinner and I have given her my word.

Keep. What, art thou asham'd of her? [65

Merr.   Nor proud of her neither, as you are of your Tyrant *Bellamira*.

Keep.   Never speak aginſt my *Bell.* she is the prittieſt little pouting tempeſtuous Rogue some- times, but 'tis soon over, and then she is so calm   [70 again, the *Halcyon* might breed upon her Lips.

Merr.   You are grown Poetical since you went into the Country.

Keep.   Prithee let me see thy Punk, thy Cockatrice, thy Harlot.   [75

Merr.   Good words, you don't know who you speak of.

Keep.   I'll set my foot againſt the door.

Merr.   You won't be such a Brute.   ⟨[*Aside*]⟩ *How shall we get rid of him ?*   [80

Keep.   I am very Rampant.

Merr.   I have that will take down your Courage. *Dangerfield* has sent me a Challenge for delivering your Eunuch and Black in his Presence.

Keep.   Why didſt thou do it in his Presence ?   [85

Merr.   'Tis paſt now, and you muſt be my Second.

Keep.   Pox on't I did not mean rampant for Fighting, I meant for th'other business, I have no malice to any man living but am wond'rous loving.

Merr.   We are to meet an hour hence, the   [90 time is short, I cannot possibl⟨y⟩ find another Friend ; besides, 'tis partly your own quarrel.

Keep.   Hang him he makes a Trade of Fighting, and kills men by the year.

Merr.   We muſt try, what Mettle he is   [95 made off.

Keep.   Let me alone, I will bring you off with Honour, and without Fighting.

Merr.   How so ?

Keep.   The Officer of the Guard is my   [100 intimate Friend, I will acquaint him with the Quarrel and get us all secur'd ; I have scap'd hitherto by his means, and yet have sent and receiv'd some

Challenges in my Life time; he saves more Blood-shed than all the Parsons in Town with their [105
Sermons against Duelling.

Merr. I have no great Lust for Fighting, if you can take it up handsomely, with all my heart, but you must about it instantly for the time is short.

Keep. I am gone, but be sure you stay at [110
home.   [*Exit.*

Merr. I knew this was a sure way to be rid of him. ⟨[*To Bellamira*]⟩ *He is gone.*

⟨*Re-e*⟩*nter* Bellamira ⟨*from her hiding-place.*⟩

Bell. And so must we, the Guard will be here presently else; You cou'd not help calling me [115
Tyrant to *Keepwell* tho you knew I was within hearing.

Merr. I must talk a little after the old rate, 'twill breed suspicion in him shou'd I change my Note all of a suddain, but I will drink him up every Night, and send him to thee so loving.   [120

Bell. Drink him down rather, pray, let him alone as he is.   [*Exeunt.*

⟨SCENE VII. *A Room in Bellamira's House.*⟩

Enter Silence *and* Eustace.

Sil. Oh, Sir, how is it between my Mistress and her Man of War?

Eust. Not so as it might be between thee and me, if thou wou'dst be rul'd.

Sil. I am rull'd by my Friends and Relations. [5

Eust. They'll undo thee *Silence*, if thou heark'nest to 'em: thou wilt spend thy Youth in Service, and in thy Age be eaten up with Children.

Sil. Better so than with the Pox: I had rather be a Coblers Wife, than the best Man's Whore [10
in the Land.

Eust. This is a wicked Principle, and has undone more young Women !

Sil. If I muſt be ruin'd, I'll be ruin'd in an honeſt way. [15

Eust. A Woman ruin'd in an honeſt way is the vileſt, contemptibleſt thing imaginable : give me a Woman ruin'd with a Coach and six Horses, a house in the *Mall*, fine Equipage ! and all this thou might'ſt be in a fair way to Compass. [20

Sil. But what of my Miſtress and *Dangerfield* ?

Eust. They are all to pieces.

Sil. About what ?

Eust. About a young Maid *Dangerfield* gave her : nothing will serve but he'll have her again. [25

Sil. She will never meet with such a Loyal, Obedient Lover, as *Keepwell*.

Eust. He is the Top Cully of the Town. But here she comes her self.

Enter Bellamira.

Bell. I believe he'll come to take her away [30 by force ; but let him offer to touch her with a Finger, I'll pluck his Eyes out. I can bear with his impertinences and big words, while they are but words ; but if he offer violence, I know what he is at the bottom, and can find those that can Cudgel him. [35

Eust. I have expeƈted you a good while here.

Bell. Do you know that *Dangerfield*'s laſt Quarrel and mine was a Concern of yours ?

Eust. He was not Jealous of me ?

Bell. No : but while I endeavour'd to reſtore [40 your loſt Siſter, to you, as I think in Conscience I ought ; I suffer'd what you see, and more from him.

Eust. You have several times talk'd to me of a Siſter of mine, loſt from our house in *Devonshire* ; but I always look't upon it as a meer Wheadle. [45

Bell. One that has an ill name, is half hang'd :

but, I assure you, I was in earneſt, as I shall make appear to you by infallible Circumſtances.

Euſt. I loſt indeed a Siſter, about twelve years since, but where she is, Heaven only knows.   [50

Bell. Yes I know she is at home.

Euſt. What at your house ?

Bell. Yes at my house : my Mother bred her, as if she had been her own, you need not be asham'd to own her.   [55

Euſt. ⟨[*Aside*]⟩ She bred her up from a Child ! I like that well : then this is not she that *Dangerfield* gave her yeſterday, and that *Lionel* Ravish'd.

Bell. I doubt not of your Gratitude, when you see her : She's a delicate Creature.   [60

Euſt. How old is She ?

Bell. Seventeen.

Euſt. The very Age that *Lionel* mention'd : I am undone again ! She had my Father's Piƈture on, when she was loſt.   [65

Bell. She has it ſtill and kisses it a hundred times a day.

Euſt. A bite by a Monky upon her left arm.

Bell. She has so. If I shew her you with these Tokens will you not thank me, and own her ?   [70

Euſt. Yes, if you have not taught her your own Trade.

Bell. By my Life, she is as innocent, as when you loſt her firſt, we ever kept a ſtriƈt hand over her. By good fortune *Keepwell* gave me a fine Eunuch,   [75 to his care I have intruſted her and charg'd him not to ſtir from her.

Euſt. ⟨[*Aside.*]⟩ Hell, and Damnation ! The Eunuch was *Lionel*. I have heard as much, Madam.

Bell. Who cou'd tell you ?   [80

Euſt. I know not : I heard in the Town, you had an Eunuch.

Bell. Now let's have a care we don't both lose

her, for this is she that *Dangerfield* gave and threatens
to take away again.   [85

Euſt.   It is too apparent, no sooner found, but
loſt, my *Isabella*: Loſt, to thy Fame thy Family for
ever.

Bell.   You seem disorder'd: are you well?

Euſt.   A little surpris'd, at the unexpeſted   [90
discovery of my dear Siſter.   But why did you not
tell me this sooner?

Bell.   I had her of *Dangerfield* but yesterday.

Euſt.   Did you not tell me you were bred up
together?   [95

Bell.   Yes, but how we firſt met, how we parted,
how *Dangerfield* got her, I will tell you at more leisure,
he threatens to take her away by force; you are not
afraid of him?

Euſt.   Of no man less.   I have a sudden   [100
Qualm come over me; I have drunk too much Wine.

Bell.   Come in I'll give you some *Mirabilis*.

[*Exeunt.*

⟨SCENE VIII.   *Outside Bellamira's House.*⟩

Enter Dangerfield, Smoothly, Bullies, *and* Link
Boyes.

Dan.   I'll teach her to provoke a man of Honour,
Culverin, *Wildfire*, and *Hackum*, follow your Leader:
Firſt I'll pull the house about their Ears.

Smoo.   Spoken like your self.

Dan.   I'll slit her Nose, then give her the   [5
Trant'vne.

Smoo.   It will be a brave revenge, and make you
Terrible through the World.

Dan.   Advance *Culverin*, with the   *Link-boyes*:
Hackum command thou the right Wing; and   [10
thou *Wildfire* the left.

Boyes. Here, here, here.

Dan. I my self will bring up the Rear, give the Sign for the on-set, and be ready to assist you with my Conduct, if need be. [15

Smoo. What a Jewel is experience in a General!

Dan. I learnt this of *Monteculi*.

Eust. What bustle is that about the door?

Sil. Oh Mistress the House is beset: we are all undone. [20

Eust. Not with Thieves, I hope.

Bell. No, 'tis *Dangerfield*; fear him not, he dares do nothing: A meer blustring Coward.

Hack. Shall we break the Windows?

Dang. Not yet my valiant Friends; I see [25 *Bellamira* at her Belcony: I'll proffer Peace; and that refus'd, make War.

Smoo. O, the difference between Man and Man! I never hear this Master of mine speak, but am the wiser for it. [30

Dan. Answer me thou Punk, thou Cockatrice, thou Man-Leech, that suck'st their Marrow, and their Mony: When I gave thee *Isabella*, didst not thou promise me two days entirely to my self.

Bell. Why you over-grown Booby, gelt [35 with muddy Ale, Brandy, and Tobacco; you had 'em and cou'd make no use of 'em.

Dan. Next did not you bring your Stallion there under my Roof, talk with him in private, and after steal away to him? [40

Bell. I had some business with him, and found you had none with me, but drinking and making my head-ake.

Smoo. Oh, Impudence! this to you, that are such a *Hercules* in Love, and War. [45

Dan. Restore me *Isabella* or I'll force her from you.

Eust. She restore her! Or you touch her! I shou'd laugh at that.

Dan. Are you her *Hector* ? I shall spoil your [50
Mirth with a Brick-bat. Come down; I'll fight
thee hand to hand in the head of my Army.

Smoo. No wise General will forsake his advantages,
you shan't expose your self so rashly.

Dan. Peace you Fool : if he comes, we'l [55
seize him ; then offer him in exchange of Prisoners,
for *Isabella*. There's a ſtratagem : he shall find I
am a Souldier.

Smoo. The greateſt I ever read of.

Euſt. I will not venture my self among your [60
Hell-hounds, but I shall find a time.

Dan. You will not deliver *Isabella* then, by fair
means ?

Euſt. Nor by foul neither : She is my Siſter, too
good to be thy Wife, and shall be no Man's [65
Servant.

Dan. I bought her young of her Friends, in
Spain.

Euſt. They had no right to Sell her; she is a
freeborn *English* Woman, and I will defend [70
her with my life.

Smoo. You speak like an honeſt Gentleman :
Bellamira has cheated my Maſter. Do not make
your self a Party, and consequently this great Man
your Enemy. [75

Euſt. Perswade that Calf he is a Lion if thou
canſt ; I scorn both him, and thee.

Dan. Then 'tis no time to talk, salute 'em with a
Volley.

Enter Merryman *and* Cuningham.

Cun. Let's give *Bellamira* a Serenade, as we [80
go by, for old acquaintance sake : she'l take it kindly.

Merr. *Dangerfield*'s there : we'l break the
Windows, call him Rogue and Rascal, and ſo go on
with our Musick to *Thisbe*.

Cun. I hate these rude Frolicks. [85

Merr. The house is beset : What's here, Scourers ?
Brick-bats mounting, and Pispots descending ?

Cun. We'l scour 'em for a Company of uncivil
Fellows, thus to diſturb Lovers at their innocent
Recreations.   [90

Merr. Strike up, we have no Drums and Trumpets,
but we'l swinge 'em by way of Lute and Violin.

L. Boys. Fall on : this is our old Maſter *Merry-
man* ; we use to light him home drunk three or [94
four times a week.   [*The Link Boyes revolt.*

Dan. If our Soldiers revolt, shift every man for
himself : This did *Pompey*, when over power'd by
Julius Cæsar, at *Pharsalia*.   [*Ex. Omnes.*

ACT V. SCENE I

⟨*Outside Bellamira's House.*⟩

Merryman, Cuningham.

Cun. This drinking does so muddle one's com-
plexion and take of one's mettle, a man the next day
is but the wrong side of himself. I was so doz'd
I was an hour about a Billet dou⟨x⟩.

Merr. We shou'd look gratefully back upon [5
the paſt pleasure and not peevishly repine at the
present suffering. What think you of a hair of the
same Dog ?

Cun. That saying has kill'd many an honeſt
fellow, but do you remember we were at [10
Thisbe's ?

Merr. Yes, and were let in ; but have forgotten
moſt of the reſt.

Cun. You are a precious Guardian ! You muſt
e'en Marry her your self, you will make her [15
fit for no body elſe, with your disorderly Frolicks.

Merr. ⟨[*Aside.*]⟩   That's it I wou'd be at.   But what said she ?

Cun.   She told me, she wond'red to see me in that disorder; squeez'd me by the hand, and bad   [20 me take more care of my health hereafter.

Merr.   Now I remember me, she said you look'd lamentably; and that, had you come alone at that time of the night, she shou'd have taken you for a Ghost; that you smelt as if you had been buri'd   [25 a Fortnight.

Cun.   She may say her Pleasure; but there are as fine Women as she of another mind : I knew when she had no better a Complexion than my self.

Merr.   When was that ?   Had she ever the   [30 Green-sickness or the Yellow Jaundies ?

Cun.   No, before she bought her Paint of the *Italian.*   I look like a Ghost !   Why, I am the same man I was twenty Years ago ; as vigorous, as Amorous, and I think as taking amongst Men and Women.   [35 I had three Maiden-heads brought me last Week by their Parents : I will leap the half Almond with you.

Merr.   Thou ma'st well be active, thou hast no more flesh upon thy back, than a Flea, and thy Bones have as much Quick-silver in 'em, as ten Bales   [40 of false Dice : They will scarce lie still when thou art dead.

Cun.   Thou art *Picqu'd* at *Thisbe*'s concern for me : Well thou art an honest Fellow ; we will not dispute about her, tho we Rally one another now and   [45 then.   I have ten as fine Women as she upon my hands at this time ; she was but my *Pisallee* : What will you say when you see me Marry'd to one of the best Fortunes about the Town ?

Merr.   I shall not wonder ; Women have   [50 another Green-sickness in their Souls, that sways 'em to the Trash of Mankind : but here comes *Keepwell*, his time of Banishment is expir'd, as filthily fine as hands can make him.

Enter Keepwell.

Keep. Sure Jealousie is the greateſt Tor-   [55
ment in the World, I have had the dismalleſt Dreams !
Methought I saw *Dangerfield* Rampant, and *Bellamira*
Couchant all Night long.

Merr. You consented, and can reasonably complain
of none but your self.   [60

Keep. I consented she shou'd make a Fool of
him, and Cozen him of *Isabella*, but no farther.

Merr. I saw her at *Knightsbridge* Garden with
him; so fine, methought they were the happieſt
Couple !   [65

Keep. Pox on their happiness.

Merr. It may end in that indeed, they say *Danger-
field* is not very sound.

Cun. Women like wanton Whelps, fawn ever on
the next that comes in their way, but, when   [70
they see an old acquaintance, they run to him for all
that; never be discourag'd.

Keep. At once I hate her, and I love her too;
The Chief thing I beg'd of her was, that she wou'd
not be seen in publique with this *Dangerfield*:   [75
she has no mercy on my Reputation.

Merr. No more than on your Fortune: be wise
and take this occasion.

Cun. All this makes for you *Merryman*: there is
no such Soaker as a Lover in affliction.   [80

Merr. I had as live drink with a Gib'd Cat: they
are alwaies Mewing and Wauling about her Incon-
ſtancy, Cruelty, or one silly thing or other.

Cun. *Dangerfield* has a sweet Calech.

Merr. There is no talk of any man now but   [85
him; the Braveſt, the moſt Generous, the moſt
accomplish'd Gentleman !

Cun. You will make *Keepwell* hang himself.

Keep. I'll fight him, my Courage is wound up,
and I will ſtrike him to the heart.   [90

Merr.　You'l have an ill time on't; he kills an Humble Bee flying with a single Bullet, rides three manag'd Horses every morning, Fences two hours after, and ſtinks of Gun Powder like the fifth of *November.*　　　　　　　　　　　　　　　[95

Keep.　Then let him be hang'd, I'll have nothing to do with him.

Merr.　'Tis she is to blame, and not he: If a man Robs my Orchard, I shall blame my Gardiner more than the Thief.　　　　　　　　　　　[100

Keep.　He has done but what the beſt Lord in the Land wou'd be proud to do: but I will mawl her, break her China, take down her Hangings, leave her no Plate but the poor Thimble she began the World with.　　　　　　　　　　　　　　　　[105

Merr.　Spoken like a man of Mettle! and shall we Sup together, and drink till daylight, as we were wont?

Cun.　Thou art one of *Keepwell*'s evil Counsellors; and if ever he and *Bellamira* piece again, I shall　[110 see thee banish'd his presence for ever.

Keep.　I will never be sober again, scarce cleanly, take Tobacco and lie in a Bawdy-house.

Cun.　*Merryman* will Compound for Less.

Merr.　Half drunk every night, and ſtark　[115 drunk once a week, is very fair.

Keep.　I'll Rout her Inſtantly.

Cun.　She has a great many Rich Cloaths, let her wear out her Livery at leaſt in your Service.

Keep.　That's well thought, let her wear out　[120 her Cloaths at leaſt in my Service as he says.

Merr.　You have almoſt worn out your self in her's: you look worse than he, that begun twenty years before you.

Cun.　Every man's Conſtitution will not　[125 run out into Fat, 'tis the Commendation of a Capon: a good Cock is alwaies lean as I am.

Merr.　A good Coxcomb alwaies thinks well of himself; why thou lean Rascal Deer, thou visible

Pox, thou Common shore of Physick, Reproach [130
of Doctors, and Ruine of Apothecari's, who Flux'ſt
away thy Flesh as often as the Adder caſts his Skin,
and art full as venemous.

Cun. I am sure you look like a full Moon or a
Fat Bawd swell'd with the Tooth Ach. [135

Merr. When I walk the Streets, men say there
goes an honeſt well natur'd Fat Fellow to drink a
bottle with, and a good Husband I warrant him.

Cun. A good Cuckold perhaps : but, the Ladies
cry foh, there goes a greasie Sot, a Chandlers [140
Shop in the shape of a man, a meer Lump, a Spunge
full of Terse : whose mouth ſtinks worse than the
Bung-hole of a Barrel, a Load of manifeſt impotency,
Guts and Garbage for the Bear-Garden.

Merr. Thou meer ſtake to hang Cloaths [145
upon, thou Scarrow, thou piece of Shrivil'd Parch-
ment, thou walking Skelleton that may'ſt be read
upon alive, can'ſt thou think any Woman so sharp
set as to pick thy rotten Bones, which are but the
leaving of Pox, Mercury and Consumption ? [150

Keep. Nay good Gentlemen, no heat, let us debate
this matter calmly ; will this Quarrel about Fat and
Lean never have an end ?

Cun. 'Tis as irreconsilable as that of the Flesh
and Spirit ; *Merryman* will never let it reſt : I [155
am alwaies on the defensive part.

Keep. You never consider your poor Friend,
toss'd as I am between the Billows of Love and
Jealousie.

Merr. Well now I have Tormented you [160
sufficiently, it goes againſt my honeſt nature to con-
ceal your happiness from you any longer, *Dangerfield*
is an ugly niggardly Rogue, and *Bellamira*——

Keep. Was she never abroad with him in Publick.

Merr. Nor in Private neither, but once [165
and they fell out ; well she loves you moſt intirely,
I cou'd never have thought it.

Cun. She was all in Tears by that time you were

on Horse-back: I had the moſt ado to Comfort her,
and, yet I said a great many pretty things to   [170
her; and never look'd better in my Life.

Merr.   I sat with her two hours and our whole
discourse was of you, how much she was oblig'd to
you, and what a dear man you were.

Keep.   I ever told you *Merryman,* you were   [175
too hard of belief and that there was such a thing as
true Love, and Conſtancy too.

Merr.   I confess my error and shall hereafter think
you can never do too much for her.   I will drink her
health in a Bumper as long as I live, for her   [180
fidelity to my Friend, and in his absence too.

Cun.   If ever you leave her she'l make her self
away, that's certain, I have heard her say so a hundred
times.

Keep.   Nay, I always thought so, and durſt   [185
never Chide, nor deny any thing; she has such a
spirit.

Enter Silence.

Merr.   But here comes *Silence,* who will tell you
more.

Sil.   My Miſtress wonders you can be so   [190
long in Town and not see her.

Merr.   What, as a whole hour?

Sil.   You wou'd not have been so long out of a
Tavern.

Keep.   I hear she is taken up with *Dangerfield.*   [195

Sil.   He's a Calf, a Blockhead, and she scorns
him.

Keep.   Do. you hear this, *Merryman?*   He's a
Calf, a Blockhead, and she scorns him.

Merr.   Did not I tell you as much: and   [200
you know I was of another mind?

Sil.   My Miſtress and *Dangerfield,* are quite
fall'n out: he gave her the pretty Maid she told
you of, and came laſt night with some drunken
Bullies, to take her away by force.   [205

Cun. I am a witness of that : *Merryman* and I drove him away, and rais'd the Siege.

Sil. My Mistress will refer all to *Merryman.*

Cun. ⟨[*Aside.*]⟩ Now they are in discourse, I will steal away to Mrs. *Thisbe,* and make my excuse [210 for last night's disturbance.   [*Exit.*

Keep. Come *Merryman,* let's see what *Bellamira* can say for her self.   [*Ex. Keep. and Sil.*

Merr. I'll follow you instantly. We were fellow Robbers ; I must keep fair with *Bellamira* or [215 she may get her own Pardon, Peach, and hang me besides I have receiv'd her fee, and am bound to plead her cause.

Enter Lionel.

Lion. I am the happiest man ! Whom shall I praise first ? Thee that laid'st the Design ; [220 my self that executed it, or Fortune that gave it success ?

Merr. You have succeeded then ?

Lion. Beyond expectation.

Merr. It was a bold design.   [225

Lion. And a fortunate one for me : I must have di'd, if I had not enjoy'd her.

Merr. I will not trouble your modesty for particulars, but why in this dress still ? Do you intend to live and die in your new service ?   [230

Lion. I cou'd live and die with my new fellow Servant, I went to *Eustace*'s, thinking to have shifted, but the house was full of Company.

Merr. Are you not afraid of being known ?

Lion. No, I met *Cuningham* and twenty of [235 my acquaintance ; they star'd at me alittle.

Enter Eustace *and* Cuningham.

Eust. Here he is, and *Merryman* with him, the vile contriver of *Isabella's* ruine. *Cunningham,* I must use your Sword.

Cun. 'Tis at the service of any Gentleman, [240

much more at yours that are my Friend.   But againſt whom ?

Euſt.   You see the man.

Cun.   What my old acquaintance *Merryman*, and that young fellow ?   [245

Euſt.   That young fellow is *Lionel*.   When you hear it, you'l say my Quarrel's Juſt, the Injury not to be pardon'd.

Lion.   My deareſt *Euſtace*!   The Man of all the World I wish'd to meet.   [250

Euſt.   And *Lionel* the Man of all the World I am bound to Curse.

Lion.   Some Villain has abus'd me to my Friend : I'll cut his Throat.

Euſt.   That Villain is your self.   [255

Lion.   Villain !   Death, I wou'd have shar'd my Fortune, my Reputation, my all, but *Isabella*, with that Man, and to be thus requited.

Euſt.   That Name has rouz'd up my Revenge : Draw and prepare for thy defence.   [260

Lion.   What means my Friend⟨?⟩ is he become my Rival ?

Euſt.   That shou'd not make this breach I'd turn the Boyish Passion out of doors, And fly to the embraces of my Friend.   [265

Lion.   Am I reported to have wrong'd you in my discourse ?

Euſt.   I'd Kick the Liar shou'd tell me so.   O that I were so happy as to doubt !   You have accus'd your self.   [270

Lion.   Of what ?

Euſt.   Of an injury so great, to me, and all our Family——

Lion.   To you ?   Whose Injuries I count my own, and shou'd alike resent 'em.   [275

Euſt.   Revenge me then upon Luſtful *Lionel*.

Lion.   Sure you are mad, for what ?

Euſt.   Why, for a Rape upon my Siſter.

Lion. I know no Sister that you have.

Eust. That's our misfortune, that thou [280 knew'st her not; far hadst thou wrong'd me with thy Will, I cou'd kill thee as men do *Wolves* and *Tigers*; but now must pay a cruel Sacrifice to Honour.

Lion. I understand you less and less.

Eust. Know then (for it is just I tell our [285 Quarrel e'r we Fight) that *Isabella* was my Sister.

Lion. What the young Maid at *Bellamira*'s! 'Tis impossible.

Eust. By certain Tokens and Circumstances, to me invincible, I know her so. [290

Lion. You amaze me!

Merr. *Lionel*, thou wert wrapt in thy Mother's Smock. Thy *Isabella*, whom thou lov'st of all the World is found the Sister of thy dearest friend. What then remains, but that you Marry her? [295

Eust. I know his Honour is too nice: nothing remains but that we Fight.

Lion. I love my *Isabella* above my Life
And all the little niceties of Honor;
And had rather call her mine than be Crown'd [300
King of all the habitable World.

Eust. Then we are ti'd in stricter Bonds than ever. Oh my best *Lionel*!

Lion. Throw not away the Treasure of thy Love, [305
Upon a Soil so Barren:—my Father——

Eust. I can easily satisfie all his scruples. She had five Thousand pounds left her by an Uncle: to which I'll add to make her worthy of my dearest Friend. [310

Lion. I know not how to speak, and yet I must.

Eust. Thou found'st her apt and easie to thy Lust: Ha,

Lion. By all that's good, I hold her Innocent, as violated Temples. [315

Eust. Wert not thou then a sacrilegious Villain?

Lion. It is confess'd.

Merr. Now you have confess'd, it is but doing Pennance in a pair of Matrimonial Sheets, and there's an end on't. [320

Eust. I was to blame, to trifle all this while. Draw.

Cun. I must have a thrust at thy fat Guts.

[*Fight.* Merr. *disarms* Cunn. *and parts the other.*

Merr. Now are thy Skin and Bones, at my Mercy.

Eust. This satisfies my Honour; but my Revenge must find some other time. [325

Lion. What if I were long since contracted to another, and to be disinherited if I went back.

Eust. You might have told me so⟨.⟩ Yet what cou'd that have done?

Lion. Perhaps you wou'd not have believ'd [330 me, and it might have look'd like Fear, till we had Fought; but now take the sad truth, and if thou wilt the Life of *Lionel*: I have been sometime since contracted to *Theodosia*, the rich Gold-smith's Daughter. [335

Cun. If that be all, you are as free as you were born. You are all men of Honour, and I'll tell you a secret, I have this Morning privately Marri'd that pretty Creature.

Lion. It is impossible I shou'd be so happy. [340

Cun. She heard I know not how, that you ravish'd a young Maid, and were in Love elsewhere: I came in the lucky minute, and am now her Husband.

Merr. In the unlucky minute to her. How came she to think of thee? [345

Cun. She did not; her Maid that Governs her, was formerly a Servant to a Mistress of mine, has often tasted of my Bounty and some other civilities have past between us.

Merr. What cou'd she find to say for thee? [350

Cun. She told her Mistress, her Father was one of my Tenants, and that I had a thousand a year in *Northumberland*, to her knowledge.

Merr. Thou art a luckie Fellow: the Women will venture Body and Soul to do thee Service [355 any way.

Cun. I had miss'd her for all that, but for a Hundred pound I gave a Nonconformiſt Parson for his good word. Cou'd I have thought the news of my Marriage with *Theodosia* wou'd have [360 pleas'd you, you shou'd have heard of it sooner.

Lion. Joy, such as thou giv'ſt me now, be ever with thee.

Cun. I was half afraid we muſt have had a Tilt.

Lion. Will you be my Advocate to your [365 offended Siſter?

Euſt. You need none, since your Designs are Honorable.

Lion. Let's embrace like Brothers: for the next Prieſt shall make us so. [370

Enter Bellamira, Silence, Betty, *and* Keepwell.

Sil. Madam, there's the Rogue that has made all this work.

Bett. I never lik'd him, he has a slie look; and a Hawks Eie with him.

Sil. 'Twas a mercy any of us scap'd. [375

Bell. Peace you Fools; he is a Gentleman, and may make her Reparation. We are undone ruin'd for ever! Your unfortunate Siſter whom I under-took to reſtore you.

Euſt. What of her? [380

Bell. She has been ravish'd, and by that Villain you embrace. But now I am asham'd to offer her thus ſtain'd and sulli'd; but 'twas no fault of mine.

Lion. Oh bring her inſtantly⟨,⟩ the *Roman Lucrece,* was not more virtuous; nor an Eſtate [385 to one in Goal for Debt more welcome, than she to *Lionel.*

Keep. Think what you do; Marry a Servant, my Father will be in Town anon.

Lion. She is the Siſter of my deareſt [390

Eustace. And above me in Wealth, as in desert.
He cannot but approve my Choice.

Keep. When you are Marri'd I'll take my pleasure
like an *Italian* elder Brother, and now my dearest,
Bellamira, we are safe for one seven years.   [395

Lion. My Father's appetite of Grand-Children
I'll undertake to satisfie, if you'l pardon my making
bold with your house.

Bell. I take it the best way, and charge it all on
Love, whose power we most of us have felt. [400
You seem a worthy Gentleman.

Lion. A poor younger Brother of your Servant
Keepwell's.

Eust. How came you to find us here?

Bell. We heard that there were Swords [405
drawn; but saw no such matter.

Enter Dangerfield *and* Smoothly.

Smooth. There she is; but so hem'd in with
friends and acquaintance, we had best let her alone.

Dan. She is a victorious Beauty, I will go and
Surrender my self to her.   [410

Smooth. Let's make honourable Conditions.

Dan. I will yield to mercy, *Hercules* did so to
Omphale.

Smooth. The Example's great.

Keep. What's that thing in Buff.   [415

Bell. 'Tis *Dangerfield*: I thought you had known
him.

Keep. He looks like a Militia Captain upon a
Training day.

Merr. You had best tell him so.   [420

Keep. My heart's too big; I can't endure to speak
to him.

Dan. Who is that next *Merryman*?

Smooth. Your Rival *Keepwell*.

Dan. I can no more endure the sight of a   [425
Rival than a fighting Cock can: Hold me, or I shall
fly in his Face.

V. i. 428.

Bell. What wou'd that fellow have?

Dan. Your Pardon, for my laſt night's rudeness; and my *Isabella*, the pritty Maid I gave you, if you please.   [430

Euſt. Name her no more: I tell thee she is my Siſter a free-born Subjeçt of *England*.

Lion. If thou doſt but name her tho in thy sleep, I'll cut thy Throat: She is my Miſtress.   [435

Merr. Speak to him, *Keepwell*: we'l bring you off.

Keep. She is to be my Siſter-in-law; and I will flea thee, ſtuff thy Skin full of Straw, and Set thee in my Cherry-Garden, if thou depart not.

Dan. I am utterly undone; if I find not some way into this Family: the less hope ⟨I⟩ see, the more I love this *Bellamira*.   [440

Smooth. What if I get you receiv'd among 'em, according to your desert?

Dan. Command me and mine for ever: I'll give thee fifty Guineas hard Money in hand, and the Sword I twice sav'd the Nation with.   [445

Smooth. Retire a little, 'tis not fit you shou'd be by, at your own Commendations. I'll try what I can do; you have been a good Maſter to me. [450 [*Exit Dang.*] I hope all this good Company believes I follow'd this Fool my Maſter more for my own sake than his?

Merr. None but himself ever doubted it.

Smooth. I have thought of it seriously, and find you can't do better than to receive this Blunderbus, my Maſter, into your Family.   [455

Keep. What? A Rival! I will as soon receive a Roaring Lion.

Smooth. Yes, such a one as he is: a Fool, a Blockhead, a Coward, a Knave that ne'r paid.   [460

Merr. For his Cowardice I can answer: he ſtood to be robb'd, like a Cow to be Milk'd.

Bell. He carri'd me to Supper, and drank himself faſt asleep by me.   [465

Cun. If he be such a one, what shou'd Ladies do with him ?

Smooth. He loves Play : you may win his Mony, and he has abundance : if he refuse to Play, you may beat him till he will.   [470

Cun. I have not heard of a more useful acquaintance, he muſt not be refus'd :

Smooth. You need not fear any Woman shou'd like him he has been impotent these seven years : when you are weary of him you may Kick him   [475 out of doors.

Euſt. He is a man of a thousand : let me intreat for him.

Keep. He shall be admitted, but if he do not prove this Fool, this Coward you speak of, you   [480 had better be hang'd.

Smooth. My life for't. Now, Gentlemen, take me into your Prot"ction, and then Eat, Drink upon, and Laugh at the Fool my Maſter.

Merr. He deserves it abundantly, for keep-   [485 ing such a Rascal.

Keep. Call in *Dangerfield*, and let him know he is receiv'd without a Negative.

Smooth. Sir you may come in, the whole Company bids you welcome.   [490

Re-enter Dangerfield.

Keep. Moſt welcome, noble *Dangerfield*!

Cun. I shall be proud of your farther acquaintance.

Merr. I shall be glad to drink a Gallon of Wine with you at the Rose, we will write you of our Club.

Bell. I never knew a Civiller person ! I was   [495 once abroad with him, and he did not offer me the leaſt rudeness.

Dan. Gentlemen if any of you want a Second, I am at your service : And Ladies, if any man speaks ill of you, or Lampoon you, I'll cut his throat :   [500 Thou haſt charm'd 'em ; I thought they wou'd have

torn me to pieces e'en now: There are Fifty Guineas
I promis'd thee.

Smooth. I hope Sir, you'l find I have deserv'd 'em;
they did not know your worth; but when I   [505
inform'd 'em of your good Qualities and Parts, I
foresaw they cou'd do no less.

Dang. Nay, I never came in any place in my
life, but when I was well known I got the Love of
Man, Woman, and Child.   [510

Bell. Now you see what a fellow this *Dangerfield*
was to be Jealous off.

Keep. Where there is no Jealousie, there is no
Love.

Bell. I have had no other Proof of your   [515
Love these two months.

Keep. Thou shalt have proofs of all kinds.

Bell. So you say alwaies.

Keep. I have been in the Country, and have
brought wherewith to pay old Scores, and will   [520
deal hereafter with ready Mony.

Bell. We muſt have a general Act of Oblivion,
now you are one of us no heart burnings hereafter.

Dan. I declare I am in Charity with all the World,
but that Fat Thief that laid on me so unmerci-   [525
fully.

Bell. He muſt be comprehended too.

Dan. I cannot in Honour, unless you lay your
positive commands.

Bell. You shall never queſtion him at Law,   [530
nor otherwise.

Dan. By these Hilts, I never will then.

Merr. Then here are the six Guineas you swore
were a hundred, your false Rings, filthy Medals,
Table book, and other Pocket-Lumber.   [535

Bell. And *Merryman* and I were the whole Dozen
of Robbers, you swore againſt.

Euſt. What, my valiant Bully, you and your man
robb'd by two; and one of 'em a Woman!

Dan. As I was going to draw, I heard a [540
voice cry, hold, hold, thy dead doing hand; strike
not: it is thy Mistress, *Dangerfield*.

Eust. You *Smoothly*, you heard this voice too?

Smooth. As perfectly as my Master, one might
have heard it to *Knightsbridge*: besides there is [545
something in a man of Honour that keeps him from
striking a Lady.

Enter Lionel *with* Isabella.

Lion. Can you forgive your *Lionel*?
He never will commit a second Fault.

Merr. Not of the same kind, I'll answer for [550
him.

Isa. My heart was your's, when we first met in
Spain.
You seiz'd the rest somewhat too rudely here:
But I am your Wife, and now am all obedience. [555

Eust. How shall I thank Heaven, and *Bellamira*
for her care of thee?

Isa. My former troubles vanish like a Dream,
And ⟨I⟩ am wak'd to perfect happiness
By that voice; Oh, my dearest Brother! [560

Eust. I shou'd have known her any where; she is
as little alter'd, as 'tis possible.

Bell. Husband and Brother I must yield to them;
but the third Joy is mine. My *Isabella* ⟨,⟩ was *Lionel*
the man thou saw'st in *Spain*? And mad'st [565
that pretty innocent discription of?

Isa. The same: I never lov'd another, and now
I never shall.

Lion. How many accidents have met, to make
this happy day! [570
The least of which is half a Miracle.

Merr. Does not your mouth water, at these
Amorous preparations?

This. Not at a greasie bit of a fat Drunkard. I
am not ambitious of holding your head in a [575

morning, or carrying you to *HampSted*, to get you a stomach to a Drunken Supper.

Merr. Your proud heart will come down, when you have faSted from Man a year longer, and been arreSted once or twice more.   [580

This. I might have gone to Goal for all my worshipful Guardian.

Merr. Oh, vanity! vanity! What Knight-Errant, do you think wou'd lay down two Hundred pound for you.   [585

This. *EuStace* knows beSt, he brought the Mony; but whoever he were that sent it, if he have but so much a year, I'll Marry him before any man in *England*.

Merr. What tho he love Wine, Women, [590 and Tobacco, and were as Fat as I am?

This. Yes, with all your faults, and as many more of his own.

EuSt. Then take her *Merryman*, she is thine, by her Confession: 'Twas his Mony that did [595 satisfie the debt, and I was but employ'd by him.

Lion. We are all Witnesses; there is no going back.

Cun. She is proof againSt all Mankind, for I have Courted her these six Months, yet never [600 cou'd obtain the leaSt indecent favour.

This. Since it muSt be so, I hope you'l prove as indulgent a Husband, as you were a Guardian.

Merr. My little charge, if thou had'St not taken pity on me I shou'd have kill'd my self with [605 Whoring and Drinking; but now I will beget Sons and Daughters till threescore.

Cun. Gentlemen your Company is so good, I had almoSt forgot I was Marry'd this Morning. *Lionel*, I hope we shall have no suit in the [610 Prerogative Court, tho I have Marry'd your MiStress.

Lion. Thou art my Redeemer, and haSt broken that Knot I shou'd have been troubled to untie.

Theodosia was my Father's Choice (her Bags were contracted to his Acres). But *Isabella*'s mine. [615

    Keep. These Roguish Fidlers smell a Wedding already; since—— They are come Let's dance——

                          [They Dance.

    Keep. My *Bell.* and I will lead a marri'd Life,
Bating the odious Names of Man and Wife;
In Chains of Love alone we will be ty'd,   [620
And every Night I'll use her like a Bride.

    Merr. Wits, Whore-Masters, Gamesters, Drunk-
    ards, Bullies,
We in our several wayes are all but Cullies.   [624

                          [Exeunt Omnes.

EPILOGUE

Like a young Wench that cou'd not well forbear,
And yet is loath her Lewdness shou'd appear.
Our modeſt Poet wou'd have made away
In private, this mere lump you see to day.
We bid him lay the Bantling at our door   5
And for th'event concern himself no more.
Poets of late with humane Sacrifice
Have feaſted you like Heathen Deities.
In every Play they serv'd you up a man
Nay some at Parties and whole Factions ran ?   10
After such fare, how flat muſt Terence *taſte ?* ⎫
Yet his plain Tales have had the luck to laſt. ⎬
While your fam'd Authors, in their life time waſt. ⎭
Ye all cry out the art of Writings loſt
Yet nicer Judgments in perfection boaſt.   15
Strange Stars ; malignant to Poetick ſtrains
Yet so productive of Judicious brains.
What if you Judge, as ill as others Write ?
And only loath for want of appetite ;
No Jew *into the* Sanhedrim *might come*   20
That had no Issue of his own at home.
For barrenness supposes cruelty
No Childless man, might others Children try.
This wholesome Law wou'd save us from the spight
Of all the furious Wits that cannot Write.   25
And you that do, we shou'd not fear your doom
If you'd Judge here but as you Judge at home ;
Now Gallants moſt of you are so well bred ⎫
French *has long since chas'd* Latin *from your head* ⎬
And Terence *yo have forgot or never read.* ⎭   30
Faith spare 'um both, leſt your chance medly Wit
Miss the Translator and the Author hit.

AN ESSAY ON ENTERTAINMENTS

Marcus Varro, in a Treatise written of the Number 1
of Guests; the Disposition and Order of an elegant
Supper; the Choice, Condition and Quality of such
as are invited; begins with their Number, which, he
says, ought not to be less than the Graces, nor greater 5
than that of the Muses : in plain English, not less than
three, nor more than nine.—They ought not to be
many, that every Man may have his turn of speaking
as well as hearing. A great Table is subject to Noise,
and Disorder; a Number of Equals cannot easily be 10
kept with in the Bounds of Decency and Respect one
to another.—Four things are principally required in
what he calls an elegant Supper.—The Guests must
be Men of some Quality, well bred, and not ill drest.—
The Place must be well chosen; retir'd from publick 15
View, and the common Disturbances of Passengers and
Business; where they may hear no Noise, but what
they make.—The Time convenient, not too late, nor
too early; for an early Supper comes too fast upon a
late Dinner; and a late Supper takes too much of the 20
Night from our natural Rest; and consequently too
much of the next Day from Business.—The Linnen,
the Room, the Servants, and what we now call the
Bufett, rather clean and neat, than pompous or magnifi-
cent : the Supper such as some of the invited may give 25
in their turn without hurting themselves.—Not all
great talkers, nor too silent; but ingenious Men,
knowing when to speak, and when to hear; rather
facetious, witty and agreeable, than contentious,
rhetorical, or eloquent : Eloquence is proper in a 30
great Assembly or Senate; Contention for the Bar or

Courts of Juſtice; but in a private Company a shorter
Way of Expression, and a quicker Turn of Wit is more
acceptable.—The Gueſts shou'd not be all old, nor all
young Men: for old Men talk of nothing but what 35
was done twenty Years ago; and young Fellows of
nothing but the Amours, the Disorders, and Debauches
of laſt Week; the Old ought to put on as much Youth
as they can on such Occasions; and the Young a
temporary Gravity, that the two Extreams may meet in 40
a third Point.—Stories ought to be sparingly ventur'd
upon, for they impose too long a Silence on the reſt
of the Company, and may offend three Ways, either
by being tedious, common, or unpleasant.—The
Conversation shou'd not role or dwell upon State- 45
affairs, private Business, or Matters of Intereſt, which
Men are apt to dispute with more Heat, Concern, and
Animosity, than is consiſtent with the good Humour
and Mirth principally intended at such Meetings; in
which we shou'd rather talk of pleasant, chearful and 50
delightful Subjeċts, such as Beauty, Painting, Musick,
Poetry, the Writers of the paſt and present Age;
whereby we may at once improve and refresh our
Wits; not wrack and torture them with knotty, rugged
and contradiċtory Disputes, occasion'd often by an 55
Affeċtation of Superiority, which is the worſt Effeċt,
and greateſt Proof of Self-conceit.—Such Men think
themselves in the right; because others will not give
themselves the vain trouble of telling them they are in
the wrong, which is oftner a Tribute paid by modeſt 60
Men to their invincible Obſtinacy, than an Acknow-
ledgment of their superiour Judgment.—Every Man
ought to be left to his liberty in point of Wine, as well
as Meat; for amongſt Men, as well as Horses, some 65
want the Curb, and some the Spur.

APPENDIX

WORKS ASCRIBED TO SEDLEY ON
DOUBTFUL AUTHORITY

THE

Grumbler:

A

COMEDY

OF

THREE ACTS.

Never before printed.

[Publisher's Device]

LONDON, printed 1719.

EDITOR'S PREFACE

" THE GRUMBLER " is a fairly close and a very able translation of the famous French farce, " Le Grondeur " by D. A. de Brueys and J. de Palaprat. As it only appeared for the first time in Briscoe's edition of 1722, it cannot be assigned to Sedley with absolute certainty, but the translation is so well done that it is highly probable that it is the work of the author of " Bellamira." It is a play that would be very suitable for performance by amateurs, and, as it was never produced at a public theatre in Sedley's lifetime, it may be supposed that he translated it for an amateur company.

The Abbé David Augustin de Brueys (1640–1723) and Jean de Palaprat (1650–1721) collaborated in a number of dramatic works in the last years of the eighteenth century. " Le Grondeur " was originally a full-dress comedy in five acts, but was cut down to its present dimensions because of the hostility of the critics. It was performed at the Théâtre Français on February 3, 1691, and was published in 12mo, Paris, 1693. It was at first a failure, but the Prince de Condé came to see it, and was so pleased that he infected the Court with his enthusiasm, and it was played before the king. Since then it has been part of the classic repertory of the French theatre. Brueys's frank comment on the play must be recorded:

> " C'est une bonne pièce. Le premier Acte est excellent; il est tout à moi; le second coussi coussi: *Palaprat* y a travaillé; pour le troisième, il ne vaut pas le diable. Je l'avois abandoné à ce barbouilleur."

" The Grumbler " was twice adapted for the stage in the eighteenth century, firstly by Garrick in 1754 (see Genest, IV. 391), and secondly by Goldsmith as a benefit for the actor, Quick, in 1773. Garrick's adaptation was never published, but a specimen scene of Goldsmith's version is printed in his " Miscellaneous Works," London, 1837, 8vo, IV. 333.

William Archer in " The Old Drama and the New " (p. 199 n.) writes of " The Grumbler " as follows:

> " *The Grumbler*, Sedley's excellent translation of *Le Grondeur* of Brueys and Palaprat, was not produced till fifty years after his death. It is significant that this gay and sparkling character-farce, crystal clear and brimful of comic invention, apparently made no appeal to the vitiated taste of the sixteen-nineties."

DRAMATIS PERSONÆ

⟨MEN⟩

Mon. *Grichard,* the Grumbler.
Aristus, his Brother.
Terignan, Son to *Grichard.*
Mondore, In Love with *Hortensia.*
Mamurra, Tutor to *Brillon.*
⟨M. *de Saint Alvar.*⟩
⟨*Fadel,* M. *de Saint Alvar*'s Brother-in-law.⟩
Brillon, Grichard's youngest Son.
⟨*Lolive,*⟩ Footman ⟨to *Grichard.*⟩

WOMEN

Hortensia, Grichard's Daughter.
Clarice, in Love with *Terignan.*
Catau, Hortensia's Maid.

Scene *Paris.*
The House of Monsieur *Grichard.*

THE GRUMBLER: A COMEDY, &c.

ACT I

SCENE I

Terignan and Hortensia, *the Grumbler's Eldest Son and Daughter.*

Ter. But, Sister, What can this Delay mean?

Hor. We shall know when my Father returns out of the City.

Ter. I must know it sooner, if it be possible.

Hor. You have sent *Lolive* to my Uncle's; and I, *Catau,* to *Clarice's* to inquire into it; they will soon be here.   [5

Ter. How tedious they are! And how great my Pain in the Uncertainty I'm under!

Hor. Here's *Catau* coming already.

SCENE II

To them, Catau.

Ter. Well! What have you learn'd at *Clarice's?*

Cat. Monsieur *Saint-Alvar* her Father was gone abroad, and *Clarice* was not stirring, But . . . .

Hor. But . . . . What?

Cat. Don't you know by my Air that I bring you good News? [5

Hor. What News?

Cat. You will both of you be marry'd this Evening. Monsieur *Saint-Alvar's* House is still full of the Preparations that are making for your Nuptials.

Hor. I told you so, Brother.   [10

Ter. I shall not be easy in my Mind 'till I hear from my Father's own Mouth, the Reason of last Night's put off.

Hor. See then if my Father be come back.   [*To* Cat.

Cat. Good: He come back! And we not hear him! Does he ever cease bawling, grumbling, and storming so long as he's in [15 the House? And are not the very Neighbours sensible whenever he comes in or goes out?

Hor. Prithee, *Catau,* assist us but to day; let him do what he will, we are resolv'd to please him.

Cat. Please him? They must be very cunning who can [20 do that: This Father of yours is a terrible Mortal, on my Word.

107

Hor. We are oblig'd to bear with him, as bad as he is.

Cat. No Servant, Male or Female, can stay with him at most above five or six Days. Whenever we want a Domestick, 'tis in vain to think to get one in the Neighbourhood, or even throughout [25 the whole City; we are forc'd to send into a Country, where they never hear of Monsieur *Grichard* the Physician. Little *Brillon* your Brother, whom he loves of all things, has had three several Masters within this Month, because they did not chastise him as he would have them. For my part, I had long since been far enough off, [30 if the Affection I have for you, . . . But here's *Lolive.*

SCENE III

To them, Lolive.

Ter. Well, What says my Uncle to you?   [*Hastily.*

Lol. [*Deliberately.*] The first thing, Sir, that he ask'd me was, Whether the honest Gentleman, your Father, to whom he had recommended me, was satisfy'd with me. I answer'd, that I was not over-well satisfy'd with him, and that for these two Days which I [5 serv'd him, it has not been possible for me . . . .

Ter. [*Interrupting.*] Well, well, let that alone; and only tell me whether he did not know for what reason my Marriage with *Clarice* has been deferr'd.

Hor. And whether he has heard any thing further concerning [10 mine with *Mondore.*

Lol. That's what I was coming to.

Cat. Why, come then and be far enough!

Lol. In the very Moment that I was inquiring about your Affairs, in comes *Clarice*'s Father, and he had not an Opportunity of [15 speaking to me.

Ter. So you learn'd nothing?

Lol. Pardon me, Sir.

Hor. He listen'd to their Discourse, I suppose.

Lol. Yes, Madam.   [20

Cat. And what did they say?

Lol. I'm going to tell you: They went aside by themselves; they nodded to me to keep at Distance; *They* fell to Whispering, and *I* heard nothing.

Cat. Well inform'd truly!   [25

Lol. Better than you think for.

Ter. But at this rate thou canst know nothing.

Lol. Pardon me, Sir.

Hor. My Uncle then told it thee, or some other, after Monsieur *Saint-Alvar* was gone?   [30

Lol. Pardon me, Madam.

Cat. How the Devil dost thou know it then?

Lol. Pray have Patience; you don't yet know half my Talents; when People have any Secrets together, they are cautious of Servants: Now I, from the Time I've serv'd, have made it my Study to [35 guess People.

Cat. Deuce take the Fool!

Lol. Yes; and I have made such Progress, that let but two Persons, whose Affairs I'm acquainted with, discourse together with some little Action, I will only look them in the Face, and will lay [40 you any Wager, by their Gestures, and the Air of their Countenance, to give you Word for Word what they said.

Cat. He's turn'd Fool!

Ter. But, to conclude, What is it thou expectest then?

Lol. That your Affairs have chang'd their Aspect. [45

Hor. How do you know?

Lol. First and foremost, because Monsieur *Saint-Alvar* wou'd say nothing to Monsieur *Aristus* while I was by.

Ter. Ah, Sister, that is but too likely.

Lol. I have not told you all yet. [50

Hor. Knowest thou ought beside?

Lol. Oh, Yes, yes, yes. Scarce had *Clarice*'s Father open'd his Mouth, but see how your Uncle reply'd. Pray observe.

　　　　　[*He makes Signs, and mimicks the Actions of a Man*
　　　　　　　　surpris'd and angry.]

Cat. What a dickens dost thou mean?

Lol. Don't you see it? Why 'tis as plain as the Sun at [55 Noon-day. Master understands me, I dare say.

Ter. My Mind sufficiently misgives me.

Lol. And Madam too.

Hor. I don't comprehend it at all.

Lol. I will explain it to you. When your Uncle did thus [60 *he mimicks the same again*] you may be sure he was surpris'd, amaz'd, and in a Wrath at what Monsieur *Saint-Alvar* had said to him: These Actions speak of themselves. Consider, if with these Gestures he cou'd say any thing but How? Have ye chang'd your Mind? What do I hear? Is it possible? [65

Ter. What said Monsieur *Saint-Alvar* to that?

Lol. He made this Reply. [*Here he Acts a Man excusing himself.*]

Cat. And what mean these Actions?

Lol. As for these, they are Equivocal.

Cat. Not at all: I think them as clear as the other. [70

Lol. Do you explain them again for a Trial.

Cat. Explain them your self, since you have begun.

Lol. This may signify that he excus'd him upon his being oblig'd to change his Resolution. Thus, I am very sorry for it, I cou'd not do otherwise, Monsieur *Grichard* wou'd have it so: Or it might [75 likewise signify, that the Absence of Monsieur *Mondore* occasion'd the deferring your Nuptials.

Cat. What? Didst thou find all that by their Gesture?

Lol. If I err a Syllable, I'll hang for't.

Cat. You're a Fool; I tell you, it cannot be. *Clarice* is the [80 only Child of Monsieur *Saint-Alvar*, who is a rich Gentleman, and your Father's Friend: *Mondore*, is a Man of Quality, whose Estate and Merit are answerable to his Birth : Your Marriages were yesterday determin'd, Word given, Contracts drawn, and nothing to do but to sign and seal. He does not know what he says. [85

Lol. I don't think I'm mistaken for all that.

Cat. And yet thou heardst nothing at all.

Lol. No, but I saw; and Mens Actions are less deceitful than their Words.

Ter. I tremble lest it shou'd prove true. [90

Cat. You stick at meer Visions; I tell you I just now saw the Nuptial Preparations.

Lol. Those Preparations perhaps are what offended Monsieur *Grichard.* You know he has a perfect Aversion for whatever is call'd Feastings, Balls, Assignations, Concerts, Diversions, and in [95 short, for every thing that is capable of inspiring Joy.

Hor. However it be, Do you go and exactly perform what my Father bade thee when he went forth, that so at his Return, he may here find no Occasion to be angry.

Cat. Adieu, Interpreter of ill Luck : Go and comment upon [100 the Grimaces of our Monkey.

[*Exit* Lol.

SCENE IV

Ter. What *Lolive* has said redoubles my Alarms.

Cat. You have not made your Father acquainted with your Love of *Clarice* ?

Ter. No, no : On the contrary he suspects I love *Nerina*, the Daughter of a Physician, whom he has no great Kindness for; [5 and the better to conform him in his Error, when he yesterday pro-pos'd to me the Beautiful *Clarice*, I pretended a great Unwillingness.

Cat. You did very well.

Hor. Neither does he know my Sentiments towards *Mondore*, and even believes that I have never seen him any more than he [10 has, because he is almost always at the Army.

Cat. So much the better; beware you don't let him know these Matches are agreeable to you; cross-grain'd Tempers, like him, are never for doing what one wou'd have them, and are always for doing what one wou'd not have them. [15

[*A knocking.*]

Hor. Somebody knocks, and smartly too : See who 'tis.

Cat. It is undoubtedly your Father : No, Heav'n be prais'd, 'tis Monsieur *Aristus.*

SCENE V

To them, Aristus ⟨and *Lolive.*⟩

Ter. Well, Uncle, How go our Affairs ?
Ar. Very ill.
Ter. Ah Heav'ns !
Hor. How Uncle ?
Ar. You⟨r⟩ Father's at my Heels, retire, leave him to me, I [5
will endeavour to reduce him to Reason.
Ter. I much fear it.
Ar. Begone, I say, and wait for me in your Apartment, I will
come, and give you an Account of every thing : Fly, he's here.
Cat. I say fly too : For here comes a Storm, a Tempest, [10
Hail, Thunder, and something worse. The Devil take the hindmost.
                              [*Exeunt all but* Lolive *and* Aristus.

SCENE VI

To them, Grichard, *the Grumbler.*

Gr. Rascal, will you always make me knock two Hours at the
Door ?
Lol. I was at work, Sir, in the Garden : At the first Stroke of the
Knocker I made such haste, I fell upon my Nose.
Gr. Wou'd thou hadst broke thy Neck, Hang-Dog; Why [5
don't you leave the Door open ?
Lol. You was angry with me yesterday, Sir, because it was open :
When it is open you are offended ; when it is shut you are offended
no less : For my part I know not what to do.
Gr. What to do !   [10
Ar. Brother will you . . . .
Gr. [*Interrupting.*] Pray be quiet. What to do !
Ar. Pray Brother, let your Servant alone, and suffer me to speak
to you concerning . . . .
Gr. Sir Brother, when you chide your Servants, you are [15
suffer'd to do it without Molestation.
Ar. We must let the Storm pass, I see.
Gr. What to do ! Scoundrel.
Lol. Sir, . . . When you go abroad, Will you please to have the
Door left open ?   [20
Gr. No.
Lol. Will you please to have it kept shut ?
Gr. No.
Lol. But, Sir . . . .
Gr. Again dost thou argue ; Sot ?   [25
Ar. Methinks, Brother, after all, he does not argue amiss : A
Man shou'd be glad to have a rational Servant.

I. vi. 28.

Gr. And methinks, Brother, that you argue very ill: Yes, a Man shou'd be glad to have a reasonable Servant but not a Servant that will reason.   [30

Lol. Oons, wou'd I had no Reason; if this be the Trade!

Gr. Will you hold your Tongue?

Lol. Sir, if you cut me as small as minc'd Meat, a Door must be either open or shut: Chuse you which you'd have it.

Gr. I have told you, ye Rogue, above a thousand Times, I'll have [35 it . . . . I'll . . . But ye Dog, Does it become you to ask me Questions? If I take you in Hand, I'll show you how I'd have it. You laugh, methinks, Mr. Lawyer?   [*To his Brother.*

Ar. I? Not at all: I know Servants do not always do as they're bid.   [40

Gr. And yet you gave me this Hedge-bird.

Ar. I thought I did well.

Gr. Oh I thought! Know Mr. Sneerer, that *I thought* is not the Language of a sensible Man.

Ar. Well, well, let us drop that, Brother, and permit me to speak [45 to you about a more important Affair, of which I should be glad . . . . .

Gr. [*Interrupting.*] No, I will first let you see how I am serv'd by this Whoresbird, that you may not afterwards come and say that I'm angry without Cause: You shall see, you shall see. Have you swept the Stair-Case, good Mr. Prater?   [*To Lol.*] [50

Lol. Yes, Sir, from Top to Bottom.

Gr. And the Court-yard?

Lol. If you find therein any more Dirt than you do here, I'll lose my Wage⟨s⟩.

Gr. You have not water'd my Mule?   [55

Lol. Sir, ask the Neighbours if they did not see me go by.

Gr. Did you give him any Oats?

Lol. Yes, Sir, *William* was present.

Gr. But you have not carry'd those Bottles of *Quinquina*, where I order'd you?   [60

Lol. But I have Sir, and brought the empty Bottles back.

Gr. My Letters, Did you put them into the Post? Hem . . . . .

Lol. You may be sure, Sir, I would not fail in that, neither did I.

Gr. I have a hundred times forbid you scraping that damn'd [65 Fiddle; and yet you was at it agen this Morning: Thrum, thrum.

Lol. This Morning, Lord Sir, Don't you remember you broke it yesterday into a thousand Pieces?

Gr. I'll be hang'd if those two Loads of Wood are yet . . .

Lol. They're pil'd, Sir: And since that, I have help'd *William* [70 to put a Load of Hay in the Loft; I have water'd every Tree in the Garden; I have sweep'd the Walks; I have dug three Beds, and was finishing another when you knock'd.

Gr. Oh! I must put this Rogue away; never did Servant make

I. vi. 75.

a Master so mad as he does me ; he wou'd kill me with Vexation : [75
Away ! Out of my Sight !

Lol. What a Devil has he been eating ?

Ar. [*Pitying him.*] Get out of his Way.   [*Exit* Lol.

SCENE VII

Ar. In Truth, Brother, you are of a very strange Humour, by
what I see ; you don't take Servants to use them, and to have the
Benefit of their Service : You only take them to have the Pleasure of
growling at them.

Gr. Bibble babble : Give the Goose more Hay !   [5

Ar. You turn away a Servant, because, in doing what you com-
manded, and even more, he gives you no occasion of chiding ; or
rather you are angry, because you have not wherewithal to be angry.

Gr. Gramercy, Mr. Counsellor ; control my Actions.

Ar. No, Brother, I did not come hither for any such Purpose ; [10
but I can't help pitying you, when I see that, with all the Reasons in
the World to be content ; you are always out of Humour.

Gr. It is my Pleasure to be so.

Ar. I see it is ! Every thing smiles upon you, you have a good
state of Health ; you have very agreeable Children ; you're a [15
Widower ; your Affairs cannot be in a more flourishing Condition ;
and yet there is never seen upon your Countenance that Tranquility
of a Father of a Family, which diffuses Joy throughout the whole
House : You incessantly torment your self, and consequently torment
all who are oblig'd to live with you.   [20

Gr. [*Aside.*] There's some Truth in this. [*Turning to* Ar.] Am
not I a Man of Reputation too ?

Ar. No body denies it.

Gr. Is there any Objections to my Morals ?

Ar. Undoubtedly no.   [25

Gr. I think I am not a Knave, nor a Miser, nor a Lyar, nor a
Babler, like you ; nor . . . .

Ar. [*Interrupting.*] It is true ; you have not any of those Vices
that have hitherto been represented upon the Stage, and which
strike the Eyes of all the World ; but you have one which poisons [30
all the Sweetness of Life ; and which perhaps is more offensive in
Society than all the rest. For in short, a Man may sometimes, at
least, live in Peace with a Knave, a Miser, or a Lyar ; but there is
not one Moment's Repose to be enjoy'd with those, whose unhappy
Temper inclines them to be always dissatisfy'd, who are put into [35
a Passion by a Trifle, and who take a wretched Delight in Scolding,
and making an eternal Noise !

Gr. I hope you have almost done moralizing : I'm sure I begin
to be tir'd with it.

Ar. I have done, Brother. Let us leave these Contests, [40 and call another Cause, They say you are going to marry.

Gr. They say! They say! Pray who are they that say so?

Ar. Some Persons who interest themselves in your behalf.

Gr. I don't care a Rush for them. The World is full of nothing but these Interesters, who at the Bottom value us no more, [45 than they do *John-a-Nokes* and *Tom-a-Styles*.

Ar. I see there's no speaking to you.

Gr. Then you may hold your Tongue.

Ar. But for your own Good, there may be some Things to be said. [50

Gr. Then you may speak on.

Ar. You had yesterday resolv'd to marry off your Children to Advantage.

Gr. May be so.

Ar. They both consented to your Will. [55

Gr. I shou'd have been glad to have seen them dare to do otherwise.

Ar. Every body prais'd your Choice.

Gr. I did not care a Pin whether they did or no.

Ar. To day, without knowing why or wherefore, all on a [60 sudden, you have alter'd your Purpose.

Gr. Why not?

Ar. After you had promis'd your Daughter to *Mondore,* you are now for giving her to M— *Fadel,* who has no other Merit, but that of being Brother-in-Law to M. *Saint-Alvar* . . . . [65

Gr. What's that to you?

Ar. And are your self for marrying the very *Clarice,* whom you promis'd to your Son?

Gr. Good! Promis'd! Let him reckon upon that.

Ar. But, Brother, Do you in your Conscience believe, that [70 the World approves of your Conduct?

Gr. My Conduct! But, Brother, Do you in your Conscience believe, that I concern my self with what the World thinks?

Ar. Mean while . . . .

Gr. Oh! Mean while. Mean while: Every body does at [75 his own House according as he pleases; and I am the Master of my self and Children.

Ar. Tho' you are Master, yet, Brother, there are many Things, which Decency does not permit to do: For suppose . . . .

Gr. O suppose, If, But . . . . I'll have nothing to do with [80 your Supposes; I've told you so a hundred Times.

Ar. But, Brother, if you wou'd but reflect upon it ever so little . . . . .

Gr. Again! I find then you are not for having me marry *Clarice?*

Ar. I'm afraid you wou'd repent of it. [85

Gr. 'Tis true, she's a more suitable Match for my Son.

Ar. Undoubtedly.

Gr. Neither do you think it a whit more fitting, that I should bestow . . . . *Hortensia* on M. *Fadel*?

Ar. He's a Fool; and I'm afraid, you wou'd make your [90 Daughter very unhappy.

Gr. Very unhappy! I think you said so. So then, you are of Opinion, I shou'd do much better to pursue my former Design?

Ar. Most certainly.

Gr. And you have taken the Pains to come hither, on [95 purpose, to tell me so?

Ar. I thought my self oblig'd to it, for the Repose of your Family.

Gr. Very well: This is your Opinion, you say then?

Ar. Yes, Brother.

Gr. So much the Better, I shall have the Pleasure to break [100 off two Marriages, and make two others against your Sentiment.

Ar. But you do not consider . . . .

Gr. And I will go this Moment, to Mr. *Rigaut* the Notary, for that Purpose.

Ar. What do you go, to . . . . .?   [105

Gr. Your Servant.

SCENE VIII

Enter to them, Brillon, Grichard'*s Son, and* Catau.

Cat. Sir, *Brillon* wou'd speak with you.

Gr. What does the idle Boy want?

Bril. Father, Father, I have made my Theme to day without e'er a Fault: There, see else.

Gr. (*Throwing the Book at his Head.*) I'll look on that presently. [5

Bril. Pray Father, look on it now.

Gr. I han't time.

Lol. You will have read it in a Moment.

Gr. I have not got my Spectacles.

Bril. I'll read it to you.   [10

Gr. 'Tis the most importunate little Fool in the World.

Ar. You had better satisfy him.

Bril. I will first read you the *English*, and afterwards the *Latin*: Men . . . . The *Latin* is not so obscure as yesterday's Theme, you may easily understand this.   [15

Gr. Rascal!

Bril. *Men who never laugh, but always scold, are like those Savage Beasts which* . . . .

Gr. (*Giving him a Box on the Ear.*) There, take that, and bid your Master give you other Themes.   [20

Cat. Poor Child.

Ar. He's finely educated!   [*Aside.*

I. viii. 23.

Bril. (*Crying.*) Yes, yes, you beat me when I do well; but I'll study no longer, not I.

Gr. If I take you in Hand? [25

Bril. The Devil take Books and *Latin*!

Gr. Stay, Sirrah, stay.

Bril. Ay, stay 'till you beat me again. There, (*Tearing his Books.*) That's for your Blow.

Gr. The Rod, Rascal, the Rod. [30

Bril. Ay, ay, the Rod, I'll go and serve my Grammar and Psalter the same Sauce. [*Exit.*

Gr. You shall pay severely for it. This little Rascal every Day abuses the Tenderness I have for him.

Cat. Ay, there's a little *Grichard*, as like his Father, as if [35 he was spit out of his Mouth, for ill Humour. [*Aside.*

Gr. What's that you mutter there?

Cat. I say, Sir, that little *Grichard* is gone out in a very ill Humour.

Gr. Is that any thing to you, Impertinence?

Ar. My Brother is in the right. [40

Gr. Well, and what if I had been in the wrong?

Ar. Be it as you will. But pray, Brother, let's return to the Business we were speaking of . . .

Gr. Have not I already told you that I'm going to Mr. *Rigaut*, my Notary; so, Sir, your Servant. But what does this Ass want [45 with me?

SCENE IX

Enter to them, Mamurra.

Ma. Sir . . . . .

Gr. What now, *Sir*? Have you nothing else to do but come hither. Go, Mr. *Mamurra*, and whip *Brillon*.

Ma. *Abiit, Effugit, Evasit, Erupit.*

Gr. What, is *Brillon* run away? [5

Ma. Yes, Sir, *Effugit.*

Gr. These Sots cannot help spitting out *Latin*. Either speak *English*, Blockheady Pedant, or hold your Tongue.

Ma. Since you will have it so, *Sit pro ratione voluntas.*

Gr. Again. Speak *English*, and be hang'd, if you can; [10 thou University Excrement.

Ma. Be it so, we read in *Arriaga.*

Gr. What a Devil has *Arriaga* to do with *Brillon*'s Flight?

Ma. Come on, then; since you will have me speak *English*, I must tell you, that you gave my Disciple a Box of the Ear very [15 improperly. He has lacerated, incendiated all his Books, and *effugit, effugit*; that Correction is necessary, *concedo*; but nothing is more dangerous than Chastisement, *sine causa*, instead of meliorating, it pejorates; and paternal and magisterial Sincerity, says *Arriaga* . . .

I. ix. 20.

Gr. Still *Arriaga.* Be gone Knave, this Minute, you, and [20
your *Arriaga,* and see you don't set Foot again within my Doors
without *Brillon.*

Ma. Sir.

Gr. Out of my Sight, I say, look for him presently.

[*Exit.* Mam.

SCENE X

Ar. You won't hear me then.

Gr. Your Servant. Here, *Lolive,* saddle my Mule; I shall return
in a Moment: I must visit a Patient that stay's for me.   [*Exit.*

SCENE XI

Ar. What a Man he is!

Cat. Who do you say so to, Sir?

Ar. If you did but know what a whimsical Design he has form'd!

Cat. I know more than you, *Rosine, Clarice*'s Chamber-Maid has
just now told me all. Can you imagine, why your Brother, since [5
yesterday has taken it in his Head to marry *Clarice?*

Ar. Beauty perhaps.

Cat. Beauty; Fiddlestick: Do you think Beauty can take such
a one as he?

Ar. What can it be then?   [10

Cat. You know, Sir, that we all advis'd *Clarice* to affect a Severity
and Roughness towards the Servants in *Grichard*'s Presence, that
she might obtain his Favour, and oblige him to consent to her Marriage
with *Terignan.*

Ar. I know it.   [15

Cat. Yesternight, your Brother was in the Room with M. *St.
Alvar,* and *Clarice* was in her's, which joyns to it: *Rosine* had com-
mitted some small Fault, *Clarice* took hold of the Opportunity to
scold at her for it. M. *Grichard,* hearing her Quarrel, abruptly left
M. *St. Alvar,* and went to help her to scold. The poor Creature [20
was call'd to some Tune, as you may well imagine, her Mistress pre-
tended to put her away; and from that Moment our Grumbler has
conceiv'd such an Esteem for her as cannot be imagin'd, and is resolv'd
to marry her himself.

Ar. Is it possible!   [25

Cat. He presently proposed it to M. de *St. Alvar.* He being an
easy Man, consented to it, on Condition that M. *Grichard* wou'd
give *Hortensia* to M. *Fadel,* his Brother-in-Law, who is burthensome
to him.

Ar. Does *Clarice* know it.   [30

Cat. She is ready to run mad about it. I just now spoke to her,
she has already complain'd to her Father, who begins to repent of it.

Ar. We must by all means break off this Match.

Cat. We have already concerted *Clarice* and *Rosine*, what's to be done; and *Brillon's* Flight makes me think of a *Stratagem*, which [35 I must put in Execution.

Ar. What do you intend to do?

Cat. I will tell you when we have more Leisure.

Ar. Let us go and inform *Terrignan* and *Hortensia* and take Measures to act in Concert. [40

Cat. Come then, our Grumbler shall be very cunning indeed, if he escapes my Snares.

ACT II

SCENE I

Lolive Solus.

What a damn'd Beast is a freakish Mule! What a plaguy Man is a morose Physician! What a hard Task a poor Servant has to please those two Animals! And how fit one is for the other! How am I out of Breath; but, thank God, I shall be so no more.

SCENE II

Enter to him, Catau.

Cat. O, are you here? I was looking for you: Where have you been?

Lol. I have been setting our cross Physician upon his cross Mule, they are at length both pack'd off, after having been very boisterous: But for a Recompence, they have given me my Discharge. [5

Cat. Thy Discharge!

Lol. Yes, M. *Grichard* spoke for both; there's no great Harm done.

Cat. I know it. But before the Day ends, I'll put thee in the way, if you have a Mind to it, to be reveng'd on him. [10

Lol. Tho' Revenge does not belong to a noble Soul, yet I am ready for any thing; you may dispose of me.

Cat. We knew we might. But first of all, go keep Watch at the Corner of the Street, and when you see our Grumbler coming, give me Notice. Here's my Mistress. [15

SCENE III

Enter Hortensia.

Hor. My Uncle and Brother are gone to tell *Clarice* to come hither.

Cat. That's well. Do you, if your Father proposes Mr. *Fadel* to you, seem to be submissive to his Will, and do not irritate him by a Refusal. [5

Hor. But if once I've said Yes!

Cat. Why, you may say no if you will; What care I?

Hor. Dear *Catau*, do not be angry.

Cat. Be rul'd then.

Hor. But if what you undertake shou'd not succeed. [10

Cat. Why then, you'd best follow your own Fancy.

Hor. How hasty you are. I fear I shall be marry'd to the most silly and ugly of Men.

Cat. You will not be without Companions in Misery. I know Women as young and handsome as you, who are marry'd to [15 Baboons of Men; but, in Return, I likewise know handsome young Fellows, who are marry'd to Apes of Women; but a good Fortune will make up that Matter; and Avarice every day makes such Matches.

Hor. The Unhappiness of others is but a weak Consolation.

Cat. Since you run so much upon Arguments, What do you [20 intend to do if, notwithstanding what I undertake, your Father shou'd persist in—giving you to M. *Fadel*?

Hor. I know not—I will die.

Cat. Die!

Hor. Yes, I tell you, die. [25

Cat. And what if you can't die!

Hor. I must obey.

Cat. Obey!

Hor. Yes, *Catau*, obey. That's all a Child that has Virtue can do.

Cat. I am not quite of that Opinion. Virtue, indeed, forbids [30 a Daughter marrying one that pleases her, against her Parents Will; but Virtue do's not forbid her opposing their Will, when they wou'd marry her to a Man she does not like.

Hor. My Father is not like others: And if once I have consented—— [35

Cat. Good; consented. Go, Madam; in Point of Marriage, a Child may say and unsay what she pleases: But we will not bring it to that; only let *Clarice* alone, and do as I wou'd have you.

SCENE IV

Enter Lolive.

Lol. Have a Care, have a Care, M. *Grichard.*

Cat. Is he come home?

Lol. No, *Will* has brought back his Mule.

Hor. And where's my Father?

Lol. A small Accident has made him light a little Way off.   [5

Cat. What Accident.

Lol. As he was going on his Mule by the Door of one of our Neighbours, a Shock-Dog, who did not like his Figure, presently began to yelp. The Mule took a Fright, turn'd half way round to the Right, and M. *Grichard*, half way round to the Left, on the Pavement. [10

Hor. Is he hurt?

Lol. No, he is now scolding at the Dog; you'll have him here in a Moment.

Hor. I'll get into my Chamber; I dread his ill Humour. [*Exit.*

Cat. He is soon come back.   [15

Lol. His Business was done before he came there, *Will* say's.

Cat. Perhaps, then, another Physician was sent for?

Lol. No, but the Patient was impatient; and seeing M. *Grichard* delay'd coming, he departed without his Order.

Cat. He found him dead, ha?   [20

Lol. You have said it.

Cat. That happens to him every day. But I expect him; get out of the Way, lest he see thee. Go tell *Clarice* to come hither quickly, she will tell you what you have to do: Hark ye, a Word in your Ear.   [*She whispers him.*] [25

Lol. Enough.   [*Exit.*

SCENE V

Enter Grichard.

Gr. Yes, you Rascal, I'll teach you to tye a Dog up.

Cat. Ay, Sir, that Rascal of a Neighbour has been told of it a thousand times; if you'll leave him to me, Sir, I'll handle him.

Gr. This Wench has something good in her. Is *Brillon* come back?   [5

Cat. No, Sir.

Gr. This young Rogue will make me mad; and that Beast his Master, where is he?

Cat. He's gone to look ⟨for⟩ him, and will not return without bringing him to you.   [10

Gr. He'll do well.

SCENE VI

Enter Footman, introducing M. Fadel.

Foot. M. *Fadel*, Sir, desires to speak with you.

Gr. Let him come in—I must talk with this young Man a little, to see if he's such a Fool as he is reported to be. Draw near, Son-in-Law that is to be . . . . . Draw near, I say.

Cat. To him. Nearer yet. My Master does not love to [5 bawl.

Fa. Humph . . . . .

> Grichard *proceeds to ask the following Questions, and looks*
> *on him at every Question, to see if he'll Reply.*

Gr. People wou'd make me believe I'm going to marry my Daughter to a Fool.

Fa. Ay!   [10

Gr. But I don't believe so, since I bestow her on you.

Fa. Hah!

Gr. And with a large Portion too.

Fa. Ho, ho!

Gr. I promis'd her to one *Mondore*, who is absent.   [15

Fa. Law ye there now!

Gr. But I prefer you before him.

Fa. To be sure!

Gr. He shall be hang'd before he shall have her.

Fa. Ha, ha, ha!   [20

Gr. And I will marry your Relation, *Clarice.*

Fa. Indeed!

Gr. Hum, ha, ho; Ay, Oy, Truly, Yes, indeed : Have you nothing else to say?

Cat. He answers you very justly.   [25

Fa. Ho, ho!

Gr. Ay, but his Style is very Laconic.

Fa. La! La!

Cat. He'll never make your Head-ach with Talking.

Gr. A great Talker is still more Troublesome.   [30

Cat. I know, Sir, above Four, who without, oh, oh, yes, and ah, ah, wou'd often have nothing to say.

Gr. I must carry him to *Hortensia*; perhaps he will speak before her.

Fa. Oh, oh!   [35

Gr. Come then.

Cat. Go and see your Mistress, Mr. Oh, oh. To what a stupid Ass is such a Girl as she to be given? But I shall hinder it.

SCENE VII

Enter to her, Terignan, Aristus *and* Lolive.

Ar. Where is my Brother ?
Cat. He's just gone into *Hortensia's* Chamber with M. *Fadel,*
they will have no long Conversation.
Lol. Can I enter ?
Cat. Yes, but make haste.   [5
Lol. *Clarice* will be here in a Moment.
            In this Scene Lol. *always looks to see if M.* Grich. *is
                        coming.*
Cat. So much the better.
Lol. I have found *Brillon.*
Cat. What then ?
Lol. I have carry'd him to my Master.   [10
Cat. You have done well.
Lol. He will go from thence without your Order.
Cat. 'Tis enough ; Has *Clarice* instructed thee in what thou art
to do ?
Lol. Yes.   [15
Cat. Go then, and get ready to play your Part.
Lol. I'll go.
Cat. I do not think M. *Grichard* knows your Face much.
Lol. He ! For twelve Days which I serv'd him, he never look'd
me in the Face ; he knows no body.   [20
Cat. Be gone, quickly lest he see thee here . . . .
                                                        [*Exit* Lol.

SCENE VIII

Enter Hortensia, *to them.*

Hor. How, I breathe ! M. *Fadel* is gone, and my Father is in his
Closet, ... very sorrowful about *Brillon's* Flight.
Cat. He shan't see him again without good Tokens.
Ter. How ?

SCENE IX

M. Grichard *at the farthest Part of the Stage.*

Cat. You shall know at a better Opportunity.
Hor. (*Perceiving M.* Grichard) Silence, there's my Father, he has
heard our Discourse, may be.
Cat. He ! Do you not know, that when his Scolding changes into
Chagrin he is now in, he neither sees, nor hears any body ? I [5
wou'd lay a Wager that he does not so much as perceive that we are
here.

II. ix. 8.

Ar. He must be prepar'd for *Clarice*'s Visit. Accost him, Nephew.

Ter. I dare not. [10

[*Each as he speaks, gets farthest off from M.* Grichard, *who is at the farther Part of the Stage.*

Ar. Do you *Hortensia.*

Hor. I am afraid.

Ar. Do you, then, *Catau.*

Cat. I'd as soon be hang'd.

Ar. But from whence can this Melancholy proceed? [15

Cat. He has not scolded at any body this Hour!

Gr. (*Walking in Anger.*) 'Tis a strange thing! I can find no body, with whom I may converse a Moment, without being oblig'd to be angry. I am a good Father, my Children make me mad. A good Master; my Servants think of nothing but angering me. A good [20 Neighbour; yet those that live near me, let loose their Dogs at me, even my Patients plague me, witness to day, one wou'd think they died on purpose to make me mad.

Ar. I must speak to him. Brother, I'm your Servant.

Gr. I am yours. [25

Ar. What makes you sorrowful?

Gr. I know not.

Hor. What ails you, Father?

Gr. Nothing.

Cat. Are you out of Order, Sir? [30

Gr. No.

Ter. Cannot one know——?

Gr. Hold your Tongue.

Cat. Will you, Sir . . . . .?

Gr. Leave me. [35

Cat. I've News that will please you, Sir; I just now saw *Clarice.*

Gr. *Clarice*! Be gone quickly. (*To* Hort.) Leave me, you too, you make me angry with your serious Airs. . . . .

[*Exeunt all but* Gr. *and* Ar.

SCENE X

Gr. As for you, if you intend to give me at present any of your foolish Counsel; you were better go home, and see if any one wants you.

Ar. No Brother, since you are absolutely resolv'd to marry, and *Clarice* pleases you, be it so. [5

Gr. You shall see what Difference is between her and your jovial Women.

Ar. I believe it.

Gr. I have need of such a one as she.

Ar. You ought to be satisfy'd.   [10

Gr. I my self am not sufficient to keep a Family in awe, and provide for Affairs abroad at the same time.

Ar. No, certainly.

Gr. Whilst I shall hold those at home in their Duty, she will go into the City to scold at the Merchant, the Butcher, the Shoe- [15
maker, the Grocer; and woe be to them that play us the least Trick. But here she comes, you shall see.

SCENE XI

Enter Clarice.

Cl. Behold me, Sir, in so great an Excess of Joy, that I cannot express it to you.

Gr. How's this! Whence proceeds this irregular Transport?

Cl. My Father, just now, granted me all that I have ask'd of him.

Gr. What did you ask of him?   [5

Cl. All that could please me.

Gr. But, what?

Cl. He has made me Mistress of all our Nuptial Preparations.

Gr. What Preparations are there to be?

Cl. How, Sir, what Preparations! Habits, Feasts, Violins, [10
Hautboys, Masquerades, Concerts; and especially the Ball, which I will have every Night for fifteen Days.

Gr. How the Devil!

Cl. You see this Suit, 'tis the worst of twelve I have bespoke. I have order'd as Many for you.   [15

Gr. For me!

Cl. Yes, but there are but two made yet, which they will bring home to Night.

Gr. For me!

Cl. Yes, Sir, Do you think I can bear you as you are? One [20
wou'd think you were in Mourning for the Patients that die under your Hands.

Gr. She is mad.

Cl. You must throw off this melancholy Equipage, and take one more gay.   [25

Gr. A more gay Habit for a Physician?

Cl. Without doubt; since we are to be marry'd, we must assume the Best Air. Are you the first that have worn a Cavalier Dress?

Gr. She raves.

Cl. For the Feast, we have two Tables of thirty Covers, I [30
myself have, just now, given Order in what Part of the Hall the Violins and Hautboys shall be placed.

Gr. But do you consider . . . . .

Cl. I have prepar'd a charming Masquerade.

II. xi. 35.

Gr. I say . . . . . [35

Cl. When we have danced about an Hour, we two will leave the Ball without saying any thing, and we will disguise our selves; I like *Venus,* and you like *Adonis.*

Gr. I lose all Patience.

Cl. How we will dance! Dancing, I must own, is my greatest [40 Delight; I have already got four Lacquies that play perfectly well on the Violin.

Gr. Four Lacquies!

Cl. Yes, Sir two for you, and two for me.

Gr. Four Lacquies! [45

Cl. When we are marry'd, we will have a Ball every Day of our Life, and our House shall be the Rendezvous of all that love Pleasure.

SCENE XII

Enter Rosine.

Ros. Madam, all your Masquerade Habits are come home; come quickly, and see them, they are the prettiest in the World.

Gr. Is not that the Crack you turn'd away yesterday.

Cl. Yes, Sir.

Gr. What! Have you taken her again? [5

Cl. I cannot do without her, she is the best humour'd Girl in the World; she is always singing and dancing.

Gr. Such as these, Madam, are but ill Servants.

Cl. That's true indeed, but I had rather be ill served, so that I have but Servants that are always gay: I think that those who [10 are about us communicate to us, in spite of our selves, either their Joy or Sadness; I hate Melancholy.

Gr. Ah, somebody has bewitch'd her since yesterday!

Ros. Come, Madam, you are impatiently expected.

Cl. Adieu, Sir, I die to see your and my Habits, I have left [15 Monsieur *Canary* at home, who stay's for me. [*Exit*

SCENE XIII

Gr. Who is that Monsieur *Canary?*

Ros. Her Singing-Master. Oh, Sir, she is a Jewel of a Woman: Most love to scold at their Servants, and to put their Husbands out of Humour. But I'll answer for her. Sir, all will go well; let every thing be as it will, she'll never trouble her self with Houshold [5 Affairs: She's the best of Women; I have served her five Years, and never saw her angry before yesterday.

Gr. But tell me, is not her Father the Cause of . . . . . . [*Exit.*

Ros. Sir, I beg your Pardon, I must go and try my Masquerade Habit. [10

SCENE XIV

Manent, *M.* Grichard *and* Ar.

They stand looking on each other for some Time.

Ar. Well Brother ?
Gr. I am amazed !   [*Aside.*
Ar. Are these the Women you made such a boast to me of ?
Gr. There is some Mystery in this.   [*Aside.*
Ar. Does he suspect the Trick ?   [*Aside.*] [5
Gr. I guess from whence this proceeds.
Ar. Perhaps you think that the Joy of her ⟨go⟩ing to be
marry'd . . . . .
Gr. Do you know, Sir, that you have the Gift of Reasoning always
wrong ?
Ar. I ?   [10
Gr. Yes, you. Monsieur *Saint-Alvar* has made *Clarice* commit
this Madness ; these Country Gentlemen love Feasts, and I remember
I have heard that old Fool say, he wou'd dance at his Daughter's
Wedding.
Ar. What, Do you believe . . . . .   [15
Gr. And I'll go and rattle that old Blockhead, as he deserves.
                                                            [*Exit.*

SCENE XV

Enter Catau.

Cat. Where is he going ?
Ar. To *Clarice*'s Father. He has taken it in his Head, that all
⟨s⟩he has said to him, does not proceed from her.
Cat. Let him go. Mon. *de Saint-Alvar* is on our Side.
Ar. It will be hard to make him renounce *Clarice*.   [5
Cat. I have more than one String to my Bow, he cannot hold
out against the Trick I shall play him : I have told it you ; our
Grumbler will soon return ; he will find no body where he is gone ;
he has only the Street to cross ; do you hide your self in the Corner
of this Room, listen to what passes, and when you think the [10
Thing carry'd far enough, come to his Succour.
Ar. But did not you say you would have no body at Home ?
Cat. I have made *Hortensia* and *Terignan* retire, and your Brother
has turn'd away all his Servants to day : But here he is, hide your
self quickly.   [15

SCENE XVI

Enter M. Grichard *and* Jasmin.

Cat.   Are you return'd, Sir, already from Mon. *de St. Alvar?*
Gr.   I did not find him at home.
Cat.   'Tis said there will be a great Ball there to Night.
Gr.   I know that twelve Pistoles are promised to the Violins, carry
them twenty four, and bid them not come this Evening.   [5
Cat.   O, Sir, that will be in vain : If *Clarice* has a Mind to have
them, she will give them fifty ; nay a hundred, if need were.   I know
the Ladies of the World, they spare nothing for their Pleasure, and
the ease with which most of them throw away Money, makes it be
suspected that it is not got too hard.   [10
Gr.   But 'tis not so with *Clarice*, Hussy.
Jas.   Sir, a Gentleman wou'd speak with you.
Cat.   Good, here comes my Man.   [*Aside.*
Gr.   Who is it?
Jas.   He say's his Name is Monsieur *Ri . . . . Ri . . . . .* [15
Stay, Sir, I'll go and ask him again.
Gr.   (*Pulling him by the Ears.*)   Take that Sirrah.
Jas.   Ahi, Ahi.   [*Exit.*
Cat.   Sir, you have torn his Hair off, so that he must now have
a Peruke, you have pull'd his Ears off ; but there are none of [20
them to be had for Money.
Gr.   I'll teach you. . . . 'Tis certainly M. *Rigaut*, my Notary,
I know who it is, let him come in : Cou'd he find no Time but this
to bring me Money?   Plague take the Importunate !

SCENE XVII

Enter Lolive, *like a Dancing-Master, and his Boy.*

Gr.   This is not my Man ; Who are you with your Compliments?
Lol.   (*Bowing often.*)   I am call'd *Rigaudon*, Sir, at your Service.
Gr.   (*To* Cat.)   Have not I seen that Face somewhere?
Cat.   There are a thousand People like one another.
Gr.   Well, M. *Rigaudon*, What is your Business?   [5
Lol.   To give you this Letter from Madam *Clarice.*
Gr.   Give it me. . . . I wou'd fain know who taught *Clarice* to
fold a Letter thus : A fine Form indeed ; a fine Gewgaw ; What
contains it.
Cat.   (*Aside, whilst he unfolds the Letter.*)   A Lover, I believe, [10
never complain'd of that before.
Gr. *Every body says I am to marry the most Bru . . . brutish of
men ; I would disabuse them, and for that Reason you and I must begin
the Ball to Night.*   She is mad.

Lol. Go on, pray Sir. [15

Gr. Reads. *You told me you cannot dance, but I have sent you the first Man in the World.*

[*Grichard* looks on him from Head to Foot.

Lol. O Lord, Sir!

Gr. *Who will teach you in less than an Hour, enough to serve your Purpose.* I learn to dance! [20

Lol. Finish, if you please.

Gr. *And if you love me, you will learn the Bourree.* The Bourree! I the Bourree! Mr. the first Man in the World, Do you know what Danger you are in here?

Lol. Come, Sir, in a quarter of an Hour you shall dance to a [25 Miracle!

Gr. M. *Rigaudon,* I will send you out of the Window, if I call my Servants.

Cat. (*Aside to* Grich.) You must not turn them away then.

Lol. (*Bidding his Boy play.*) Come, brisk. This little Pre- [30 lude will put you in Humour; Must you be held by the Hand, or have you some Steps?

Gr. Unless you put up that damn'd Violin, I'll pull your Eyes out.

Lol. Zoons! Sir, if you are thereabouts, you shall dance presently.

Gr. *Shall* I dance, Villain. [35

Lol. Yes, by *Jove,* shall you dance. I have orders from *Clarice* to make you dance, she has paid me, and dance you shall: Don't let him go out.

[*He draws his Sword, and puts it under his Arm.*

Gr. Ah! I'm dead, What a Madman has this Woman sent me!

Cat. I see I must interpose; stay you there, Sir, let me speak [40 to him: Sir, pray do us the Favour to go and tell Mon. *de St. Alvar....*

Lol. 'Tis not he that sent me; I will have him dance.

Gr. The Rascal, the Rascal!

Cat. Consider, if you please; my Master is a grave Man.

Lol. I'll have him dance. [45

Cat. A famous Physician!

Lol. I'll have him dance.

Cat. You may fall sick, and stand in need of him.

Gr. (*Taking her aside.*) Yes, tell him, that when he will, without costing him a Farthing, I'll bleed and purge him his Belly full. [50

Lol. I have nothing to do with that, I'll have him dance, or's Blood. . . .

Gr. The Rascal! (*muttering*).

Cat. Sir, I can't work upon him, that Madman will not hear Reason; some Harm will happen, we are alone. [55

Gr. 'Tis very true.

Cat. Look on him, he has an ill Phiz.

Gr. He has so (*Trembling*).

Lol. Make haste.

II. xvii. 60.

Gr.   Help, Neighbours, help!   [60

Cat.   Ay, you may cry for Help; Do you not know that all your Neighbours wou'd be glad to see you robb'd, and your Throat cut. Believe me, Sir, two Bourree Steps may save your Life.

Gr.   But if it shou'd come to be known, I shou'd be taken for a Fool!   [65

Cat.   Love excuses all Follies; and I have heard M. *Mamurra* say, that when *Hercules* was in Love, he spun for Queen *Omphale*.

Gr.   Yes, *Hercules* spun, but *Hercules* did not dance the Bourree, and of all Dances, 'tis that I hate most.

Cat.   Well, you must tell him so, the Gentleman will teach   [70 you another.

Lol.   Will you have a Minuet, Sir?

Gr.   A Minuet? No.

Lol.   The Gavotte?

Gr.   The Gavotte? No . . . .   [75

Lol.   The Passvy?

Gr.   The Passvy! . . . . No.   [*Passpied.*

Lol.   What then? (Here he names half a Dozen Dances:) The Trocanny, Tricotez, Rigadon? Come, chuse, chuse.

Gr.   No, no, no, I like none of them.   [80

Lol.   You wou'd have a grave, serious Dance, perhaps?

Gr.   Yes, a serious one, if there be any, but very serious.

Lol.   Well, the Courante, the Bocane, the Sarabande?

Gr.   No, no, no.

Lol.   What the Devil then will you have? But make haste,   [85 or Death! . . . .

Gr.   Come on then, since it must be so, I'll learn a few Steps of the . . . . . the . . . . .

Lol.   What of the . . . . . the . . . . ?

Gr.   I know not what.   [90

Lol.   You mock me, Sir, you shall dance the Bourree, since *Clarice* will have it so; or . . . . .

SCENE XVIII

Enter Aristus.

Gr.   Oh!

Ar.   How's this?

Gr.   Here I'm . . . .

Ar.   What do I see!

Gr.   This Insolence wou'd . . . .   [5

Ar.   My Brother learn to dance!

Gr.   I tell you, this Villain . . . . .

Ar.   At your Age!

Gr.   But when you're told . . . . .

Ar. People will laugh at you. [10
Gr. Ah! Here's another . . . .
Ar. I will not suffer it.
Gr. What the Devil, Won't you hear me, eternal Pratler, inde-
fatigable Squaller, I tell you, this Knave will make me dance by
Force. [15
Ar. By Force!
Gr. Yes, by Force.
Cat. Yes, Sir, the Bourree.
Ar. And who made you so bold, Sir, as to come hither?
Lol. Sir, Sir, I come from a considerable Person; and I'll go [20
tell Madam *Clarice*, how those she sends are received. [*Exit.*
Gr. I can no longer hold, I must go to that old Fool, *St. Alvar*,
and rattle *Clarice*, her Father, and all I find there. [*Exit.*

SCENE XIX

Manent Aristus, Catau.

Cat. There he's gone; What say you of *Lolive*?
Ar. I say he's a very clever Fellow. I believe he's now off of
Clarice.
Cat. This is not all, we must bring him to his first Design; where-
fore we must go upon our Business, and not lose a Moment. [5

ACT III

SCENE I

Lolive, Catau.

Cat. What do you want here? Why have not you taken your
other Equipage? If M. *Grichard* shou'd return . . . . .!
Lol. He is still to scold at *Clarice* and *Fadel*.
Cat. He may suprise you, and know you.
Lol. He know me,⟨!⟩ you cannot imagine the Virtue which [5
fine Cloaths have in changing such as we. To turn on the Heel, and
wear a lac'd Coat, is sufficient to make above four that I know forget
themselves.
Cat. What have you to say to me then?
Lol. A great many Things concerning what you wou'd have [10
me do.
Cat. Say them quickly then.

Lol. Since *Mondore* is arriv'd, let him use his own Servants to . . . .

Cat. He has brought with him but one *Valet de Chambre*, of whom we have already made the Chaplain, whom we have sent [15 to M. *Grichard*. None but you can finish what you have begun.

Lol. I cannot.

Cat. Coward!

Lol. Consider all you make me undertake in one Day. *Brillon* serves your Designs; you make me steal him away; you fear lest [20 *Mamurra* shou'd speak, you make me keep him shut up; you cause me to terrify a very honest Physician, who may catch a Fever by it.

Cat. He may cure himself.

Lol. And thou wilt have me give him a yet hotter Alarm.

Cat. You are sorely hurt indeed? Are you not well paid for [25 the Lesson of Dancing, you gave him?

Lol. I am so.

Cat. Shall you not be doubly so for this second Expedition?

Lol. I believe I shall.

Cat. And have you not the Pleasure to be revenged of a [30 Man, who has turn'd thee away without a Cause?

Lol. No, my Reputation is dear to me.

Cat. Oh, be it so, no body intends to take it away; but remember, that if you do not effect what you have promis'd *Mondore*, you may be sure of a thousand Stripes. [35

Lol. But if I do it, and M. *Grichard* discovers me, Do you think he'll spare me?

Cat. In this Case, perhaps you will risque some small Trifle; but on that Side the Blows are uncertain, and on *Mondore*'s Side very sure, as well as the fifty Pistoles he has promised you, if you serve [40 him.

Lol. This deserves a little Reflection; I see that on all Sides, I run the risque of the Cudgel; What Side shall I take? Beaten, perhaps, by M. *Grichard*, and certainly beaten by M. *Mondore*: Criminal, in not doing what I promised; criminal in doing it. [45 All I have to do, is to chuse which Cudgel I'll have.

Cat. You have stated the Case right.

Lol. Well, I must hesitate no longer, Cudgel for Cudgel; I must determine in favour of that which is accompany'd with a Lenative of fifty Pistoles: But whose Security am I to have? [50

Cat. Whose! *Mondore*'s, who wou'd give all Things, rather than lose what he loves: *Terignan, Hortensia, Clarice, Aristus*; Are you content?

Lol. No.

Cat. How so? [55

Lol. No, I tell you, give me a Security which I may take bodily.

Cat. Me, then?

Lol. Thee?

Cat. Me.

Lol. I take it.   [60

Cat. Go then, and get ready. [*Exit* Lol.] So, now our Affairs are on a good Foot, and if our Lovers are happy, the Obligation will be all to me.

SCENE II

Enter M. Fadel.

Cat. But what do I see? Does that Ninny *Fadel* come to put any Obstacle to our Designs? He shall not long be troublesome to me, if the Questions are no longer than my Answers.

Fa. I want your M. *Grichard.*

Cat. You?   [5

Fa. He went by my House.

Cat. He?

Fa. But he did not find me there.

Cat. No?

Fa. He serv'd me a fine Trick to day.   [10

Cat. Oy!

Fa. He will not give me *Hortensia.*

Cat. La, La!

Fa. And I come to tell him, I don't care a Pin.

Cat. Law ye there now!   [15

Fa. I'll marry into a better Family.

Cat. To be sure.

Fa. I might wait long enough for his Daughter.

Cat. Good.

Fa. Did he think he had a Fool to deal with?   [20

Cat. Ho, ho!

Fa. I'll soon shew him that I am not . . . . .

Cat. Ah, ah!

Fa. Don't fail to tell him . . . . .

Cat. No.   [25

Fa. I scorn him.

Cat. Yes.

Fa. And he shall repent of it.   [*Exit.*

Cat. Ha, ha! So, I'm deliver'd of this importunate Fool. Now let's go and tell my Mistress of *Mondore*'s Arrival; but here he [30 himself comes. O Heavens! What Imprudence! Cou'd you not wait for *Hortensia* at *Clarice*'s? Why do you come here?

SCENE III

Enter Mondore.

Mon. 'Tis an Hour since I heard speak of you; Where is that Ardour you express'd at my Arrival? I see neither your Mistress, nor You, nor the Man you should have sent me.

III. iii. 4.

Cat. He is at *Clarice*'s already, and *Hortensia* will be there soon. I'm going to tell her : Go quickly, and stay for her there.   [5

Mon. But make haste.

Cat. Go, I say.

Mon. Make haste then.

Cat. Why don't you make haste your self ?

Mon. If you knew how tiresome the Time is to me !   [10

Cat. If you knew how you confound me !

Mon. Come soon at least.

Cat. Begin then by your Absence ; How foolish are those who are in Love ! 'Tis enough to cool my Inclination of serving them. Be gone, I say, plague on you ; here comes M. *Grich.* He has   [15 seen us together, we cannot avoid him ; What shall we do ? Stay, by good Fortune, he don't know you : Consult him about the first Thing that comes in your Head, he'll soon send you packing, and then you may come back to me : Let the worst come to the worst, I'll send *Aristus* to bring you off.   [20

Mon. Let me alone, I'll talk to him in such a Manner, that he shall soon drive me away.

SCENE IV

Enter M. Grichard.

Gr. Who is that Man ? Another Dancing-Master ?

Cat. What say you ! Take care he don't hear you ; he's a Man of the first Quality, who upon some extraordinary Ilness wou'd have your Advice.

Gr. Let him make haste.   [*Exit* Cat.]   [5

SCENE V

Gr. What is your Business ? Of what Disease do you complain ? You have a healthy Countenance.

Mon. 'Tis true, Sir ; neither am I ill.

Gr. You have a Mind to be so then ?

Mon. No, Sir.   [5

Gr. Tell me quickly then, what your Business is ?

Mon. I know, Sir, that you are a very able Man.

Gr. No Panegyrick.

Mon. I believe you are ignorant of none of the Secrets of . . . .

Gr. I am ignorant of the Secret of freeing my self from the   [10 Importunate ; but well, to the Secrets ?

Mon. You have no time to lose.

Gr. I have lost some already.

Mon. I have but one Word to say to you.

Gr. Why, you have spoken above a hundred already.   [15

Mon. I have heard that there are Secrets to cause Love, that certain Draughts are given, a sort of Philters, which . . . .

Gr. What the Devil ! Who do you take me for ?

Mon. For a very learned, honest Man.

Gr. And you ask me for Secrets to make you be loved ?   [20

Mon. Oh no, Sir, Thanks be to Heaven ; Nature has sufficiently provided me for that.

Gr. Here's a Fop !

Mon. There are three or four Women, who incessantly trouble me, pretending they are in Love with me. I love elsewhere [25 to Madness : There are Secrets to cause Love ; pray teach me one to cause me to be hated.

Gr. By those who love you to Distraction ?

Mon. Yes, Sir.

Gr. Take . . . . . .   [30

Mon. Very well.

Gr. But two or three Times . . . . .

Mon. I hear.

Gr. Your time with 'em, is as bad as you have with me, I'll engage they'll hate you worse than the Devil. Adieu.   [35

Mon. Thank you.   [*Exit.*

SCENE VI

Enter Aristus.

Gr. He took me but in an ill Time to hear his Trifles. I am in Despair about *Brillon*'s Flight. Well, Do you bring me any News of that young Rascal ?

Ar. *Catau* is gone to look him ; but you will not go to morrow ?

Gr. At the break of Day.   [5

Ar. You mean after you have taken Care about M. *de St. Alvar*'s Business. ?

Gr. I have already taken all the Care I shall take about it.

Ar. How so ?

Gr. I'll hear no further about it.   [10

Ar. I'm amazed at you, Brother ; yesterday you were resolved to give *Terignan* to *Clarice* and *Hortensia* to *Mondore*. This Morning, you yourself wou'd marry *Clarice*, and give your Daughter to M. *Fadel*, and this Evening you will do neither.

Gr. No, no, no, by all the Devils, no !   [15

Ar. Thus have you changed your Mind three Times in one Day.

Gr. I'll change it thirty Times, if I please ; and that People may come no more to trouble me about it, I am very glad I did engage my self in your Presence to go into the Country to morrow to see the sick Lord, who did me the Honour to send his Chaplain to me.   [20

III. vi. 21.

Ar. But at least before you go, you ought to make some Reconciliation with M. *de St. Alvar.*

Gr. I shall not trouble my self in it.

Ar. He has powerful Friends.

Gr. I defy them.   [25

Ar. You have given him your Word.

Gr. Let him keep it.

Ar. He has already told you to your Face, that he knew how to make you keep it.

Gr. I fear him not.   [30

Ar. He has been at Charge about the Nuptials.

Gr. Why did he put himself to it?   [Cat. *peeps.*

Ar. You may be forced to pay Damages, and witty Interest too.

Gr. Well, you won't pay them for me.

Ar. No, but . . . .   [35

Gr. After what I have seen of *Clarice*, even tho' it shou'd cost me all I have; and tho' all the World shou'd intermeddle, I'd rather be hang'd, roasted, broil'd, any thing, than be marry'd to that Creature.

SCENE VII

Enter Catau.

Cat. Ah. Sir!

Gr. What's the Matter?

Cat. *Brillon* has listed himself a Soldier.

Gr. Listed himself a Soldier!

Cat. Yes, Sir, listed to go to the War.   [5

Gr. To the War!

Ar. (*To* Cat.) No, no! They jest with you.

Cat. Gentlemen, I spoke my self to the Serjeant and Captain.

Gr. The Rascal!

Ar. What a Misfortune 'tis!   [10

Cat. Ay, Sir, a great one.

Gr. The Captain, whoever he be, is a Rogue, and he ought to be cashier'd for listing Boys of fifteen Years old; they want able bodied Soldiers now.

Cat. So I told him, Sir. He answer'd, that was true, they [15 wanted such for *Flanders*, to *Piedmont*, or *Germany*; but as for him, he was permitted to list young Boys.

Gr. Boys! A Rogue!

Cat. Yes, Sir, he says he has Orders to carry 'em so far, that before they come thither, they shall all have Beards.   [20

Gr. Where the Devil will he carry them?

Cat. Hold, Sir! For fear I should forget, I got it written upon that Paper.

Gr. To . . . . To *Madagascar* . . . . *Brillon* to *Madagascar* !

Cat. They say, Sir, 'tis not far from t'other World. [25

Ar. 'Tis undoubtedly, Brother, for that Colony you have heard speak of. The Boy is surely lost.

Cat. [*Weeping.*] Alas, Sir, I just saw the poor Child, they have already dress'd him in green, with a Grenadier's Cap ; (*Laughing*) and . . . . they have taught him to drum. One can hardly [30 forbear Laughing at it, and Crying at the same time.

Gr. Where does that damn'd Captain lodge, I'll go and rattle him ?

Cat. He does not lodge, he always encamps.

Gr. Come, carry me to the Place where you saw him : I [35 must go find out that Turk.

Cat. Have a Care of your self !

Gr. Why, what's the Matter ?

Cat. Well, Sir, you may go if you please ; but I shou'd at least advice you to make your Will, and take your Leave of your [40 Patients first.

Gr. Why so ?

Cat. The Captain, Sir, wants Physicians to carry 'em into that Country.

Ar. Physicians ! Take care of your self. [45

Gr. What an unfortunate Day is this to me . . . . . 'Twas the only one of my Children that promis'd any thing !

Cat. 'Tis true ; he was already as like you, as two Drops of Water.

Gr. Thou must go thither with Money, and . . . . . .

Cat. Sir, they will list me too, the Serjeant wou'd have [50 taken me, if I had not been too quick for him. He says, they have Orders to carry Women thither too.

Gr. Why these are terrible Listers !

Cat. M. *Mamurra* went thither to seek *Brillon* : By his Language he was taken for a Physician ; for you know, he talks like a Fool, [55 and was presently shopp'd up. I did not see him ; but I heard him scold in a Chamber, where he swore in *Latin*, as if he had been possess'd ; to morrow Morning they set out.

Ar. You must send some body thither quickly.

Gr. But who can we find who will be safe from being listed ? [60

Cat. Desire him to go. [*Aside to* Grich.

Gr. Him ?

Cat. Yes, him. He will run no risque, they don't want Lawyers in that Country.

Gr. We cou'd do well enough without 'em here . . . . . [65 Go then, and at any Rate . . . .

Ar. I will spare nothing, and will bring *Brillon*, or lose my *Latin*.

Gr. You'd lose no great Matter.

Cat. Sir, the Captain is still at his Uncle's.

Ar. His Uncle ? [70

III. vii. 71.

Cat. M. *de St. Alvar.*

Gr. What, is that Captain the Nephew he has so often mention'd?

Cat. Yes, Sir, and he was to go to take his Leave of him; I believe he's there now.   [75

Ar. I'll run, that I may not miss of him; 'tis but a little Way off, I'll bring you an Answer in a Moment.

SCENE VIII

Cat. I'm afraid, Sir, they won't restore you your Son.

Gr. Why not? Hussy.

Cat. The Captain despises Money, he's a Marquiss of three thousand a Year. He has a Prince's Equipage, and his Men told me, that the King has given him the Government of *Madagascar.*   [5

Gr. Sure all the Devil's in Hell to day are let loose against me.

Cat. (*Aside.*) Not all yet . . . . . How griev'd I am for the poor Child.

Gr. 'Sdeath! If the sick Lord I'm to visit to morrow, was at *London,* I'd make that Captain know . . . . . But what does this   [10 Soldier want here?

SCENE IX

Enter Lol. *dress'd like a Soldier, with a Halberd.*

Cat. Ah, Sir, 'tis the Captain's Serjeant.

Gr. Perhaps he's come to restore me *Brillon.*

Lol. *Brillon?* No.

Gr. (*Aside trembling.*) Oh, oh, 'tis that Knave for a Dancing-Master.   [5

Cat. (*After having gone up to, and look'd on him.*) 'Tis he himself, Sir, I did not know him at first.

Lol. Yes, Sir, since I had the Honour to see you last, a Halberd was offer'd me; I am no longer *Rigaudon*: I am now M. *de la Motte,* at your Service.   [10

Gr. Plague take you.

Lol. I come to desire you, Sir, not to be angry with me for my last Visit.

Gr. The Devil take you.

Lol. However, if you have any thing on your Mind, that . . . . . [15

Gr. M. *Rigaudon,* or M. *de la Motte,* which you please: Be gone quickly, and trouble me no longer.

Lol. I likewise come, Sir, to give you Warning from my Captain, not to make him wait to morrow Morning.

Gr. What do you mean by this?   [20

Lol. I mean, Sir, you must be ready to go to morrow Morning by four a Clock.

Gr. Who, I ?

Lol. Yes, you, Sir.

Cat. You take him for another sure . . . . [25

Lol. No, Child, no; Is not he M. *Grichard*? You shall go from hence to *Brest*, Sir, in my Captain's Coach; and from thence, you shall embark in good Company.

Gr. What Nonsense you talk !

Lol. No Nonsense, Sir, Did you not promise the Man my [30 Captain sent just now, to go to morrow Morning ?

Cat. You equivocate, Sir, my Master promis'd to go with the Chaplain.

Lol. Right, why there's the Business. That is the Chaplain of our Regiment. [35

Gr. Oh ! I'm lost.

Cat. But 'tis to see a sick Lord in the Country, whom he promis'd to go to.

Lol. Why right again. That Country is *Madagascar* : A good Country; and that Lord is the Viceroy of the Island : A brave [40 Man.

Gr. What have I done ! What have I done !

Lol. 'Sblood, you shall be his chief Physician; I give you my Word on't.

Cat. What, Sir, Must *You* go to *Madagascar* too ! [45

Gr. I shall run mad.

Lol. He shall certainly go; he has given his Word on it in Writing, and my Captain will make him march.

Gr. I can hold no longer. Go, Rogue, tell thy Chaplain, Captain, Viceroy, and all thy *Madagascarians*, that they shall not mock [50 the Fury of a Physician.

Lol. Sir, Sir, you are a Man of Honour; and since you have engaged your self to go, Go you shall . . . .

Gr. Yes, Villain, I'll *Go*; but it shall be to assemble the Faculty.

Lol. And I the Regiment; we'll try who'll have the best on't. [55

Gr. This Affair interests all my Brethren.

Lol. Ah, Sir, if you cou'd but bring one of them with you, 'twou'd be good Service. There would be but too many of 'em in *London*.

SCENE X

Enter Aristus.

Ar. They are absolutely resolv'd not to restore your Son.

Cat. Ay; that is not all.

Ar. How !

Cat. My Master too must go to *Madagascar*.

III. x. 5.

Ar. What, my Brother !   [5

Cat. He has engag'd himself to it; he is trick'd, you were present, that Chaplain ⟨. . .⟩

Ar. Ah, I see how it is : What Treachery !

Lol. Sir, you are deceiv'd, he'll make his Fortune in that Country; they are not yet undeceiv'd as to Physicians there, as they are   [10 here.

Gr. The Villain !

Lol. 'Tis the best Place in the World for Men of his Profession.

Gr. The Traytor !

Lol. From thence comes all the Specifick Drugs.   [15

Gr. The Blockhead !

Lol. What Pleasure will it be for a Physician to see himself at the Source at Cassia, Sena, and Rhubarb.

Gr. I must strangle the Rascal.

Lol. (*Presenting his Halberd.*) Halt there. Adieu, Sir; if [20 you are not at my Captain's to morrow Morning by four a Clock, you shall have thirty Soldiers lodg'd at Discretion here at five. So, Sir, your Servant, 'till I see you again.   [*Exit.*

Cat. Sir, I suspect something which I must search further into. There's some Cheat in't.   [*Exit.*

SCENE XI

Ar. See, Brother, what your ill Humour costs you, the Blow you gave *Brillon* is the Cause of all this. The young Rogue went and listed himself, and has given room to the Trick that is plaid you; you will find it hard to disintangle your self; I have told you a thousand times, that your cross Temper wou'd draw upon you . . . . [5

Gr. We are seeking Means to hinder *Brillon* and me, from being carry'd to *Madagascar*, and the Itch of moralising takes you.

Ar. As for me, I can't see what Means will do where Money fails; all that can be used in Ills that are without Remedy is Patience. Mean while Prudence will . . . .   [10

Gr. What a Man you are ! Know, Sir Brother, I had rather go a thousand times to *Madagascar*, to *Siam*, to *Monomotapa*, than hear such unseasonable Morals. 'Tis what you were reproved for t'other Day at the Bar, you prattled an Hour upon the ancient *Babilonians* when the Law was about a *Goat* that was stolen : I am mad [15 when . . . .

SCENE XII

Enter Terignan, Hortensia *and* Catau.

Ter. Father, I have found out the Trick that has been play'd you, I have discover'd from whence all this proceeds; and I come to

tell you, that it lies in you only, not to go to *Madagascar*, and to have
my Brother again without its costing you a Farthing.

Gr. How ?   [5

Ter. M. *de St. Alvar* is the Cause of all.

Ar. M. *de St. Alvar* !

Ter. He himself : By ill Luck he is nearly ally'd to the Captain . . . .

Gr. I know he is his Uncle ; proceed.

Ter. He went and complain'd to his Nephew, that you had   [10
broken your Promise, and that was the most sensible Affront cou'd
be offer'd to a Gentleman.

Gr. Curs'd old Rogue !

Ar. He said right indeed, that he cou'd find Means to be reveng'd.

Ter. The Captain swore he wou'd carry away You and my   [15
Brother, unless you marry'd *Clarice*.

Gr. I ! I marry that Coquet ! I had as lief be marry'd to the
Opera.

Ter. I'll go then and tell him so.

Ar. Stay, Nephew. Let us take an Expedient that may   [20
content every body, it must certainly be indifferent to them which
of you two marries *Clarice*.

Ter. Ah, Uncle, I understand you.

Ar. And *Hortensia* must have the Captain.

Hor. What, Shall I marry a Man that will carry me to the   [25
End of the World.

Cat. Go, go, Madam, I know Women, who shew their Husbands
more Countries than . . . . But the Contracts are drawn, and here
come our People.

Last SCENE ⟨XIII⟩

Enter to them, M. Rigaut, *at the further End of the Stage,* M. de St.
Alvar, Clarice, Mondore, Brillon *and* Mamurra.

Mon. Sir, upon the Promise given me on your Part, there's your
Son, whom I bring you with Pleasure.

Gr. You have used me . . . . But, no more of that ; we will
talk of that another time : Where's my Writing ?

Mon. I will restore it you, when you have sign'd the two   [5
Contracts.

Gr. Let's sign then.

Ma. Sir !

Gr. Oh ! Get you gone to *Madagascar*.

Br. Do, pray Father, let me go with the Marquis.   [10

Gr. Peace, Sirrah.

Al. Come, Sir, let us sign if you please ; you must begin.

Gr. Do you begin, if you will.

III. xiii. 14.

Al. (*Signs.*) Don't let us lose time in useless Compliments, 'tis
late.   [15

Gr. (*Signs.*) Well, let me sign.

Ter. Father, I declare howsoever . . . .

Gr. Only sign, I say.   [Ter. *signs.*

Hor. I will not go to . . . .

Gr. Make haste, or I'll shew who's Master.   20
                                              [She *and* Clarice *sign.*

Rig. M. *Mondore* now is only to sign.

Mon. I do willingly.

Gr. *Mondore* ! What means this ?

Cat. Yes, Sir, 'tis *Mondore.* He it was, who by my Order, listed
you and *Brillon.* 'Twas I, who made him a Marquis and the [25
Governour of *Madagascar.* Now since he has his Wish, he renounces
those Titles.

Gr. Damn'd *Abigail* ! I'll choak thee : You Hussy ; it is so, Is it ?

⟨*Cl.*⟩ Sir, she has only obey'd your Will : Yesterday you were
resolv'd to give her to *Mondore* ; you have given her to him [30
to day ; What have you to complain of ?

Mon. Sir, the Honour of your Alliance and Love . . . .

Gr. Fiddlestick of Honour and Love . . . . I rave, I burst ;
I'm sold, cheated, betray'd, Assassinated on all sides ; but thou shalt
be hang'd, execrable Forgery !   [35

Rig. Sir, you shall hang no body, these two Contracts were drawn
by your Order yesterday, you have sign'd them to day.

Ar. (*Smiling.*) Brother, if you had been of another Humour,
we shou'd have taken other Measures.

Gr. Zoons, it shall cost the Lives of above four . . . . .   [40
                                                           [*Exit.*

Cat. Of his Patients he means, I suppose ; but let us go and
rejoyce, and the Grumbler may hang himself if he will.

FINIS

POEMS AND TRANSLATIONS ASCRIBED TO SEDLEY ON DOUBTFUL AUTHORITY

From Kemp's Collection, 1672.

XCIV

DISTICH

Although no Art the Fire of Love can tame,
'Tis oft extinguish't by an equal flame.

XCV

The painted Apples that adorn,
  Of yon'd fair Tree, the Airy top,
And seems our dull approach to scorn,
  From their weak Stalk must one day drop;
  And out of reach of Mortals plac't,   5
  Be the vile food of Worms at last;
  Thus ends of Humane things the Pride,
  Borne down Times ever-flowing Tide.

Thy matchless Beauty, that we all
  Now with such heat and passion court,   10
Though kept from worthy Lovers, shall
  Confess its Tyranny but short:
  Then do not Love with Anger meet,
  Nor cruel be, to seem discreet;
  Shunning what nature does intend,   15
  Things seldom meet a nobler end.

From Stephens's Miscellany Poems, 1685

XCVI

UPON THE SLIGHTING OF HIS FRIENDS LOVE

Love guides my hand, and shews me what to write,
That (thou) mayst know 'tis she that doth Indite.
When Love's concern'd to make her language known,⎫
She doth by Numbers soft, and sweet, bemoan ⎬
(Thy silence) enough to make her sigh and groan. ⎭   5
She fears that thy sweet Natur's wing'd away,

142

Because not touch'd, by its enlivening Ray :
She doubts some Veil has overspread its Light,
Which threatens more than an Aegyptian Night ;
Wherein nought but sad mournful Clouds appear,   10
Enough to strike thee into endless fear.
When she on every side doth cast an Eye, ⎫
To see (perhaps) if once she might descry ⎬
Her pleasing, look'd for Object passing by. ⎭
There's nought appears, her Vigilance is vain ;   15
Her careful Eye is recompenc'd with pain.
Then down she sinks, bereav'd of her sweet breath
The only sign, that now she's seiz'd with Death.
Weep now ye Heavens ; and let each pearly tear
Accompany mounting grief, and trembling fear.   20
For since Love's dead, the Beauty of our Isle,
Its more than madness to attempt a smile ;
This rather would become some pompous, nuptial train,
Than him, whose Heart feels griefs insulting pain.
When once a Jewel's lost, how careful is each Eye,   25
In prying out this Author of our misery ?
No less is he depriv'd of courting rest
When Love has left a drooping, panting Breast.
Curs'd be that Person, who has chas'd thee hence,
Heaven, with this black crime, can ne're dispence !   30
Curs'd be that time, that e're she fix'd on thee,
The Mother of such unheard of Cruelty.
Curs'd be that place, in which she did impart
Her amorous smiles, her most alluring Art.
In fine a Curse all Curses else above   35
On her, that dar'd to stab our darling Love !
May never once Loves Charms attend thee more,
Till thou attones for what is done before.
What have I said ! this, this, can never be
Done by the hands of basest Treachery.   40
No, no : we must the Gods above implore,
Who only can the dead, to life restore.
Be propitious then, ye ruling Pow'rs above,
And send us back our hence departed Love.
That we may see her raise a tow'ring frame ⎫   45
Adorn'd with lustre from her radiant flame ⎬
Too great to be exprest by empty name. ⎭
Bless us but in this, and then shall we ⎫
In reverence bow, a lowly thankful Knee, ⎬
Before the throne of your own sacred Deity. ⎭   50
Our words, like well tun'd Instruments shall be,
Breathing forth nought but grateful Harmony
Our Actions, they shall pay you Tribute, too,
For all is yours, when once we are blest by you.   54

From Poetical Recreations, 1688

XCVII

UPON A GENTLEWOMANS REFUSAL OF A LETTER FROM ONE SHE WAS INGAGED TO

Not hear my *Message*, but the *Bearer* shun !
What hellish *Fiend* inrag'd could more have done ?
Surely the *Gods* design to make my Fate
Of all most wretched, and unfortunate.
'Twas but a *Letter*, and the *Words* were few,   5
Fill'd with *kind wishes*, but my *Fate's* too true.
I'm lost for ever banish'd from her sight,
Although by *Oaths* and *Vows* she's mine by right.
Ye *Gods !* look down and hear my *Sorrows* moan,
Like the faint *Echoes* of a dying groan.   10
But now is't possible so fair a *Face*
Shou'd have a *Soul* so treacherous and base,
To promise *constancy*, and then to prove
False and unkind to him she vow'd to love ?
Oh, Barb'rous *Sex !* whose Nature is to rook   15
And cheat *Mankind* with a *betraying look*.
Hence I'll keep guard within from all your *Charms*,
And ever more resist all fresh *Alarms ;*
I'll trace your windings through the darkest *Cell*,
And find your *Stratagems*, though lodg'd in *Hell.*   20
Your gilded *Paintings*, and each treacherous *Wile*,
By which so eas'ly you *Mankind* beguile ;
Winds are more *Constant* than a *Womans* Mind,
Who holds to none but to the present kind :
For when by *absence* th' object is remov'd,   25
The time is gone and spent wherein she lov'd.
And is it not the very same with me,
To slight my *Love*, when I must absent be ?
Perhaps sh' has seen a more atracting Face,
And a new *Paramour* has taken place,   30
And shall my injur'd *Soul* stand *Mute*, and live,
Whilst that another reaps what she can give ?
Glutted with *pleasures*, and again renew
Their past delights, although my claim and due.
Oh, no, my Soul's inrag'd, revenge calls on,   35
I'll tear her piece-meal e'er my fury's gone ;
Stretch out my *Arm* all o'er th' inconstant stain,
And then cleave down her treach'rous *limbs* in twain :
The greatest *plagues* Invention e'er cou'd find,
Is not sufficient for th' *inconstant Mind.*   40
I think I have o'ercome my Passion quite,

And cou'd not *love*, although 'twere in despight.
As for the *Man* who must enjoy my room,
He'll soon be partner in my wretched doom ;
He by her *Faith*, alas, no more will find,   45
Than when she swore to me to prove most kind.
Therefore I'll leave her and esteem her less ;
And in my self both *joy* and acquiesce.
But oh, my *Heart*, there's something moves there still,
Sure 'tis the vigour of *unbounded Will*.   50
Too much, I fear, my *Fetters* are not gone,
Or I at least again must put them on.
Methinks I feel my *Heart* is not got free, ⎫
Nor all my *Passions* set at liberty, ⎬
From the bright glances of her am'rous *Eye*. ⎭   55
Down *Rebel-love*, and hide thy boyish Head,
I'm too much *Man* to hear thy follies plead :
Go seek some other *Breast* of lower note ;
Go make some Old decrepit *Cuckold* dote :
Begone I say, or strait thy *Quiver*, Bow,   60
And thou thy self fall to destruction too.
And oh, I'm gone, my *Foes* have all got ground,
My *Brains* grow giddy, and my *Head* turns round.
My *Heart's* intangled with the *Nets* of Love ;
My *Passions* rave, and now ye *Gods* above   65
Help on my doom, and heave me to your Skies ;
Look, look, *Mervinda's* just before my Eyes :
Help me to catch her e'er her *Shadow* fly,
And I fall downward from this rowling *Sky*.   69

XCVIII

SONG

The *Prodigal's Resolution*

I

I am a lusty lively Lad,
    Arriv'd at One-and-Twenty ;
My Father left me all he had,
    Both Gold and Silver plenty.
Now He's in Grave, I will be brave,   5
    The Ladies shall adore me ;
I'll Court and Kiss, what hurt's in this ?
    My *Dad* did so before me.

II

My *Father*, to get my Estate,
   Though selfish, yet was slavish;   10
I'll spend it at another rate,
   And be as leudly lavish.
From *Mad-men*, *Fools*, and *Knaves* he did,
   Litigiously receive it;
If so he did, Justice forbid,   15
   But I to such shou'd leave it.

III

Then I'll to Court, where *Venus* sport,
   Doth revel it in plenty;
And deal with all, both great and small,
   From twelve to five and twenty.   20
In Play-houses I'll spend my Days,
   For there are store of Misses;
Ladies, make room, behold I come,
   To purchase many Kisses.   24

XCIX

SONG

The *Doubtfull Lover* Resolv'd

Fain wou'd I *Love*, but that I fear,
I quickly shou'd the *Willow* wear:
Fain wou'd I Marry, but Men say,
When *Love* is try'd, he will away.
Then tell me, *Love*, what I shall doe,   5
To cure these Fears whene'er I Wooe.
The *Fair* one, she's a mark to all;
The *Brown* one each doth lovely call;
The *Black* a Pearl in fair Mens Eyes,
The rest will stoop to any prize.   10
Then tell me, Love, what I shall doe,
To cure these *Fears* when e'er I Woe.

Reply

Go, Lover, know it is not I
That wound with fear or jealousie;
Nor do Men feel those ⟨killing⟩ smarts,   15
Untill they have confin'd their *Hearts*.
Then if you'll cure your *Fears* you shall
Love neither Fair, Black, Brown, but all.   18

C

SONG

The Cavalier's Catch

I

Did you see this *Cup* of *Liquor*,
    How invitingly it looks;
'Twill make a *Lawyer* prattle quicker,
    And a *Scholar* burn his Books:
'Twill make a Cripple for to Caper,   5
    And a *Dumb Man* clearly *Sing;*
'Twill make a *Coward* draw his Rapier,
    Here's a Health to *James* our *King.*

II

If that here be any *Round-head,*
    That refuse this *Health* to pledge;   10
I wish he then may be confounded,
    Underneath some rotten *Hedge,*
May the *French Disease* o'er-take him,
    And upon his *Face* appear,
And his *Wife* a *Cuckold* make him,   15
    By some *Jovial Cavalier.*

CI

SONG

I

Evadne, I must tell you so,
    You are too *cruel* grown;
No *smiles* nor *pity* you bestow,
    But *Death* in ev'ry *frown.*
My *Love,* though *chast* and *constant* too,   5
    Yet no relief can find;
Curst be the Slave that's *false* to you,
    Though *you* are still *unkind.*

II

Were you as merciful as fair,
    My *wishes* wou'd obtain;   10
But *love* I must, though *I despair,*
    And perish in the pain.

If in an *Age* I can prevail,
I happy then shall be;
And cou'd I live, I wou'd not fail   15
To wait Eternally.

From Buckingham's Miscellaneous Works, 1704

CII

THE ROYAL KNOTTER

I

Ah happy People ye must thrive
Whilst thus the Royal Pair does strive
    Both to advance your Glory;
While he (by's Valour) conquers *France*,
She Manufacturers does advance,   5
    And makes Thread-fringes for ye.

II

Bless'd we! who from such Queens are freed,
Who by vain Superstition led,
    Are always telling Beads;
But here's a Queen, now, thanks to God,   10
Who, when she rides in Coach abroad,
    Is always knotting Threads.

III

Then hast, victorious *Nassau*, hast,
And when thy Summer Show is past,
    Let all thy Trumpets sound: 15
The Fringe which this Campain has wrought,
Tho' it cost the Nation scarce a Groat,
    Thy Conquests will surround.   18

CIII

ADVICE TO LOVERS

I

Damon, if thou wilt believe me,
    'Tis not Sighing round the Plain,
Songs and Sonnets cann't relieve thee,
    Faint attempts in love are vain.

II

Urge but home the fair Occasion,   5
   And be Master of the Field ;
To a powerful kind invasion
   'Tis a Madness not to yield.

III

Love gives out a large Commission,
   Still indulgent to the brave ;   10
But one Sin of large Omission,
   Never Woman yet forgave,

IV

Though she swears she'll ne'er permit you,
   Cries you're rude, and much to blame,
Or with Tears implores your Pity,   15
   Be not merciful for shame.

V

When the fierce Assault is over,
   Chloris soon enough must find
This her cruel furious Lover
   Much more gentle, not so kind.   20

CIV

AGAINST HIS MISTRESS'S CRUELTY

I

Love, How unequal are thy Laws,
   That Men that least endeavour
Thou favour'st, and neglect'st the Cause
   Of those that most persever !

II

What careless Lovers have been blest,   5
   Untouch'd with Grief and Anguish,
Since cruel *Sylvia* charm'd my Breast,
   Unmov'd to see me languish !

III

I find my fatal Error now
   In thinking e'er to move her,   10
Too great the Difficulty grew
   For any mortal Lover.

IV

But what Advantage can it bring
That I at last perceive it ?
'Twas rash to undertake the thing, 15
And 'tis too late to leave it.

CV

THE PETITION

Oh *Lycidas,* why thus alone
With Arms a cross, dost sigh and moan ?
Can thy *Cosmelia* prove unkind,
Or ought prevail to change her Mind ?
She was, she is great Nature's Pride ; 5
In Goodness, to the best ally'd
In her bright Eyes such Beauties Shine,
Mercy would make her all divine ;
O ye propitious Powers above,
That gently do incline to love, 10
Convey into her Breast soft Fire,
Amorous Thoughts, and kind Desire.
But if it be decreed by Fate,
That I must love, and she must hate ;
Ah ! let her not Disdain to give 15
A Tear, when I no longer live.

From the Diverting Post, 1704

CVI

By Sir *Charles Sidley.* Written Extempore

The Noble Man, why he's a thing
Thats next in Honour to the King ;
But if his Lordship's Knave or Fool,
At best he's but a Noble Tool,
Either to work with or be wrought on, 5
As odd a thing as can be thought on :
What signifies an empty Word,
His Grace, his Highness, or my Lord,
Saving your Presence, not a T——d.
'Tis Virtue stamps his Character, 10
And adds a lustre to his Star.

From Poems on State Affairs, 1705

CVII

A FABLE

In Aesop's Tales an honest Wretch we find,
Whose Years and Comforts equally declin'd;
He in two Wives had two domestick Ills,
For different Age they had and different Wills
One pluckt his Black Hairs out, and one his Grey,   5
The Man for quietness did both obey,
Till all his Parish saw his Head quite bare,
And thought he wanted Brains as well as Hair.

The Moral

The Parties hen-peckt *W——m*, are they Wives,
The Hairs they pluck are thy Prerogatives;   10
Tories thy Person hate, the Whigs thy Power,
Tho much thou yieldest, till they tug for more,
Till this poor Man, and thou, alike are shown,
He without Hair, and thou without a Crown.   14

From Briscoe's Edition of 1707

CVIII

ON THE HAPPY CORYDON AND PHILLIS

Young *Coridon* and *Phillis*,
Sat in a lovely Grove,
Contriving Crowns of Lillies,
Repeating toys of Love,
   And something else, but what I dare not name;   5
But as they were a playing,
She ogled so the Swain,
It sav'd her plainly saying,
   Let's kiss to ease our pain, and something else.
A thousand times he kist her,   10
Laying her on the Green;
But as he further prest her
   A pritty Leg was seen, and ——
So many Beauties viewing,
His Ardor still increast,   15
And greater Joys pursuing,
   He wander'd o'er her Breast, and ——
A last effort she trying

His Passion to withstand,
Cry'd, but 'twas faintly Crying,   20
 Pray take away your Hand, and ——
Young *Corydon* grown bolder,
The Minutes wou'd improve,
This is the time, he told her
 To shew you how I Love, and ——   25
The Nymph seem'd almost dying,
Dissolv'd in amorous Heat,
She kiss'd, and told him sighing,
 My Dear, your Love is great, and ——
But *Phillis* did recover,   30
Much sooner than the Swain,
She blushing ask'd her Lover,
 Shall we not kiss again, and ——
Thus Love his Revells keeping,
Till Nature at a stand,   35
From talk they fell to sleeping,
 Holding each other's Hand, and——

CIX

ON A LADY THAT DID NOT LOVE APPLES

Happy our Race; and blessed all Mankind,
Had but *Eve*'s Palate been, like yours, refin'd,
Nor meanly stoop'd, while in her natures Pride,
To taste the poorest Fruit, that Heav'n deny'd.
But nought tempts Woman, more than a Restraint,   5
Access deny, and strait on that they're bent;
And had your Coyness, in her place been found,
The Devil had strove in vain to give the Wound.
Tho' cast his Serpents Skin, to be more fair,
Tho' dress'd like Beau, and courted with an Air,   10
For where Man fails, the Devil must sure dispair :
In vain, he'd strove your Virgin Heart to Storm,
We'd all been sav'd, had you her part perform'd.
But since long time will not that change allow,
Be but a second Eve, and save us now.   15

CX

ON FRUITION

None, but a Muse in Love, can tell
The sweet tumultuous joys I feel,
When on *Cælia's* Breast I lye,
When I tremble, faint, and dye;

Mingling Kisses with Embraces,　　　　　5
Darting Tongues, and joyning Faces,
Panting, stretching, sweating, cooing,
All in the extasie, of doing.　　　　　　8

From Briscoe's Edition of 1722

CXI

TO CELINDA

Celinda, think not by Disdain,
　　To vanquish my Desire
By telling me, I sigh in vain
　　And feed a hopeless Fire.
Despair it self too weak does prove,　　　5
　　Your Beauty to disarm,
By Fate I was ordain'd to Love,
　　As you were born to Charm.　　　　8

CXII

A SONG

Celinda

Prithee tell me, faithless Swain,
Why shou'd you such Passion feign,
　　On purpose to deceive me?
So soon as I to love began,
　　Then you began to leave me.　　　　5

Damon

Celinda, you must blame your Fate,
Kindness has its certain Date,
　　E'er we the Joys have tasted,
Had you not then with feigned Hate
　　Love's kindest Hours wasted.　　　　10

Then weep no more, nor sigh in vain,
But lay your Baits to catch again
　　A more deserving Lover;
For know, a Slave who's broke his Chain
　　You never can recover.　　　　　　15

CXIII

CUPID'S RETURN

Welcome, thrice welcome to my frozen Heart,
  Thou long departed Fire,
How could'st thou so regardless be
Of one so true, so fond as me,
Whose early Thought, whose first Desire   5
  Was pointed all to thee?
When in the Morning of my Day,
  Thy Empire first began,
Pleased with the Prospect of thy Sway,
  Into thy Arms I ran;   10
Without Reserve my willing Heart I gave;
Proud that I had my Freedom lost:
Contending which I ought to boast
The making thee a Sov'reign, or my self a Slave.

Still I am form'd to execute thy Will,   15
  By me declare thy Power and Skill;
My Heart already by thy Fire
  Is so prepar'd, is so refin'd,
    There's nothing left behind
    But infinite Desire.   20
O! would'st thou touch that lovely Maid,
(Whose Charms and thine I have obey'd)
    With such another Flame,
  The Heav'n that would appear in me,
Wou'd speak such Goodness dwelt in thee;
    Thy Bow, thy Art,   25
  No more need guide thy Dart;
No Art so stubborn but at that would aim.

THE PASTORALS OF VIRGIL

THE PREFACE

As the chief Aim of Poetry ought to be the copying of Nature, so the principal Design of Translation should be the Resemblance of its Original.

That this may be most nearly and compleatly taken, 'tis requisite, beside our Author's Language, to know his utmost Meaning and Intention, and as far as possible the very Disposition and Frame of his Mind, and Temper of his Genius. For Authors generally in their Works give in some measure an Image of themselves; and every one has something in him particularly remarkable and distinguishable from all others.

And though a too servile or pedantic following is by all means to be avoided, because it necessarily cramps the Vigour and Gracefulness required in a good Translation; yet a just Translator ought by no means farther to deviate in any respect, than that Necessity compels him; and whoever has most of the Likeness of every particular Part with an equal Share of the Beauty and Force of the whole, undoubtedly shews the noblest Skill, and is the most accomplish'd, and happy in his Performance.

How far I have succeeded here, I must leave others to judge.

Yet since an earnest Zeal to do some right to this incomparable Author has engag'd me in this Undertaking, I hope the candid and ingenious will forgive me the Faults I may have committed, if they are not many or considerable.

CXIV

THE FIRST PASTORAL

T⟨ity⟩rus Melibæus

Melibæus

You *T⟨ity⟩rus !* in the cool refreshing Shade
Of a broad *Beach*, thus negligently lay'd,
In your sweet Pipe and rural Muse delight.
We forc'd, alas ! from our dear Country's fight
And pleasant Fields, in sad Distress to fly,   5
Are doom'd in woful Banishment to lie :
You undisturb'd here sing your am'rous Lays,
And make the Groves sound *Amaryllis* Praise.

Tityrus

This Leisure 'twas a God bestow'd : for he,
Oh *Melibæus !* shall be such to me ;   10
Oft shall his Altar with Devotion due,
The streaming Blood of my young Lambs imbrue.
He suffer'd as you see my Herds to stray,
And will'd that on my Pipe, I shou'd securely play.

Melibæus

I envy not thy Case, but wonder much,   15
While of our Plains the sad Distraction's such ;
See ailing thence, I my *She-Goats* convey.
This, *Tityrus !* I can hardly drag away,
Amid'st the Hazels, as I came along,
She yeaning unexpectedly two young ;   20
(The Hope of my unhappy Flock) has left
On the hard Stone of ev'ry Help bereft.
This sad Mischance, was I not stupid grown !
My blasted Oaks had oftentimes made known,
And often from a hollow Holm the *Crow*   25
Did on the left the coming Mischief show :
But yet oh ! *Tityrus !* I pray disclose
The God who this distinguish'd Favour shows.

Tityrus

The City they call *Rome*, as yet unknown,
I thought, oh *Melibæus !* like our own,   30
(Fool that I was) whither we us'd to go,
And oft the young-ones of our Flock bestow,
So Whelps I had perceiv'd, were like their Damms,

And like the Mother Ews, the tender Lambs :
So little Things I did compare with great,　　　　35
But other Cities this excels in State,
Rising o'er all, as Cypresses exceed
The creeping Osier, or the binding Reed.

Melibæus

And what was the prevailing Cause that drew
Your mind this great aspiring *Rome* to view ?　　　40

Tityrus

'Twas Liberty, which tho', it scarce appear'd,
When the *grey* Hairs were sprinkled in my Beard,
Long look'd-for kindly did arrive at last,
When *Galatea's* early Love was pass'd,
And *Amaryllis* did my Heart possess ;　　　　45
For dallying with the first, I must confess,
No hope of Liberty, nor Care had I
T' increase my Store, or gain a fit Supply,
To cure my Wants ; tho' often of the best,
Pass'd from my Folds, and store of *Cheese* was press'd.　50
Unprofitably to the City sent,
For what I got, I there profusely spent.

Melibæus

Oh *Amaryllis !* little guess I had
For whom you pray'd, for whom you was so sad ;
For what Occasion, for whose sake so long　　　55
Th' ungather'd Apples on their Branches hung.
Tityrus was hence ; oh *Tityrus !* thy lov'd Name,
The Springs, the Pines, nay Bushes did proclaim.

Tityrus

What shou'd I do ? what cou'd I hope to be
By other means from lasting Service free ?　　　60
Nor cou'd I think to find another, where
A fav'ring God so ready to my Prayer !
Here *Melibæus !* I beheld him here,
The Youth for whom our Altars twice a Year
Shall smoke with Incense. He (when I address'd)　　65
Kindly and soon, thus answer'd my Request.
Go Boy ! be still on Rural Works imploy'd,
And hold whatever ye before enjoy'd.

Melibæus

Oh bless'd old Man ! thy Lands shall then endure,
And all Possessions still to thee secure ;   70
And large enough shall for thyself be found,
Tho' *Stones* and *Reeds* o'erspread the nearest Ground :
Thy *Flocks* from *Beasts* of *Prey* no harm shall find
Nor catch Infection from their neighbouring kind.
Oh fortunate old Man ! who may abide   75
Thus sweetly by this noted River's side,
Here with Delight thy leisure Time employ,
And of these sacred Springs the cool enjoy.
Here from the bord'ring Hedge the passing *Bees*,
Thy Ears shall with continual Murmurs please,   80
Soft Sleep invite, and give thy Labours ease.
The Pruner from the lofty Mountain there,
With chearful Songs shall chace intruding Care :
Here thy lov'd Pidgeons shall delight thy view,
There on sweet Elms the *Turtles* sweetly coo.   85

Tityrus

Therefore the *Stags* shall mounting feed in Air,
And Occeans sinking, leave their Fishes bare
On the dry Sands, the *Parthians* from their home,
And hardy *Germans* shall be forc'd to roam,
And to each others Land in Exile come,   90
Before the Figure of this Youth depart,
And quit Possession of my grateful Heart.

Melibæus

But we must hence dispers'd and driven go
To sultry *Africk*, and to *Scythia*'s Snow,
Part must with speed repair to spacious *Crete*,   95
And near the swift *Oaxis* take their Seat :
Part must on *Britain*'s barb'rous Land be hurl'd,
Amongst a Race divided from the World :
Yet when a long unhappy Time is pass'd,
Oh ! may I see my Country's Bounds at last,   100
And pleas'd, and wond'ring visit once again
My poor thatch'd Dwelling where I us'd to reign !
Shall a vile Soldier these neat Fields command ?
This Harvest bless a wicked barb'rous Hand ?
Oh fatal Strife ! from thee what Sorrows flow ?   105
From thee what Ills we wretched People know ?
See who the Fruits of all our Toil possess,
Now graft thy Pears, fond Swain ! thy *Vineyards* dress !
Hence ye *She-goats !* once prosp'rous and my Care,
Begone, henceforth stretch'd on the Grass, I ne'er   110
Shall see ye hanging on a Rock afar ;

Henceforth no Verses shall I sing, nor more
Protect and feed ye as I did before.

Tityrus

With me this Night however chuse to stay,
Forgetting Care yourself reposing lay   115
On the green Leaf, and of our present Fare,
(*Curds, Chessnuts, Apples*) take a welcome Share,
For see the Village Tops begin to fume,
And vaster Shadows from the Mountains come.   119

CXV

THE SECOND PASTORAL

The fair *Alexis* was his Master's Joy,
And *Coridon* lov'd the delicious Boy,
But failing of his Hope, he daily go's
Where *Beachen* Boughs a constant Shade compose,
There to the Woods and Mountains thus alone,   5
Makes in imperfect Strains his fruitless Moan.
Cruel *Alexis !* must my Verse and I
Be thus disdain'd by thee ?   Ah ! must I die,
Thro' thy Unkindness most unhappy made ?
Now Cattle seek the cool refreshing Shade,   10
And *Thestylis* sweet Herbs do's mixing beat
For weary Mowers vext with Toil and Heat ;
But while in eager Search of thee I run,
With me beneath the persecuting Sun,
The *Grashoppers* from ev'ry Bush bemoan   15
Their Case, and grate my Ears with a harsh Tone ;
Had it not better been for me poor Swain ⎫
Of peevish *Amaryllis* to sustain   ⎬
The direful Anger and the proud Disdain ? ⎭
Better had I *Menal⟨c⟩as* made my Care ?   20
Tho' swarthy he ; tho' thou as Lillies fair !
Oh Youth ! tho' bless'd with ev'ry blooming Grace,
Trust not too much to thy inticing Face.
White Blossoms from the Trees neglected fall,
The black uncomely Berry's sought by all.   25

Me you despise, *Alexis !* nor incline
To know what *Choice* and plenteous *Stores* are mine ;
A thousand *Lambs* I call my own each Day,
That scatter'd o'er *Sicilian* Mountains stray ;
Plenty of Milk in Summer fills my Pails,   30
Not even in the Winter-Season fails ;
Nor sweet *Amphion* singing to his Herd,
Cou'd be for Voice before myself prefer'd.

Nor am I free from Grace, I lately stood,
And view'd my Image in the briny Flood,   35
When not a Breath of Wind disturb'd the Sea,
Not *Daphnis* in his Form surpasses me,
And him (thyself a Judge) I cannot fear,
If like ourselves, our Images appear.

Oh! that with me, you wou'd these *Shades* admire,   40
And to our humble Cottages retire,
Pursue the *Harts*, and to the verdant Boughs,
Consent to drive the wanton *Goats* to brouze;
To the delightful Groves confine your Will,
And strive with me to rival *Pan* in Skill.   45
Pan, first, the Shepherd's Pipe and Skill improv'd;
By *Pan* the Sheep and Shepherds are belov'd;
With the melodious Pipe thy Lip to gall,
Grudge not, fair Youth! nor think it harm at all:
What, that this pleasing Art he might have known,   50
Wou'd not *Amyntas* willingly have done?

A Pipe of seven unequal Reeds I have,
That me of old, *Dametas* dying gave;
Take this last Token of my Love, said he,
And prosp'rous may it ever prove to thee,   55
The Fool *Amyntas* did with Envy see.
Beside two *Kids*, I in a Valley found
Their *Skins* ev'n now with white are *sprinkled* round
A Yew's swoln Udders twice they daily drain,
And both for thee still carefully remain.   60
Yet *Thestylis* to gain them often try's,
And she at last may have the hop'd-for Prize,
Why shou'd she not, since you my Gifts despise?

Come hither fairest, dearest Youth! and see
The lovely Presents here in Store for thee;   65
Behold the courteous Nymphs in Baskets bring
The choicest Beauties of the blooming Spring,
For thy Delight, pale Lillies and the blue
Soft Violets; the bright *Narcissus* too,
To which they Heads of sleepy Poppies joyn,   70
And Leaves of the sweet smelling *Anethine*.
Then having nicely cull'd each chosen Flow'r,
With each most fragrant Herb they dress thy Bow'r:
I joyning too will here employ my Care,
And downy Peaches for thy Tast prepare;   75
To these I'll add Chessnuts the most approv'd,
Such as my beauteous *Amaryllis* lov'd,

And waxen Plumbs, a Fruit deserving Praise :
Thou Myrtle ! too I'll crop, and Laurel-Spraies,
So plac'd, that both may grateful Scents dispence,   80
And mingling fully, entertain thy Sence.

   Oh *Coridon !* thy clownish Gifts forbear,
For thy mean Presents will *Alexis* care ?
Or were thy Off'rings ne'er so worthy ; yet
Wou'd *J⟨ola⟩s* in such to thee submit ?   85
What have I done ? in mentioning that Name,
How is my rash unwary Tongue to blame ?
A Southern Wind to blast my Flow'rs I bring,
And plunge the *Boars* into the christal Spring !
Whom fly you ! frantic Youth ? ev'n Gods have made   90
With Joy their Dwellings in the Sylvan Shade ;
Here *Trojan Paris* liv'd : let *Pallas* go
To Tow'rs that to her Art their Structure owe ;
There let the Warrior-Goddess proudly rest
The peaceful Groves of all things please me best.   95
Fierce *Lionesses* urg'd by strong Desire,
Pursue *He-Wolves* to quench their raging Fire ;
The *Wolves* themselves with hungry Appetite ⎫
Pursue the *Goats ;* green Leaves the *Goats* invite, ⎬
Thou me, *Alexis !* all things seek Delight. ⎭   100

See Ev'ning comes ; from Toils the Cattle cease,
And by the setting Sun the Shades increase ;
Yet do's my Pain its lasting Fury prove :
For oh ! what Measure can be found in Love ?

Ah ! *Coridon !* what wretched Frenzy's thine ?   105
Behold, at home, a tender blooming Vine
Ly's half undress'd ; haste thither, and apply
To useful Things, lay fruitless Wishes by ;
If this *Alexis* scorns you, you may find
Some other Youth to your Endeavours kind.   110

CXVI

THE THIRD PASTORAL

Dametas, Menalcas, Palæmon

Menalcas

Tell me, *Dametas !* whose'n Sheep these are :
Do's *Melibæus* own them ?

Dametas

No, my Care,
Ægon employs; if you wou'd understand
They're his late giv'n.

Menalcas

To an unhappy Hand;
For while he courts *Næera*, fearing she 5
Disdaining him, shou'd better think of me,
To bribe her Favour from his Master's Store;
Twice in an Hour he milks the Cattle o'er,
And thus he drains the Moisture from the Damms,
And of their Food defrauds the little Lambs. 10

Dametas

Yet softly thus to Elders; I know too,
Pert Youngster! Who did you now? what with you;
The rank *He-Goats* appear'd the Deed to blame,
Turning their Heads another way for Shame;
I noted well the sacred Place and Time, 15
But th' easy Nymphs by laughing pass'd the Crime.

Menalcas

'Twas when they saw this envious Hand of mine
Break *Micon*'s Shoots, and cut his tender Vine.

Dametas

Or at th' old Beachen Trees, when you thought fit
To *Daphnis* here to set your manly Wit, 20
Whose broaken *Bow* and *Shaft*, your Malice show'd, ⎱
For when you saw them on the Boy bestowed, ⎰
You griev'd, and from that time a *Grudge* you ow'd, ⎰
And if your Spleen had not been satisfy'd,
E'er this *Menalcas!* You had surely dy'd. 25

Menalcas

What shall we Masters do, when Varlets we
Audacious find to such a high Degree?
Did I myself not see you: Thou, most vile!
(*Lycisca*, barking greatly all the while,)
Attempt a *Goat* of *Damon*'s to betray, 30
And slily from the Flock to bear away?
And when I cry'd Ho! where now flies he to?
Tityrus! take care, observe your Cattle! you
Did close behind the Hedges sneaking lie.

Dametas

Pray can you tell me, strict Accuser ! why,   35
When he in singing was by me out-done,
He shou'd not yield the *Goat* I fairly won ?
The *Goat* you saw was mine (if you must know) ⎤
Damon himself confess'd it to be so,   ⎬
But did deny he cou'd the Due bestow.   ⎦   40

Menalcas

You him in singing ! such a wond'rous Deed !
Was you e'er Master of a waxen Reed ?
You *Ignoramus* ! who on the high Ways
Did use to squander miserable Lays,
And with a tuneless Pipe and senseless Song   45
Suit the dull Fancy of the gaping Throng.

Dametas

Then will you that we present Trial make
Of both our Skills ?   This Heifer here I stake,
Lest you refuse, and think the Prize too mean ;
Know in a Day, twice at the Pail she's seen,   50
Two Young besides she nurses, Stripling ! say
What Wager now with me you chuse to lay ?

Menalcas

As at this time my Circumstances are,
To wager from the Flock, I do not dare,
I have at home a Father, whom I fear,   55
And a Step-Mother that is too severe,
Twice in a Day, my Charge they numb'ring see,
Both the grown Cattle, and the young ones he,
But since the mad Man you're resolved to play,
What yourself shall worthier own, I'll lay   60
A Beachen Cup, with curious Carving grac'd, ⎤
By spreading Vines and Ivy 'round embrac'd, ⎬
Two Figures in the mid'st are neatly plac'd. ⎦
Conon and what's his Name ?   The Man that drew
The World and all its various People shew,   65
The Times when Harvest shou'd begin and end ;
And when the Ploughman at his Task shou'd bend ;
The Work Divine *Alcim⟨e⟩don*'s :   I keep
This up, as yet untouch'd by mortal Lip.

Dametas

And this *Alcimedon*, whom you have nam'd,   70
Two Cups for me has in like manner fram'd ;

The Rims *Acanthus* twining do's embrace, ⎫
The middle Part *Orpheus* appears to grace, ⎬
And following Woods, the sweet Musician trace. ⎭
These too, like you, with Care I hidden keep,   75
Nor to their Edges yet have laid my Lip;
Nevertheless, you'll small occasion find
To praise the Cup, if you the Heifer mind.

Menalcas

No where shall you escape this live-long Day,
Where e'er you slip, I'll follow strait away;   80
Our Diff'rence now, let any fairly try;
Let any Man be judge who passes by.
See there *Palæmon*, from this time I shall
Teach your bold Tongue more humble Words to all.

Dametas

Come on Pretender! and your utmost try, ⎫   85
I'm ready, and the worst you can defy, ⎬
Nor ever do I any basely fly. ⎭
But, Friend *Pal⟨æ⟩mon!* ponder well withal
Our present Cause; the matter is not small.

Palæmon

Then let your Skill be mutually express'd,   90
While here upon the tender Grass we rest,
The Trees now bloom, and each delightful Field
Do's now its choicest Sights and Odours yield,
Leaves crown the Woods, and in its Beauty's Prime,
The Year now reigns; most lovely is the Time.   95
Begin *Dametas!* and *Menalcas!* you ⎫
Shall in alternate Strains his Steps pursue, ⎬
Alternate Verses please the Muses too. ⎭

Dametas

Be your first Off'ring, Oh ye Muses! *Jove's*, ⎫
Jove fills the World, and ev'rything improves; ⎬   100
He gives us Plenty, and my Verses loves. ⎭

Menalcas

And me his Favour bright *Apollo* shows, ⎫
His Gift the Laurel ever with me grows, ⎬
He the sweet ruddy *Hyacinth* bestows. ⎭

Dametas

A wanton Lass, brisk *Galatea*, me ⎫   105
With Fruit allures; then passes swiftly she ⎬
And hides; yet wishes that I first shou'd see. ⎭

Menalcas

But scarce from me will kind *Amyntas* go,
Who freely comes and haunts my Dwelling so,
That not our *Dogs*, now *Delia* better know.   110

Dametas

My *Venus* soon shall have a Gift; for I
Lately a *Pidgeon's* Nest observ'd on high,
I mark'd the Place, and have it in my Eye.

Menalcas

Ten Wildings I have sent my lovely Friend,
'Twas what I cou'd; yet further I intend,   115
Ten more to morrow carefully to send.

Dametas

How oft has *Galatea* bless'd my Ear?
What has she say'd? ye gentle Breezes! bear
Some Part to Heav'n, that all the Gods may hear!

Menalcas

Small is thy valu'd Kindness in this Case   120
Amyntas! while the savage Boar you chace,
I hold the Nets, nor view thy comely Face.

Dametas

Hither (for this is my Birth's joyful Day)
Send *Phillis, Jolas!* and when I slay
A Heifer for my Fruits, come thou thyself away.   125

Menalcas

Of all my Loves, fair *Phillis* is the Head,
She Tears at my Departure kindly shed,
And oh! a long Farewell fair *Jolas!* she said.

Dametas

To Folds the *Wolf*, winds to tender Tree,
Show'rs to ripe Fruits most dreadful ever be,   130
And *Amaryllis* when inrag'd to me.

Menalcas

The Moisture's lov'd by Grain that's newly sown
Wean'd *Kids* to *Shrubs*, young are to *Sallows* prone,
Amyntas is my Choice, and he alone.

Dametas

Pollio the Ditties of my rural Reed, 135
My Verse tho' humble condescends to heed,
A Heifer Muses! for your Reader feed.

Menalcas

And Verses freely flow from *Pollio*'s Hand,
Pollio himself the Muses do's command :
Feed a fierce *Bull* that butts and spurns the Sand. 140

Dametas

Whom *Pollio* loves, may he all Pleasures know,
Each where to him, let plenteous Honey flow,
And prickly *Thorns, Arabian* Sweets bestow.

Menalcas

Who *Ticko*'s empty Verse imagin's fine ;
Oh lib'ral *Maurus !* may be pleas'd with thine, 145
The same may milk *He-Goats* and *Foxes* joyn.

Dametas

Ho, ye rash Boys ! who here so heedless pry ;
For Strawberries and Flow'rs hence quickly fly,
Lo ! a fell *Snake* hid in the Grass do's lie.

Menalcas

My *Sheep !* forbear approaching, I advise,
Who comes too near the Bark, not safely try's ; 150
For see the *Ram* his Fleece this instant dry's.

Dametas

My *Goats*, oh *Tityrus !* from the River bring,
When Time shall make it a convenient Thing,
I'll wash them all in yonder Chrystal Spring. 155

Menalcas

Boys ! drive the *Sheep* to some protecting Shade,
Lest, for their Milk, vain Trial shou'd be made ;
(Dry'd up thro' Heat) and we as late betray'd.

Dametas

How lean a *Bull* in a fat Field I view ?
This Love, alas ! do's mortal Things undo, 160
Ruins the Herd, the wretched Herdsman too.

Menalcas

These tender *Lambs!* their Misery ne'er sprung ⎫
From Love, their Skins scarce on the Bones are hung, ⎬
What evil Eye has thus bewitch'd my Young. ⎭

Dametas

Say in what Land the Heav'ns open lye ⎫   165
Three Ells alone? (to the observing Eye,) ⎬
And for thy Skill with great *Apollo* vye. ⎭

Menalcas

Say in what Land? if thou hast found declare, ⎫
Where growing Flow'rs the Names of Monarchs wear, ⎬
And from all Rivals lovely *Phillis* bear. ⎭   170

Palæmon

Me for a Judge, but illy you provide
A Cause of so great Moment to decide,
The *Heifer* both deserve, and all who fear
A Love that's kind, or prove a too severe;
Now let the River's running be restrain'd   175
Enough, my Boys! this time the Meads have gain'd.

CXVII

THE FOURTH PASTORAL

Sicilian Muses! yet a higher Strain,
Let's sing mean Shrubs and Bushes on the Plain,
Delight not all; arise, and try to prove
The Woods deserving of a Consul's Love.
　　Now! now! the last auspicious Times behold,   5
By the *Cumean*'s sacred Verse foretold,
A glorious Race of Ages is begun,
And now springs forth successively to run;
The Virgin now returns, and *Saturn*'s reign
Is to the joyful World restor'd again.   10

　　See a new gracious Progeny descends
From the high Heavens! at whose appearance ends
This Iron Age, and a new golden Race,
With ev'ry Virtue crown'd, assumes its Place.
Oh chast *Lucina!* speed the glorious Birth,   15
For now thy own *Apollo* reigns on Earth.

And thou transcendant Infant! shall be born
In *Pollio*'s Rule! his Consulship adorn!
Thence shall the wond'rous Time its Date begin,
And thou our Guide, if of our former Sin   20
Some Print remains, they shall be ras'd by thee,
And Earth from Dread of future Guilt set free.

He shall a God's exalted Life receive,
And like the Gods and mingled Heroes live,
Viewing and view'd by each, and Man's vile Race,   25
Shall sway and alter with Paternal Grace.

Thou Child! when born from the neglected Earth
Choice Herbs and Flowers shall derive their Birth,
With voluntary speed, *She-Goats* shall come,
Their Udders stretch'd with Milk undriven home,   30
And wand'ring Herds (no careful Keepers near)
Securely feed, nor the grown *Lions* fear.

To thee the Field its blooming useful Store
Shall offer, baneful Herbs shall be no more,
No more the lurking fiery Serpent's Sting   35
Shall sudden and severe Destruction bring,
In common Ways *Assyrian* Sweets shall spring;
But when advanc'd in Years, thyself shall read
Of Heroes Fame, and each paternal Deed,
Extracting thence their Virtue's hopeful Seed,   40
By soft Degrees the yellow-waving Corn
Arising, shall th' extended Plains adorn;
On Hedges purple Grapes in Clusters grow,
And from hard Oaks delicious Honey flow.

Yet still of ancient Fraud there shall remain   45
Some Signs, and bold and greedy Men for Gain
Shall tempt the Billows of the raging Main.
Cities shall be with Walls begirt around,
And the sharp Plough in Furrows tear the Ground.
Another vent'rous *T⟨iphy⟩s* shall appear,   50
An *Argo* its elected Heroes bear,
New Wars and Sieges shall Mankind annoy,
And great *Achilles* shall again to *Troy*.

But when at full-grown Manhood thou shall be,
The most successful shall renounce the Sea,   55
The Ships shall sail for mutual Wares no more,
But all things shall abound on ev'ry Shore,

No Plough shall vex the Ground, nor Hook the Vine,
The lab'ring Cattle shall the Yoke decline,
Nor more forc'd painful Servitude shall know,   60
Nor Wool its various Dyes dissembling show;

But lordly *Rams* shall in the flow'ry Mead
In Robes of native Purple proudly tread,
And sweat beneath unborrow'd State, the *Lamb*
Shall gaily prancing to its bleating Dam,   65
Repair in *Crimson* that the lib'ral Field
To grace the Wanton shall unsought for yield.

The *Parcæ* shall with joynt Consent agree
To keep thy Ages Thread from Mixture free,
And when they have the happy Clue begun,   70
Shall bid it smoothly and securely run.

Advance! advance! thy Time is now at hand,
Receive thy Honours and supream Command,
Thou precious Offspring of the Gods above!
Thou bless'd and vast Munificence of *Jove*!   75
Behold the World by sinful Weight oppress'd,
Inclines to yield; Earth, Sea, and Heav'n distress'd,
Require thy Help: Lo! Nature lifts her Voice,
And all things at th' approaching Age rejoyce!

Oh wou'd my Life endure; cou'd I but raise   80
My Skill to suit thy Due, thy lofty Praise;
Tho' *Thracian Orpheus* did with me contend,
Not *Thracian Orpheus* shou'd in Verse transcend,
Nor *Linus* in sublimer Raptures fly,
Tho' each had his Illustrious Parent by,   85

Orpheus Caliope to grace his Song,
Linus Apollo ever fair and young!
Shou'd *Pan* ev'n in *Arcadia* vye with me,
Ev'n in *Arcadia Pan* shou'd vanquish'd be!

Begin, oh little Boy! with Smiles to know   90
Thy Mother; this small Recompence bestow
On her, who has ten tedious Months so late,
With nauseous Ilness born thy growing weight.
Begin, oh little Boy! with gracious Mind,
Who smile not on their Parents ne'er shall find   95
A courteous God at Board, in Bed, a Goddess kind.

CXVIII

THE FIFTH PASTORAL

Mopsus Menalcas

Menalcas

Oh *Mopsus !* since thus luckily we meet,
Thou good to pipe, I Verses to repeat :
Why sit we not in this delightful Shade,
Which Hazles mixt with lofty Elms have made ?

Mopsus

As you exceed in Years and Worth, to you   5
I must *Menalcas !* give Precedence due,
Whither a lovely Seat we chuse to take,
Where wanton *Zephyrs* waving Shadows make,
Or in yond Cave round which the clasping Vine,
Loaden with Purple Grapes do's sweetly twine.   10

Menalcas

Amyntas only of our Mountain Swains,
Presumes to equal thy delicious Strains.

Mopsus

And what if that bold Swain presume to do
Yet more, and equal great *Apollo* too ?

Menalcas

Mopsus ! begin, if either *Alcon*'s Praise,   15
Or Loves of *Phillis* have employ'd thy Lays :
Or wou'd you the Disputes of *Codrus* try ? ⎫
Begin, thy *Goats* shall brouze securely by, ⎬
And *Tityrus* guard them with a watchful Eye. ⎭

Mopsus

No, but the Verses that I lately made, ⎫   20
And on the Bark of a green Beech display'd, ⎬
And nicely measur'd, and exactly weigh'd, ⎭
I'll try ; then let *Amyntas*, if he dare,
The Skill you boast he has, with mine compare.

Menalcas

As much as Shrubs in Sight and Value yield   25
To the pale Olives that adorn the Field,
As the mean Swallow that neglected grows

In Scent and Beauty to the blushing Rose.
(If I may claim a proper Judge to be)
So much *Amyntas* must submit to thee.   30

Mopsus

' But now my Boy ! thy Commendation wave,
For see already we've approach'd the Cave.

The pitying Nymphs thro' ev'ry Grove and Plain,
Bewail'd th' untimely Fate of *Daphnis* slain,
Did vast Regret and Lamentation show,   35
Ye Hazles, and ye Streams, confess'd their Woe !
When his dear Mother (most of all distress'd)
His bleeding Corps in strict Embraces press'd,
She did (with Rage and Sorrow fill'd) exclaim,
And all the Gods and Stars severely blame;   40
In those sad Days no lab'ring Swain for Drink
Drove his fed Ox to the cool River's Brink :
The Brooks were then by Cattles Feet unstain'd,
And hung'ry Herds their needful Food disdain'd ;
That furious *Lions, Daphnis !* mourn'd thy Fate,   45
The Woods and unfrequented Hills relate.

By *Daphnis* taught *Armenian* Tygers drew
The peaceful Chariot ; *Daphnis* did renew
The Rights of *Bacchus* and religious Chear,
And deck'd with Ivy wreaths the trembling Spear.   50

As spreading Vines o'er other Trees have Place
In goodly Show, as them their Product grace :
As lusty *Bulls* the lowing Herds adorn,
And Fields are beautify'd by standing Corn,
Thou wert the Grace of thine ; in Sorrow due   55
To thy sad Fate, ev'n from the Plains withdrew,
Pales herself with great *Apollo* too.

Where oft the golden Grain we us'd to strow
Wild Oats and Darnel now insulting grow ;
Where once the soft blue Violet appear'd,   60
And once its Head the Daffodilly rear'd,
With mingled Scent and Beauty sweetly grew,
Now Burs and bristly Thistles vex the View.

Let Earth be strow'd with Leaves, and let a Shade
Be o'er the Brooks and murm'ring Fountains made,   65
Ye Shepherds ! thus *Daphnis* himself commands,
And claims this Service from your grateful Hands ;

Then to his sacred Memory with Care
Erect a Tomb, and place these Verses there,
' I *Daphnis*, known hence to the starry Sky, 70
Kept a fair Flock, but fairer much was I.'

Menalcas

Oh Bard Divine ! thy Verses charm me so,
Not they a more delicious Pleasure know,
Who rest on tender Grass their weary Limbs,
Or quench their raging Thirsts in running Streams. 75
Thy Master's Skill thou hast not only gained
With warbling Pipe, but with thy Voice obtain'd.
Oh glorious Youth ! each way compleatly bless'd,
Equal to him thou shalt be now confess'd !

Such as they are, I'll now repeat my Lays 80
To thee, and *Daphnis* to the Stars we'll raise :
Daphnis we'll place among the Stars, for he
Good Will and Favour also bore to me.

Mopsus

Then such a Gift, what wou'd I rather chuse ?
The Youth was worthy of the choicest Muse : 85
And *Stimicon* much my Desire has rais'd,
Who to me lately these thy Verses prais'd.

Menalcas

The candid *Daphnis* th' unaccustomed Seat
Of Heav'n surveys, and far beneath his Feet,
Beholds the passing Clouds with vast Surprize, 90
And num'rous Stars that glitt'ring grace the Skies ;
Therefore a mighty Transport fills the Plains,
Pan and the rural Nymphs, and rustick Swains,
And gen'rous Mirth each where *unbounded* reigns,
Now prouling *Wolves* neglect their Rage and Wiles, 95
The Net no more the tim'rous Deer beguiles ;
All Hatred, Fraud, and fierce Contention cease.
Daphnis loves Leisure and the Joys of Peace.

The high rough Hills to Heav'n their Voices raise,
The hollow Rocks rejoycing sound his Praise. 100
The very Shrubs advance his Name on high,
And, oh *Menalcas !* he's a God, they cry.
Then to thy own, oh ! kind and gracious be,
Four goodly Altars here erected see ;
Receive, oh *Daphnis !* Adoration due, 105

Two Altars are thy Right, *Apollo*'s Two ;
Two Bowls of Milk will I before thee lay,
And two of Oil, a yearly Off'ring pay,
And being first with gallant Chear supply'd.
In cooling Shades in Summer's sult'ry Tide,   110
In Winter's Season by the Fire's side !
New Wine in plenteous Streams I'll pour to thee,
That like the Liquor of the Gods, shall be,
Dametas then a chearful Lay shall sing,
And *Lictius Egon* make the Vallies ring :   115
Alph⟨e⟩sibæus too shall featly trip
In antic Jiggs, and like a Satyr skip.

    These things shall to thy Honour e'er be paid,
When to the Nymphs our solemn Vows are made,
And when of rural Gods we crave the usual Aid.   120

    While *Boars* on Mountains Tops delight to stray,
While in the Silver Streams the Fishes play,
While *Grashoppers* are fed with Morning Dew,
And *Bees* their Toils in flow'ry Fields pursue.
Thy Honour, Name and Praise with ev'ry Swain,   125
Shall in Request eternally remain.

    As still to *Bacchus* and to *Ceres* we
Offer our Vows ; the Husbandman to thee,
The fame with Zeal shall yearly give, and thou
Shalt claim th' Observance of each offer'd vow.   130

Mopsus
    What for such Lines, what Gift shall I bestow
On thee, that my Esteem may fitly show ?
For not the coming of a Southern Breeze,
That softly stealing Whistles thro' the Trees,
Cou'd with its rustling Noise delight me more,   135
Nor Billows striking on the sounding Shore,
Nor Streams that trickle from a steepy Hill,
And stony Vallies with their Murmurs fill.

Menalcas
    But let me first a grateful Present make,
This Pipe in Token of my Friendship take.   140
Two Strains this taught me ; *Coridon* the Fair
Alexis lov'd, his Lord's delicious Care.
And, tell *Dametas !* whose'n *Sheep* these are ?

Mopsus

Take thou this Crook that from me oft in vain
Antigenes, tho' lovely, strove to gain,   145
Deserving not *Menalcas !* to be scorn'd,
With equal Knots and shining Brass adorn'd.

CXIX

THE SIXTH PASTORAL

My Muse first sported with *Sicilian* Strains,
Nor blush'd *Thalia* in the *Woods* and *Plains*
To dwell, when aiming at sublimer *Things*,
War's wastful Fury, and the Deeds of Kings ;

Apollo gently whisper'd in my Ear,   5
And thus he said, rash *Tityrus !* beware,
Sheep and low Strains best suit the *Shepherd*'s Care.
Thus, while oh ! *Varus !* other Bards proceed
To sing thy Fame, and tell each dreadful Deed,
Inferior Aims provoke my Muse's Lays,   10
And yet not wholly she despairs of Praise,
While she ingraves on ev'ry Tree thy Name,
While *Varus !* thee ev'n lowly Shrubs proclaim ;
For he whose Lines thy worthy Mention bear,
Is sure of *Phœbus* the peculiar Care.   15

Proceed, ye Muses, in his usual Guize
Chromis and *M⟨n⟩asylus* by Chance surprize
Silenus, in a Cave to sleep compos'd,
With Fumes of yester's Wine and the God was doz'd :
High hung his Pitcher old and in decay,   20
And fall'n far off his rosy Garland lay ;
With Joy (for oft the Sire in vain believ'd,
Had both the Youths with promis'd Verse deceiv'd).
Approaching softly, they secure his Hands,
With his own Wreath transform'd to sudden Bands.   25
Herself to these the beauteous *Ægle* joyn'd
A Nymph ! the fairest of the wat'ry Kind ;
And as awak'd he casts around his Eyes,
With Mulb'ry's Juice his Front and Temples dies.

He smil'd at their Design ; for what he said,   30
For what Offence am I your Pris'ner made ?
Lose me, presumpt'ous Boys ! without Delay,
The promis'd Verses instantly I'll pay
To you, the Nymph I'll please another way.

He then began, and from the *Woods* and *Lawns*,   35
A num'rous Croud of *Satyrs* and of *Fawns*
Rejoycing come, ev'n savage Beasts attend,
And stubborn Oaks their lofty Branches bend.
Parnassus ne'er more joyfully restor'd
The sounding Strains of its harmonious Lord,   40
Nor *Rhodope*, nor *Ismarus* before
At *Orpheus*'s wond'rous Skill were ravish'd more,
Than all things here united, did admire
The high exalted Strains of this experienc'd Sire.

He sung, how when thro' the vast Void compell'd,   45
The Seeds of Earth, Sea, Fire, and Spirits held
Their casual way, productive as they flew, ⎫
All things from these their Forms and Beings drew, ⎬
And hence the World's delightful Order grew ! ⎭
Then Earth appear'd, and hard'ning by Degrees,   50
Rear'd its fair Head above surrounding Seas,
With a young Offspring grac'd ; the glorious Sun
Then his ætherial Course began to run,
And Clouds exalted o'er the Land, to pour
The fruitful Blessing of a plenteous Shower ;   55
Then Woods arose and Beasts a lonely Way,
(Few yet and Strangers) o'er the Mountains stray ;
Then *Saturn*'s happy Reign the Song pursu'd,
And how Man's Race was in the World renew'd.
Prometheus's Theft and Punishment it nam'd,   60
And how the parting Mariners exclaim'd
For lovely *Hylas*, in the Fountain drown'd,
While *Hylas ! Hylas !* all the Rocks resound.

And thou, *Pasiphae !* who a happy Queen
Might have been stil'd, if Herds had never been,   65
A snowy Bullock here thy Care do's prove,
And has the Gift of thy unnat'ral Love.

Ah ! wretched Dame ! in thee what Madness reigns ?
The *Prætides*, who roving fill'd the Plains
With feigned Lowings, never did require   70
Such Mates, nor burn'd with such a foul Desire,
Tho' each for Horns explor'd her tender Brow,
And fear'd the Yoke and Labour of the Plough⟨.⟩

Ah, wretched Dame ! thou do'st the Mountains pass
In fruitless Search, while on the springing Grass   75
Heedless he feeds, or else perchance is lay'd
Beneath a spreading Oak's refreshing Shade,

Or follows some fair Heifer of the Herd,
Who is before unhappy thee preferr'd.

Oh, all ye Nymphs ! of ev'ry Stream and Grove,　　　80
Bound, bound his Course, restrain his roving Love,
With all your Might the careless Wand'rer stay,
And to her longing Eyes the Fugitive convey.

The Sire then sung the swiftly-running Maid
Stopp'd in her speed, by golden Fruit betray'd,　　　85
The Song did then the Sisters Fate display
Of him, who rashly aim'd to rule the Day,
Mourning his Lot, them sudden Barks inclose,
And each with speed a weeping Alder grows.

He sung how *Gallus* by a Muse convey'd　　　90
A grateful Journey to *Parnassus* made,
Rising to whom the sacred Choir express'd
A full Respect, and *Linus* thus address'd.
Receive this Pipe delicious Bard ! he said,
On which before th' *Ascræan* Shepherd play'd,　　　95
Who did the Rage of Savage Beasts restrain,
And charm the Mountain Ashes to the Plain ;
This the *Grynæan* Grove⟨'⟩s arise shall tell,
That *Phœbus* most may there delight to dwell.

Why shou'd I either *S⟨c⟩ylla*'s Tale relate ?　　　100
Or taught by Fame declare the latter's State ?
Who in the Sea a lov'ly Maid is plac'd,
But barking Monsters rave beneath her Waste,
That cause in passing Mariners such dread,
And often on their broken Limbs are fed.　　　105
How *T⟨e⟩reus* chang'd the various Song, express'd
The Rape of *Philomel* the horrid Feast ;
How since in Woods sad *Philomel* complain'd, ⎱
Progne (her Breast with filial Blood yet stain'd) ⎰
Now hovers o'er the Palace where she reign'd. ⎰　　　110

What e'er the God of Verse divinely thought,
Eurotas heard, and to the Laurels taught
Silenus sings, the Valleys all around
In Ecchos to the Skies convey the Sound,
Nor did the length'ned Song receive its End,　　　115
'Till driven Sheep did to the Cottage tend,
And slow unwilling Night from Heav'n descend.

CXX

THE SEVENTH PASTORAL

Daphnis by Chance his Seat reposing took
Beneath the Covert of a spreading Oak,
And *Coridon* and *Thyrsis* thither led
Their Flocks, that joyning now together fed :
She-Goats fair fruitful *Coridon* did keep,   5
The Charge of *Thyrsis* was his bleating Sheep,
Both in their Prime ! and both *Arcadian* Swains !
Both apt and ready at alternate Strains.

Now while I for my tender Myrtles made
A Fence from Cold, unhappily had stray'd   10
My *Goat* the Husband of the Flock, and I
Seeking th' unlucky Truant *Daphnis* spy,
When me again he had rejoycing spy'd,
Hither, oh *Melibæus !* haste, he cry'd,
Safe be thy *Goats !* and if Affairs permit,   15
In this cool Shade a while, I prithee sit,
Hither will come thy Bullocks thro' the Meads
To drink, and here behold, with waving Reeds
The River *Mencius* ouzy Banks are crown'd,
And from the sacred Oak the murm'ring *Bees* resound.   20

What shou'd I do in this Uncertainty ?
I had not *Phillis*, nor *Alappe* nigh,
Who from the Call of their inviting Damms,
Might now secure at home my weaned Lambs,
And Numbers on the crowded Plain appear,   25
These youthful Shepherds fam'd Dispute to hear ;
I idly too prefer their light Affairs
Before my Bus'ness, and more serious Cares.

The Shepherds then began to try their Skill
In Strains alternate, which the Muses will,   30
I shou'd remember ; thus his Art each shows,
These *Coridon* recites, and *Thyrsis* those.

Coridon
Ye lov'ly Muses ! my Delight ! incline
To grant my Lays a Harmony divine ;
Like those of charming *Codrus*, let them be,   35
Who is in worth *Apollo !* next to thee,
Or if my Prayer unkindly is deny'd,
My pipe shall on this sacred Oak abide.

Thyrsis

Arcadian Swains ! around my Temples place
An Ivy Wreath, that *Codrus* in Disgrace,   40
May burst with Spight, or if malicious Praise
From his ill Tongue, too high my Value raise :
With *Baccar* bind my Brows (a sacred Charm)
Your growing Poet to secure from Harm.

Coridon

This rough *Boar*'s Head with Favour *Delia !* see,   45
That little *Micon* now devotes to thee,
Who do's with this submissively impart
The branchy Horns of a long-living *Hart*,
If this proves well, thou shalt be wholly plac'd
Of smooth *Punicean* Stone, with Buskins grac'd.   50

Thyrsis

This Bowl of Milk and Cakes, *Priapus !* take,
A slender Present, that I yearly make.
Thy Care, my Garden is a little Spot,
A Marble Statue therefore's now thy Lot ;
But if thy Blessing shall increase my Told,   55
Thy Marble Statue shall be chang'd to Gold.

Coridon

Oh *Galatea !* sweeter far to me,
Than Honey of the choice *Hyblæan Bee*,
Whiter than *Swans* that swim the Chrystal Streams,
And fairer than the clasping Ivy seems ;   60
If thou for *Coridon* hast kind Concern,
Come ! come ! when ever my fed *Bulls* return.

Thyrsis

May I to thee more bitter seem than Rue,
More course than Fuz, than Seaweed abject too,
If this one day do's not to me appear,   65
(To weary me) more tedious than a Year,
Not yet suffic'd, what will ye ever feed ?
Hence ye gorg'd *Bullocks !* home, for shame, with speed.

Coridon

Ye murm'ring Fountains ! and thou tender Glade !
More soft than Sleep, thou sweet refreshing Shade !   70
By you protected, let my Cattle shun
The Summer's Heat that is ev'n now begun :

Lo! Warmth ev'n now is in th' encreasing Year,
And budding Gems upon the Vines appear.

Thyrsis

Here store of Fuel do's the Flames provoke,   75
The Posts are blacken'd by continual Smoke;
Here we the Rage of *Boreas* safely mock,
As *Wolves* despise the Number of the Flock;
Or, as the rapid Streams impetuous Force,
The useless Bank that wou'd obstruct its Course.   80

Coridon

Here stands the Juniper! rough Chessnut grows,
And Apples fallen from their loaded Boughs,
Each where appear, the Fields with Joy are crown'd,
And Mirth and Pleasure are dispens'd around;
But from these Mountains shou'd *Alexis* go,   85
Even the Rivers wou'd refuse to flow.

Thyrsis

The Sun with scorching Beams the Meadows fires,
Thro' blasting Air the Verdure all expires,
Ev'n *Bacchus* to his own denys his Aid,
Nor yields the gen'rous Vine a needful Shade: 90
When *Phillis* comes, will bloom the Trees and Flow'rs,
And Rain descend in joyful plenteous Show'rs.

Coridon

The Poplar to *Alcides* grateful proves,
The curling Vine gay youthful *Bacchus* loves,
The Myrtle pleases well Love's beauteous Queen: 95
Apollo likes his Laurel ever green;
But while the Hazle, *Phillis!* is thy Care,
None than the Hazle shall be thought more rare.

Thyrsis

The Ash in Woods do's ever fairest seem,
The Pine in Gardens, Poplars by the Stream;   100
The Firr of lofty Mountains is the Pride:
But wou'd'st thou charming *Lycidas!* abide
More often here, thy Grace my Boy! would be
Far more conspicuous than the fairest Tree.

Thus, *Thyrsis* did contend, but all in vain, }   105
Vanquish'd by *Coridon*, who on the Plain,
Is since that Time our most applauded Swain.

CXXI

THE EIGHTH PASTORAL

Damon, Alph⟨e⟩sibæus

Sad *Damon*'s and *Alph⟨e⟩sibæus* Muse,
At which the Herd admiring, did refuse
Their needful Food, amaz'd the *Lynxes* stood,
And the chang'd River sto⟨p⟩p'd its rapid Flood,
The melancholly and the magic Strains   5
Of these we'll sing, that charm'd the wond'ring Plains.

And thou who do'st our rough *Timavus* awe,
Or o'er th' *Illyrian* Seas extend thy Law,
Shall ever come that Day's auspicious Date,
When I thy glorious Actions shall relate?   10
It shall, and I o'er all the World disperse
Thy Praise, fit only for the tragic Verse
Of *Sophocles*, take from my willing Hand,
What now derives its Birth from thy Command;
And 'round thy Temples let thy Ivy twine, ⎫   15
And there with thy victorious Laurels joyn, ⎬
For first and last my Labours shall be thine. ⎭
Now scarcely from the dawning Skies withdrew ⎫
The Shades of Night, and left expos'd to view, ⎬
The tender Grass o'erspread with grateful Dew; ⎭   20
When on a blasted Olive as reclin'd,
Thus *Damon* utter'd his despairing Mind.

Damon

Haste *Lucifer!* the ling'ring Day constrain,
While of false *Nisa* injur'd I complain,
And call the Gods to testify my Woe;   25
And tho' in vain my Rage and Grief I show,
Unhelp'd, yet must I to my latest Hour
Invoke them still, and blame Love's cruel Pow'r.

Begin with me, while injur'd I complain,
My mournful Flute! a soft *Menalian* Strain.   30

Menalus has its Groves and speaking Pines,
It ever to the Lover's Moans inclines;
The shepherds⟨'⟩ kindly hears, great *Pan* is there,
Who makes the tuneful Pipe his constant Care.

Begin with me, while injur'd I complain,   35
My mournful Flue! a soft *Menalian* Strain.

Nisa to *Mopsus* is in Wedlock joyn'd,
What may not Lovers now expect to find?
Now *Mares* may match with *Griffins* void of Fear,⎫
And in succeeding Ages shall appear   ⎬   40
Mingling to drink, the Hound and tim'rous *Deer*.⎭
Haste, *Mopsus!* haste, and with officious Care
Oh happy Man! the Marriage Rites prepare,
Scatter the Nuts, thy Bride is present, see,
And th' Evening Star do's *Æta* quit for thee.   45

    Begin with me, while injur'd I complain,
My mournful Flute! a soft *Menalian* Strain.

Of what a worthy Man art thou the Bride?
Proud Maid? so full of Scorn for all beside,
Who hate my Pipe and *Goats*, and so are scar'd   50
At my rough Lip, and long bristly Beard.
And think the Gods thy Business will allow,
Nor more regard each mortal thing than thou.

    Begin with me while injur'd I complain,
My mournful Flute! a soft *Menalian* Strain.   55

I call to mind once with your Mother you   ⎫
Came to our Orchard; there I first did view   ⎬
Thy growing Charms, was your Conductor too.⎭
Then twelve Years old! my tender Arms cou'd stretch.
Up to the Boughs, and nearest Apples reach,   60
I gaz'd and dy'd! what Error did betray
My Soul, and steal me from myself away?

    Begin with me, while injur'd I complain,
My mournful Flute! a soft *Menalian* Strain.

Now know I what is Love, the rugged *North*   65
In Mountains, Rocks, or Desarts brought him forth;
Or *Ismarus*, or ⟨*Rh*⟩*odope*, sure fed
Him young, or farthest *Garamentes* bred:
His Birth or Breeding here he cou'd not find;
Nor is he of our Blood or gentle Kind.   70

    Begin with me, while injur'd I complain,
My mournful Flute! a soft *Menalian* Strain.

Oh savage Love! by thy Instruction led,
Her own dear Childrens Blood a Mother shed;
This in the Mother was a cruel Deed,   75
And impious Love the Cruelty decreed,
Which of the two did most pernicious prove?
Was she more cruel, or more impious Love?

Impious was Love the Mother cruel too,
Each in Extreme, and neither did out-do ! 80

   Begin with me, while injur'd I complain,
My mournful Flute ! a soft *Menalian* Strain.

From *Sheep* let *Wolves* now fly possess'd with Fear,
Let Oranges on rugged Oaks appear,
And ev'ry Alder the *Narcissus* bear. 85
Let from mean Shrubs the choicest Honey flow,
And hideous Owls of Swans the Rivals grow ;
Let rustic *Tityrus Orpheus !* change to thee ;
Let ev'ry Wood in him an *Orpheus* see,
And let him with the *Dolphins* an Orion be. 90

   Begin with me, while injur'd I complain,
My mournful Flute ! a soft *Menalian* Strain.

O'er all things let th' unbounded Ocean flow :
Adieu, ye Woods ! with sudden speed I'll go,
And from some Mountain plunge into the Sea ; 95
Take thou this last and dying Legacy.

   Now cease with me, for I no more complain,
Cease, my sad Flute ! thy soft *Menalian* Strain.
Thus, *Damon* his unhappy Fortune mourn'd,
And what *Alphesibæus* then return'd, 100
Ye Muses ! to my Memory recall ;
For all things cannot be perform'd by all.

Alph⟨e⟩sibæus

   Bring Water forth, and 'round this Altar twine
Green Ivy, and the tender springing Vine,
To these male Frankincense and Vervin joyn. 105
That my lost Husband, I by Magic Skill
May gain, and turn his Sences to my Will,
Reduce the Wand'rer to his Nuptial Vow,
All needful Things but Charms are present now.

   Bring from the Town my mighty magic Charms ! 110
Bring *Daphnis* home to my forsaken Arms.

The mighty Force of magic Charms can make
Ev'n the Moon her heav'nly Sphere forsake
Circe by Charms transform'd *Ulysses* Friends,
Their Force the deadly Snake to pieces rends. 115

   Bring from the Town my mighty magic Charms !
Bring *Daphnis* home to my forsaken Arms.

This Ribbon of three divers Hues I wind
Three times about, then to thee first, thus bind,
And 'round this Altar thrice this Image bear;   120
Odd Numbers to the God delightful are.

 Bring from the Town my mighty magic Charms!
Bring *Daphnis* home to my forsaken Arms.

Make *Amaryllis!* make immediately,
Three Knots of various Colours each, and cry,   125
I th' everlasting Bonds of *Venus* tye.

 Bring from the Town my mighty magic Charms!
Bring *Daphnis* home to my forsaken Arms.

As now by one and the same Fire this Clay
Grows harder, and this Wax dissolves away,   130
Such thorough me, let perjur'd *Daphnis* prove,
So let him harden and dissolve with Love;
Besprinkle Meal, and then with Brimstone fire
These Laurel Leaves, as magic Rites require;
Daphnis inflames my Soul, and in return   135
Against false *Daphnis*, I this Laurel burn.

 Bring from the Town my mighty magic Charms!
Bring *Daphnis* home to my forsaken Arms.

As a stray *Bullock* thro' the Woods do's go
Weary and wand'ring, and oppress'd with Wo;   140
At last in vain attempting many Ways,
Himself despairing on the Grass, he lays,
By frequent Lowings mourns his lost Estate,
Not knowing whither to return, tho' late.
Let wand'ring *Daphnis* such Distress endure,   145
Nor from my Hands obtain a needful Cure.

 Bring from the Town my mighty magic Charms!
Bring *Daphnis* home to my forsaken Arms.

These Garments (sometimes worn) perfidious he
Dear Pledges of himself bequeath'd to me,   150
These now beneath this Threshold I bestow
In thee, oh Earth! these Pledges *Daphnis* owe.

 Bring from the Town my mighty magic Charms!
Bring *Daphnis* home to my forsaken Arms.

This Poison, and these Herbs that vastly grow   155
In *Pontus*, *Mæris* did on me bestow;
By such a *Wolf* I've seen him oft become,
Then hide in Woods, and from the dismal Tomb,

The ghastly Scepter often make appear, ⎫
And often Fields of Corn with Fury rear, ⎬ 160
And into other Fields transplanting bear. ⎭

    Bring from the Town my mighty magic Charms !
Bring *Daphnis* home to my forsaken Arms.

Bring Ashes *Amaryllis !* forth with speed, ⎫
Then mark which way the flowing Stream do's lead, ⎬ 165
And with it backwards cast them o'er thy Head. ⎭
Look not behind ; thus *Daphnis*, I'll surprize,
He scorns the Gods, and all my Charms defies !

    Bring from the Town my mighty magic Charms !
Bring *Daphnis* home to my forsaken Arms. 170

See, of their own accord (while I delay
To bear them hence) the Coals new Flames display,
Which trembling from the Altar now ascend,
It shou'd, I think, some prosp'rous thing portend :
I know not certainly the Meaning ; hark, 175
Our *Hylax* at the Door begins to bark ;
Do we vain Lovers, but ourselves deceive
By Dream, or may I what I wish believe ?

    Now cease ! now cease ! my mighty magic Charms !
Daphnis returns to my desiring Arms. 180

CXXII

THE NINTH PASTORAL

Lycidas, Mæris

Lycidas

    Whither away, my Friend ! ho ! *Mæris !* ho !
This leads to Town, say whither dost thou go ?

Mæris

    Oh *Lycidas !* how are our Hopes deceiv'd ?
Things are as once we cou'd not have believ'd ;
All is my own, the rugged Souldier says, 5
Hence ancient Rustics ! march with Speed your Ways.

    Forc'd to submit, yet with a heavy Heart
(For Fate and Force change all things) we depart,
And these two *Kids* t' appease his furious Mood
Now send ; and may they never do him Good. 10

Lycidas

I'm sure, I heard from where these Hills ascend,
And their mean Summits gently sloaping bend,
As far as thence the passing Eye can reach,
Ev'n to the Water and the broken Beach;
All your M⟨e⟩nalcas had secur'd from Wrong,   15
And safely guarded by his charming Song.

Mæris

'Twas so reported, but alas! what Charms
Have Verses *Lycidas!* for martial Arms?
Here all the Muses gentle Graces fail,
As *Doves* must fly when furious *Hawks* assail,   20
And had not from a hollow Holm, the *Crow*
On the left hand forewarn'd me to forego
All new Debates; not *Mæris* on this Plain
Had been, and our *Menalcas* had been slain.

Lycidas

How? cou'd in any so much Baseness be?   25
Were all our Comforts almost lost with thee?
Thou dear *Menalcas!* who the Nymphs shou'd sing? ⎱
Who strow the Ground with blooming Herbs, or bring ⎬
Delightful Shadows o'er the chrystal Spring? ⎰

What Verses lately did I slily view, ⎱
And softly read, as little heeding you ⎬   30
Near to my darling *Amaryllis* drew. ⎰

'Oh *Tityrus!* going hence a little way,
'Let not my *Goats* 'till my returning stray,
'But feed them near this gentle River's brink,   35
'When fed, then drive them to the Flood to drink,
'And driving them along yourself take care,
'And of the rough *He-goat* who Butts beware.

Mæris

Ay! or what he to *Varus* did repeat,
Which th⟨o'⟩ imperfect I remember yet,   40
Varus! if *Mantua* keeps from Ruine clear;
'(*Mantua* to sad *Cremona*, ah! too near)
'The *Swans* sweet Voices shall declare thy Fame,
'And to the Stars exalt thy glorious Name.

Lycidas

So may thy *Bees* from harmful Yews be freed,⎫
So may thy *Cows* within the flow'ry Mead ⎬   45
Their Udders fill, and ever safely feed. ⎭
If thou hast ought begin, the Muse has shown,
Ev'n me some Favour, I some Verses own :
The Shepherds call me Poet, but I know   50
I merit not the Title they bestow ;
Aim not at *Varus*, nor at *Cinna*'s Ear,
But like a gabling *Goose* among the *Swans* appear.

Mæris

'Tis *Lycidas !* what now imploys my Mind,
And I am aiming secretly to find,   55
Which, if I can remember, I'll rehearse,
Nor is it worthless or ignoble Verse.

' Haste hither *Galatea !* what Delight
' Can in the raging Deep thy Stay invite ?
' Here blooms the purple Spring in all its Pride,   60
' And sweetly by the curling River's side :
' The bounteous Earth distributes various Flow'rs,
' Here woven, compose delicious Bow'rs ;
' The Poplar too in lov'ly green array'd,
' Yields to the Cave both Gracefulness and Shade.   65
' Haste hither ! let the Billows vainly roar,
' And madly beat on the resounding Shoar.

Lycidas

Say what I heard you sing one Night alone,
The Tune I yet retain, the Words are flown.

Mæris

' *Daphnis !* regard not any ancient Sign,   70
' Lo ! *Cæsar*'s Star do's now proceeding shine ;
' This shall to Corn and Fruits Perfection give,
' And make the luscious Grape its purple Hue receive.
' Now *Daphnis !* on thy Fruits employ thy Care,
' Thy Childrens Children shall the Blessing share.   75

Time conqu'ring all things do's our Minds destroy,
I well remember when I was a Boy,
My Voice at my Command wou'd sweetly run,
And oft sing down a lingring Summers Sun ;

Now I forget, my Voice, as it has been,　　　　80
Is nothing too, *Wolves* first have *Mæris* seen;
But all these things, and more than I forget
Menalcas to thee often will repeat.

Lycidas

You by Excuse, but my Desire increase, ⎫
And lo! to thee, now *Ocean*'s Murmurs cease, ⎬　85
And ev'ry Wind is gently hush'd to Peace. ⎭
We're now half Way, for lo! before our Eyes,
Bianor's Sepulchre begins to rise.
Let's sit and sing in this refreshing Shade,
That with green Boughs the lab'ring *Hinds* have made,　90
Let us, I prithee, rest a while, lay down
Thy *Kids*, we'll yet be time enough at Town;
Or if you fear e'er Night the coming Rain,
Let's go together singing o'er the Plain,
'Twill seem by far more short and easy Way,　　95
As thus we spend the time, and that we may
Go thus together singing on the Road,
I'll lend my help to ease thee of thy Load.

Mæris

Cease now my Boy! and our Affair let's Mind
When e'er he comes, plenty of Songs we'll find.　　100

CXXIII

THE TENTH PASTORAL

Oh *Arethusa!* this my last Work aid,
Some Verses for my *Gallus* must be made,

And what *Lycoris* may herself peruse, ⎫
Who for the sake of *Gallus* can refuse ⎬
His proper Right, the Tribute of a Muse? ⎭　　5

So may thy Stream beneath *Sicania*'s Sea, ⎫
In everlasting Ease and Safety be, ⎬
Nor *Doris* mix her briny Waves with thee. ⎭

Then let's begin, and while my *Goats* (my Care)
Securely feed; oh! *Gallus!* We'll declare　　10
Thy anxious Love, we sing not quite in vain,
The Groves shall answer to the mournful Strain.

Ye wat'ry Nymphs! what Woods or Mountains strove⎫
To check your Help, when *Gallus* thus did prove ⎬
The fatal Victim of unworthy Love? ⎭ 15
Parnassus never had your Course withstood!
Nor *Pindus* high! nor *Aganippe*'s Flood!
Ev'n from the Laurels trickling Tears distill'd,
And flowing Grief the Shrubs and Bushes fill'd,
Pine-bearing *Menalus* Compassion felt, 20
And Stones of cold *Lycæus* seem'd to melt,
As stretch'd beneath a lonely Rock he lay,
The straggling *Sheep* around their Master stray.

Oh Bard divine! think it not shame to keep,
Like us on humble Plains the fleecy *Sheep*, 25
His snowy Flocks the fair *Adonis* fed,
And unrepining to the River led.

Upilio and the Neat-herds thither drew,
And smear'd with Winter-Mast *Menalcas* too,
All shew'd Concern, and whence arose thy Flame, 30
With Pity ask'd, to thee *Apollo* came.
Gallus! what Madness fills thy Mind, (he cries)
Thy false *Lycoris* with another flies
To distant Realms, and unrelenting go's
Thro' horrid Wars and everlasting Snows! 35
Sylvanus came, and on his Head was fixt
A Fennel Wreath, with quiv'ring Lillies mixt.
Pan came *Arcadia*'s God, (by us descry'd)
His Cheeks and Temples were with Crimson dy'd,
Says he, what measure can in Love be shown? 40
Not Love as yet has any Measure known!
Fierce Love to flowing Grief no Bounds allows,
As *Goats* are ne'er suffic'd with verdant Boughs!
As *Bees* are ne'er suffic'd with Store of Flow'rs,
Or rising Grass with Streams or frequent Show'rs. 45

He mourning, thus reply'd, *Arcadian* Swains,
Record my Fate in your melodious Strains,
This let your Hills resound, your Songs alone
Are fit to make the Dying's Sorrow known!
How wou'd my Bones enjoy more perfect rest, 50
If by your Pipes my Passion was express'd?
And oh! that Fate had me like you decreed
To dress the Vines, or bleating Flocks to feed;
That I had been on the delightful Plain,
A chearful Shepherd of your tuneful Train: 55
To *Phillis*, or *Amyntas* made my Court,

Or any other of the rural sort,
Tho' brown or black, they yet might yield Delight,
Not Violets, nor Berries please the Sight !
Among the Sallows and the Vines we'd lay'd   60
Our careless Limbs, and innocently play'd ;
Phillis had crown'd my Head with Wreaths of Flow'rs,
With pleasing Songs *Amyntas* bless'd the Hours.

By these cool Fountains ! in these shady Groves !
(The proper joyful Scene of mutual Loves)   65
In these soft Meadows so profusely gay !
With thee *Lycoris !* cou'd I chuse to stay,
And well-delighted pass an Age away !

Now frantic Love keeps me in horrid Arms,
Expos'd to War's fierce Rage and hostile Harms,   70
While most unkindly and perversly you
(Nor am I willing to believe it true)
Over the lofty *Alps* perpetual Snow
To *Rhenus*'s Coasts and dreary Regions go,
Ye bleaky Winds ! your wonted Rigour spare ;   75
Ah ! hurt not, vex not the too vent'rous Fair,
And thou sharp *Ice !* her tender Limbs forbear.

I'll go, and with *Sicilian* Pipe rehearse
My once compos'd, yet long-neglected Verse,
Amidst the Dens of savage Beasts I'll be,   80
And carve my Flame on ev'ry tender Tree,
The lonely Wilds my hopeless Love shall know,
And as the Trees increase, the Love shall grow.

Then *Menalus*, I'll tred with eager Pace,
And mixing with the Nymphs, pursue the Chace,   85
Or hunt wild *Boars*, nor sharpest Colds shall stay
My steps, as 'round *Parthenian* Hills I stray.

And now, methinks, with op'ning *Hounds* I fly
Thro' sounding Woods that echo to their Cry ;
Over *Cydonia*'s Plains and Mountains go,   90
Rush thro' the Brakes, and bend the *Parthian* Bow,
As if such Toils cou'd cure my painful Mind,
Or any chosen Way the Means cou'd find,
Oh rigid Pow'rs of Love ! to calm thy Rage,
Or human Ills thy Fierceness cou'd asswage.   95

And now my Thoughts (averse to all of these,)
Not Nymphs, nor Woods, nor charming Strains can please :

The cruel God our Labours cannot change,
Not tho' o'er *Thrac⟨i⟩a*'s bleaky Realms we range,
To *Heber*'s frozen Waters shiv'ring go,   100
In depth of Winter press *Sithonia*'s Snow,
Or when the Sun do's to the Scales incline,
Drive our scorch'd Flocks beneath the Tropic Line.

    The World is with his Pow'r and Presence fill'd,
Love conquers all, and we to love must yield !   105
Here cease ye sacred Muses ! nor prolong
Beyond due Limits the devoted Song,
These mournful Verses, shall to *Gallus* prove
A grateful Token of my zealous Love,
My Love to *Gallus !* that do's hourly show   110
Increasing Force as springing Alders grow.

    Now let's arise ! for often by the Shade,
The Singer's Voice is hoarse or feeble made ;
The Shades of Junipers unwholsome are,
Shades hurt the Fruits, 'tis Ev'ning⟨,⟩ leave your Fare,   115
Ye fill'd *She-goats*, and to your home repair.

CXXIV

A PINDARIQUE ODE

Written in a Garden

I

Blest Shade ! where I securely stay,
    And taste the Fragrance of the Plain ;
Which wanton *Zephyr* does convey
    In his refreshing Play,
To chear the panting Flock, and panting Swain.   5
    Here on this flow'ry Carpet laid,
By Nature's Hand, in Nature's Pride array'd ;
    My Soul, unus'd to balmy Ease,
        By Sympathy at Rest,
        Is lull'd within my Breast,   10
Unhurt by Care or Sorrow's worse Disease.

II

So have I seen the warb'ling Lark,
When Winter's cheerless Frosts were o'er,
And noisy Bear has ceas'd to roar,
    The Day no longer cold, nor dark,   15
The narrow Compass of a Cage forget,
And broadling o'er a Turf, in silent Pleasure sit.

Here Solitude and gentle Ease combine
   To give a Taste of Joy divine;
   Here every Object seems design'd,   20
Whither thro' blooming Groves or flow'ry Meads we stray,
   To drive Anxiety away,
And help Philosophy to cure the Mind.

            III

   With Joy I hear the tuneful Choir,
   Which now are hov'ring o'er my Head;   25
   Whilst I beneath supinely spread,
Their various Notes, and little Cares admire:
   The Bird that sits upon this Bough,
   Fearless by me to be distress'd,
   Pursues the Building of her Nest;   30
   Sure she by Instinct knows me now:
   But my harmonious Friend, beware,
   In me tho' safely you confide,
   Thy Nestlings for the future hide;
All are not gentle, nor thy Work would spare.   35

            IV

I feel, ah! lovely Seats, I feel your Influence, ⎫
   That native Truth, and Innocence,   ⎬
Which liv'd, e'er Virtue was deprav'd by Sense; ⎭
E'er momentary Trifles, transient Joy,
   Did Man's Posterity destroy;   40
   E'er foul Oppression had its Rise,   ⎫
   When all was blissful Paradise,   ⎬
Before the Birth of Law, or its curs'd Parent Vice. ⎭
   Oh! Let me here, kind Fate, remain
   Upon this harmless, happy Plain;   45
Secure of peaceful Virtue and Content,
   In no inglorious Ease and Banishment.

            V

   The Sun withdraws his genial Ray,
   And reddens in the Western Sky;
   The wand'ring Rooks do Homeward fly,   50
And, 'till the Morn appears, forsake the Prey
The Nightingale her mournful Story trills
      In yonder Hawthorn Shade;
      The Bleating Sheep are laid;
And on the Earth the nightly Dew Distills: 55
   The Shepherd hasts to sound Repose,
   Such sleep the Guilty never knew;
'Till *Phœbus* shall again his Beams disclose,
     Blest Solitude, Adieu.   59

CXXV

THE FALL

I

As *Chloe* o'er the Meadow past,
    I view'd the lovely Maid;
She turn'd and blush'd, renew'd her Haste,
And fear'd by me to be embrac'd,
    My Eyes my Wish betray'd.   5

II

I trembling felt the rising Flame,
    The Charming Nymph pursu'd;
Daphne was not so bright a Game,
Tho' Great *Apollo*'s Darling Dame,
    Nor with such Charms endu'd.   10

III

I follow'd close, the Fair still flew
    Along the Grassy Plain,
The Grass at length my Rival grew,
And catch'd my *Chloe* by the Shoe,
    Her Speed was then in vain.   15

IV

But Oh! as tott'ring down she fell,
    What did the Fall reveal?
Such Limbs Description cannot tell,
Such Charms were never in the *Mall*,
    Nor Smock did e'er conceal.   20

V

She shreik'd, I turn'd my ravish'd Eyes,
    And burning with Desire,
I help'd the Queen of Love to rise;
She check'd her Anger and Surprize,
    And said, Rash Youth, retire.   25

VI

Be gone, and boast what you have seen,
    It shan't avail you much;
I know you like my Form and Mien,
Yet since so insolent y'have been,
    The Parts disclos'd you ne'er shall touch. 30

CXXVI

TO *PHILLIS*: WHO SLIGHTED HIM

Since you no longer will be kind,
  But my Embraces shun,
Bacchus shall ease my am'rous Mind,
  To his embrace I run.

Wine gives a Pleasure unrestrain'd,   5
  Dispells the frantick Spleen;
Tho' Wishes cannot be attain'd,
  Looks still are joyful seen.

The God within his gladsome Cave
  No Care nor Grief allows;   10
He laughs to Scorn the Sober, Grave,
  And Sighing Lover's Vows.

Then, *Phillis*, do whate'er you can,
  I dully will not pine,
I'll ne'er forget I am a Man,   15
  But seek my Cure from Wine.

That sullen Look, and hasty Kiss,
  That Air reserv'd and coy;
That cold Denial of the Bliss
  Shall not my Ease destroy.   20

If you no more can love like me,
  Why should it give me Pain?
Frail Woman will inconstant be,
  Nor Art their Will can chain.

As well I might cross Winds deplore,   25
  At rising Tempests rave,
As hope a wav'ring Mind to cure;
  Nature its Course will have.

Then welcome more enduring Joys,
  Long shall my Doctor be,   30
A Club of Witty, Toping Boys,
  And Love, adieu to thee.

CXXVII

SOPHRONIA'S *ANSWER TO A COXCOMB*

I

Satisfy your self, fond Youth,
　I can believe you love;
I know the Charms of Wealth and Youth
　Are Charms which you approve⟨.⟩

II

Regardless of my Wit, and Mind,　　　　　　　5
　With Truth and Virtue fraught,
To meaner Beauties you are kind,
　By Lust or Int'rest taught.

III

But know, the Person I shall choose,
　Must have a Taste like mine;　　　　　　　10
I never shall consent to loose
　The Charms in which I shine.

IV

To other Nymphs your Vows address,
　Your sordid Accents, prate
Of Airs, Complexion, Mien and Dress,　　　　15
　And cringe your empty Pate.

V

You're handsome, fine, can caper, sing,
　Of Coxcombs lead the Van;
Yet have not Sense, the only thing,
　That I can like in Man.　　　　　　　　　20

CXXVIII

TO CLARISSA

Upon dirtying her Lodgings

Dust from my earthy Surface fell,
And soil'd the fair *Clarissa*'s Cell;
Clarissa's Eyes have Pow'r Divine,
And with uncommon Lustre shine;
I'm form'd of sordid Earth, which must,　　　5
When shin'd upon, be turn'd to Dust;

This *Phœbus* meaner Force can do,
Who is not half so bright as You;
Be not severe then in your Doom,
Since from your Self my Fault did come;   10
'Twas Wonder, when so near the Ray,
I did not moulder quite away;
She smiles, forgives; I feel the Pain,
Be angry, Charming Nymph, again;
Better to dye, than thus endure   15
What, You, ah Cruel! will not cure.

CXXIX

A Lady, asking the Author's Opinion of two Gentlemen, her Lovers,
occasioned the following Lines

With decent Carriage, and an artful Stile,
The prudent *Cynthio* does the World beguile,
And hides the Satyr underneath the Smile.

Not so *Astolpho*, gen'rous and sincere,
He ne'er at common Failings is severe;   5
Open his Words, and undisguis'd his Soul,
He let's no trifling Humour spoil the Whole:
Ne'er sooths the harmless Foibles of Mankind,
Vainly, inhumanly, to laugh behind;
Wisely, at nobler Merit, he aspires,   10
And more the Name of Man, than Wit desires.

Teach me, kind Heav'n, to make so good a Choice;
Let Truth alone inspire an honest Voice:
Far from me keep the frothy Part of Wit;
Let me be dull, —— but not an Hypocrite.   15

CXXX

SONG

I

Unveil, divinely Fair, your Eyes,
And from the downy Bed arise;
Ah! did you *Strephon*'s Love partake,
You would not sleep, but ever wake.

II

Hence, hence, dull God of Sleep, away,   5
Let my *Celinda* bless the Day:
Insensibly, you close those Eyes,
At whose each Look, a Shepherd dyes.   8

CXXXI

SONG

I

Since Wine, Love, Musick, present are,
 Let's banish ev'ry Doubt and Care;
This Night is ours, and we'll enjoy,
 To Morrow shall not *Now* destroy.

II

Let us indulge the Joys we know   5
 Of Musick, Wine and Love;
We're sure of what we find below,
 Uncertain what's above.   8

CXXXII

SONG

I

Young *Strephon*, who thro' ev'ry Grove,
Had chas'd the fleeting God of Love,
Met *Hymen* once, who cross'd his Joy,
And chain'd the Am'rous Captive Boy.

II

Happy the Swains, who only stray   5
Where Love and Pleasure lead the Way;
Where *Hymen*'s Arts can never move,
And Love receives no Tye, but Love.   8

CXXXIII

SONG

I

Why flies *Clarissa* from her Swain,
 Regardless of Desire?
The Wanton sees his Pain,
And, of the Conquest vain,
 Derides the Love-sick Fire.   5

II

Beware, ah! Cruel! Tempt not Fate,
    Nor with Love's Arrows Toy;
Tho' now unhurt, Elate,
You'll surely find, too late!   10
    There's Danger in the Boy.

CXXXIV

THE MINOUET

A Song

I

My lovely Charmer, will you Dance
    With *Strephon*, your obedient Slave;
She look'd the kind consenting Glance,
    And then her snowy Hand she gave.

II

The Youth with Joy the Nymph receiv'd,   5
    And gently press'd her tender Palm,
'Till Musick's Sound the Hand reliev'd,
    And robb'd him of his healing Balm.

III

The Am'rous Swain, thro' eager Haste,
    Both *Time* and *Measure* did disdain :   10
Twice careless, he the Figure trac'd,
    And snatch'd the snowy Hand again.

IV

The blushing Maid his Flame approv'd,
    And with like gen'rous Passion mov'd,
Again, they round the Figure glow'd,   15
    Then turn'd, and curtsy'd; *Strephon* bow'd.

CXXXV

THE TOPER

A Song

I

Let's Tope and be Merry,
Be Jolly and Cheary;
    Since here is good Wine, good Wine.

Let's laugh at the Fools,
Who live by dull Rules,
   And at us Good-Fellows repine.   5

II

Here, here, are Delights,
To amuse the dull Nights,
   And equal a Man with a God;
To enliven the Clay,   10
Drive all Care away,
   Without it a Man's but a Clod.

III

Then let us be willing
To spend t'other Shilling,
   For Money we know is but Dirt;   15
It suits no Design,
Like paying for Wine,
   T'other Bottle will do us no hurt.   18

CXXXVI

VENUS AND *ADONIS*: OR THE AMOUR OF VENUS

Omnia vincit Amor ————
           Virgil.

In *Ida*'s Grove a secret Place there lies,
That seems secure from *Man*'s and *Heav'n*'s Eyes:
No raging *Heat* but *Love*'s cou'd this invade
Ever protected by a grateful Shade
With rising Grass the plenteous Earth is Spread,   5
And various Flowers form a fragrant Bed:
Close by a softly-stealing Stream complains,
As if it self endur'd a Lover's Pains.
Around the Turtles, gently moaning seem,
And mix their Murmurs with the purling Stream.   10
Venus distress'd in Pallaces above,
Found no Content while absent from her Love;
The Residence of Gods cou'd yield no Joy,
Without the Presence of the lov'ly Boy:
She therefore left Heav'n's Courts (oppress'd with Cares,)   15
And to this humble, quiet Seat repairs.
Here now she seeks (her Comfort and Delight,)
The Youth, who must each soft Regard requite;
But ah! No Youth appears to bless her Sight.

The appointed Time was pass'd, th' exalted Sun   20
To th' utmost Summit of his Course was run ;
Yet still *Adonis*, with an eager Pace,
Thoughtless of Heat, or Rest, pursues the Chace ;
Thoughtless of Danger, or her kind Embrace.
But She (in whom nothing can Love controul   25
Love ! The sole Joy and Essence of her Soul,)
Full of Desire, cannot her self contain,
But thence as Winds sweep o'er the stormy Main,
She swiftly springs . . . stops ev'ry Nymph and Swain,
Some Tidings of the ling'ring Boy to know,   30
And where, and how employ'd, and why so slow ?
   Her Voice and Eyes, and eager Steps proclaim
The fierce Impatience of the heav'nly Dame.
So flies the wounded Deer along the Plains,
Seeking Redress . . . while of its cruel Pains,   35
The fatal Cause fixt in it's Side remains.
   To ev'ry Hill that a far Prospect makes
Thro' pathless Ways, a desp'rate Flight she takes,
In frantick Mode, her loose dishevell'd Hair,
Toss'd by the Winds, her Limbs expos'd and bare,   40
Careless of Beauties that so meanly charm,
And heedless in his Cause of ev'ry Harm.
   Much Pains th' impatient Goddess dos' imploy
In fruitless Search of the neglectful Boy.
Weary'd at length with Toil, and faint with Heat,   45
Repairs again to her cool shady Seat,
Hoping in Sleep's inviting Arms to find
A Solace, to relieve her harrass'd Mind,
And faint Idea of that Bliss to gain,
For which, she waking fought so much in vain.   50
   Now, now to needful Rest she's softly lay'd
In the Recess of the most secret Shade,
The ravish'd Earth, it's grassy Carpet spreads,
And new sprung Flowers nod their fragrant Heads.
Twine round her Limbs, and grateful Odours give ;   55
But far more grateful Odours thence receive.
The Breezes ev'ry part with Kisses greet,
And by those Kisses make their Breaths more sweet ;
The Trees in circling Crouds behold the Sight,
And shake their leafy Limbs, and tremble with Delight.   60
   The curling River in a vast Amaze,
Restrains his murmuring Flood, and stops to gaze ;
Transported, views the Grace of ev'ry Limb,
And grasps its dear Resemblance in his Stream.
Each am'rous Turtle far more am'rous grows,   65
And in tumultuous Moans its Passions shows⟨.⟩

Her heavenly Charms all but *Adonis* fire,
Whole Nature sees with Wonder and Desire !
  The little Love's in silent, solemn State,
With due Obedience on the Goddess wait,   70
Part guard, Her sleeping with the strictest Care,
The Rest to seek the Darling Youth prepare.
  Thus *Venus* do's her ardent Mind employ
The dear, the beauteous, wild, and wand'ring Boy,
Tho' shy t' embrace, tho' careless yet t' enjoy :   75
At least some fancy'd Blessing to procure
From Hind'rance, and from Interruption sure.
But ah ! No cautious Dealing can delude
Close Envy, nor her jealous Sight exclude :
For whom shou'd simple Love securely blind,   80
Contrive, or act what Envy cannot find ?
She slily lurking, this Intrigue do's know,
Disclosing all to Love's severest Foe.
And now th' abstemious Goddess of the Groves,
Cruel *Diana*, conscious of their Loves,   85
With Fury burns, and to pursue her Hate,
Had search'd the Volume of eternal Fate ;
(For Fate all Actions sways, his Laws confine,
All aims, and curb even the Pow'rs Divine.)
Its brazen Leaves all Mortals Dooms comprize   90
In Characters of various Hue and Size ;
The smaller still each happy Doom express,
Which human Malice (as it can) makes less
A sanguine Dye, and sullen Black unfold
The bad . . . . the Prosp'rous are display'd in Gold,   95
So deeply writ, that neither Force nor Skill
Can fully raise Them, both the good and ill
Slow Care, Discretion and Advice are by,
And all the bad t' abolish vainly try.
  Here for *Adonis*'s Doom the Goddess pry's   100
With dire Intent . . . and while her Hands and Eyes,
  With Expedition, yet with Caution move,
She finds the Pages of disastr'ous Love.
There sees his sudden Lot in sanguine Hue,
Engraven deep, the Characters yet new.   105
And scarcely dry, the woful Deed reveal,
And seem an Image of the Case they tell,
How in small Time assaulting on the Plain
A furious Boar, the Hunter shou'd be slain.
  At this well pleas'd, she smil'd, and cry'd *Caress*,   110
Thy Youth, fond *Venus* ! thy Delight possess ;
But short's th' allotted Time, and I the Joy
Of that short time shall labour to destroy.

This said, with furious Haste the Path she trod, ⎫
(And *Mind* with *Vengeance* fraught) to sleep's abode, ⎬   115
There took a Fantom from the drowsy God.   ⎭
Fram'd like *Adonis*, in that dismal State,
To which he quickly must be doom'd by Fate.
This Envy had in Keeping to convey
With speed to where expecting *Venus* lay.   120
    And now soft Sleep with welcome sweet Surprize ⎫
Approaching *Venus* shuts her radiant Eyes;   ⎬
Yet ah ! full Conquest anxious Thought denies,   ⎭
By sudden Fits she shakes it from her breast
With fearful sad prophetick Dreams oppress'd.   125
    No sooner had soft Slumber seiz'd the Dame, ⎫
(Ever within her Thoughts) *Adonis* came,   ⎬
But how surprizing ! How unlike the same ?   ⎭
His Eyes distorted ! stupid ! gastly ! stare,
Pale were his Cheeks, and clotted was his Hair ;   130
His feeble Limbs with Dirt besmeer'd around,
And Blood in Streams flow'd from a direful Wound :
From's Lips Words broken and imperfect, fell, ⎫
Some mournful Tale, he stamm'ring, seem to tell, ⎬
He sigh'd, and bad eternally Farewel.   ⎭   135
    Th' astonish'd Goddess vast Endeavours made
To grasp the dear, the lovely, dismal Shade :
But all alas ! were vainly loss'd in Air,
Waking, she finds no sad Resemblance there.
    O'er all the gloomy Grove with Care she pry'd,   140
But when no true *Adonis* she descry'd,
Again, t' inviting Sleep her self resign'd ;
Again, the gastly Vision haunts her Mind :
Again, with Blood and Dirt obscene appears :
Again, the dismal long Farewel she hears :   145
    Then, rising puts the horrid Dreams to Flight,
And frees her from the dire distracting Sight :
But oh ! th' Impression still remains behind,
And with vast Doubts and Fears, torments her Mind.
    As grievous Cares the Tender Mother seize,   150
Who from her Arms, and such indulgent Ease,
Her Life's Delight ! her Age's Hope ! for Gain,
Her only Son ! has ventur'd on the Main.
When told by Fame, that on some rocky Coast,
The hapless Youth with all his Wealth is loss'd ;   155
Such now of *Venus* seems the wretched Case ;
Such weighty Grief in her sad Mind takes Place.
    But now the Loves (by ranging all around,)
The long'd-for and lamented Youth had found ;
And by his Side, in close Attendance came,   160

And introduc'd him to the wishing Dame :
Upon the dear delicious Boy she fly's,
As swift as Lightning flashing from the Skies,
Or as the Glances of her brighter Eyes :
Her circling Arms upon his Neck she flung,   165
And with fixt Kisses on his Lips she hung.
   A while the Transport of the present Joys,
All Thought of future, or of pass'd destroys ;
But when her Flame (that Grief more raging made)
By softest Dalliance was in Part allay'd,   170
Reflecting on her Dream, she silence broke,
And sighing thus, the tempting Goddess spoke :
   Forbear, regardless Youth ! at length forbear ;
Nor prosecute with Beasts an endless War,
Thy *Venus* do's in all the Danger share.   175
Or, if, alas ! thy too licentious Mind
Is still to vig'rous *Sylvan* Sports inclin'd,
At least, dear Youth ! be cautious in thy Way,
Fly ! fly with Care each furious Beast of Prey ;
Ne'er arm'd with Launce provoke the raging *Boar*,   180
And dread the *Lion*'s most tremendous Roar :
From the rough *Bear*'s rude Grasp, oh ! swiftly run,
The *Leopard*, and the cruel *Tyger* shun ;
With strict Regard, oh ! ever such avoid,
Lest all my Joy shou'd be with thee destroy'd :   185
But Nets, or fleetest *Hounds* for *Deer* prepare,
Or chace the crafty *Fox*, or tim'rous *Hare* :
Mix Safety ever with thy Sports, be wise,
And ne'er approach where Danger may arise.
   For oh ! a dismal Dream, portending Ill,   190
Do's all my Soul with wond'rous Horror fill ;
Some mighty Mischief now impending shows,
And seems to threaten with unusual Woes :
What Apprehensions hence my Peace destroy,
And even in thy Presence, blast my Joy ?   195
How will they then, while thou'rt hence surprize,
What countless Store of Jealousies will 'rise ?
Oh ! what Mistrust ? What Terrors will impart
A constant Anguish to my aching Heart ?
Be ever careful, and afford me Rest,   200
For both our sakes, *Adonis* ! this Request :
Let not thy Mind be tempted to refuse,
Nor slight a Goddess, when she humbly sues.
   Yet oh ! most happy and secure to live,
To Love and Me, all, all thy Moments give.   205
I not with *Juno*, covet boundless Reign,
Nor strive with *Pallas* on the fatal Plain,
Such Triumphs, such dire Victories to gain :

Nor with *Diana* to the Chace inclin'd.
Do's thy affected Sport delight my Mind.   210
I all my Thoughts on Love alone employ,
That yields the truest and sublimest Joy;
Of all Diversions, only this is mine,
And dearest Youth ! let it be ever thine;
Let's bid to ev'ry vainer Thing, Adieu,   215
You only bless'd in Me, and I in You.

Here by increasing soft Concern possess'd, ⎫
She ceas'd to speak, and ardently she press'd ⎬
His Hand, and Looks, and Kisses plead the rest. ⎭
But ah ! the Sallies of a roving Mind,   220
No soft Endearments, or Entreaties bind :
Still in his Thoughts the wild Infection reigns,
He Freedom loves more than Cælestial Chains :
Nor can th' greatest Beauty of the Skies,
With all her Fondness and her Grace suffice;   225
But as young Striplings from the watchful Eye,
Break wildly forth, and to their Pastimes fly;
Their Friends, and their secure Abodes neglect,
And Counsel, and 'forewarning Care reject :

He vent'rously again the Chace pursues,   230
And Fearless in the Woods his Haunts renews;
Too soon, alas ! forsakes her safer Arms,
Heedless of her Advice, and all her Charms,
Spurns at the Pleasures of his blissful State,
Perversly blind, and rushes on his Fate.   235

EXPLANATORY NOTES

LIST OF SIGLA USED IN EXPLANATORY AND TEXTUAL NOTES

(Catch Titles from the Bibliography are given, see pp. 235–261.)

K = Kemp's Collection, 1672, 8vo. Bibliography, No. 9*a*.
A = Miscellaneous Works, 1702, 8vo. ,, ,, 30.
B1 = The Poetical Works, 1707, 8vo. ,, ,, 36.
B2 = The Poetical Works, 1710, 8vo. ,, ,, 37.
B3 = The Works, 1722, 2 vols. in 12mo. ,, ,, 40.
B4 = The Works, 1776, 2 vols. in 8vo. ,, ,, 41.
B5 = The Works, 1778, 2 vols. in 12mo. ,, ,, 42.
G = Gildon's New Miscellany, 1701, 8vo. ,, ,, 29.
Gent.'s Journ. = "The Gentleman's Journal," 1691/2–4. 4to.
    Bibliography, No. 24.
I = D'Urfey's "The Intrigues at Versailles," 1697, 4to. Biblio-
    graphy, No. 26.
Com. = Commendatory Verses, 1700, fol. Bibliography No. 28.
W = Wit and Mirth, 1719, 8vo. ,, ,, 39.
SP = Poems on Affairs of State, 1698, 8vo. ,, ,, 27.
D1 = Dryden's Miscellany, 1684, 8vo. ,, ,, 16*a*.
D2 = Dryden's Miscellany, 1692, 8vo. ,, ,, ,,
D3 = Dryden's Miscellany, 1702, 8vo. ,, ,, 16*b*.
V = Buckingham's Miscellaneous Works, 1704, 8vo. Bibliography,
    No. 32.
P = Poetical Recreations, 1688, 12mo. Bibliography No. 21.
Q, Q1, Q2, etc. = Quarto editions of plays.
Ff. = Folio editions of the "Happy Pair," 1702 and 1705.
etc. = "and all subsequent editions."

EXPLANATORY NOTES TO·
BELLAMIRA, or the MISTRESS

BELLAMIRA

The Preface to the Reader, l. 8. A Friend

Malone (quoted by Genest, I. 455) says that this was the dramatist, Thomas Shadwell, who dedicated his translation of the Tenth Satire of Juvenal to Sedley in the same month as the production of " Bellamira." See " Sir Charles Sedley," pp. 168–171.

Prologue, l. 11. *Bully-rocks*

Originally this word was a term of familiar endearment, as in Shakespeare's " The Merry Wives of Windsor," I. iii., where the older form " bully-rook " is found. Afterwards it came to mean a hectoring ruffian. *Woodcock*, in Shadwell's " The Sullen Lovers " (4to, 1668), however, still gives it the old sense.

l. 15. *Perruque comb'd . . . Pocket tortoise stir'd*

There are many contemporary allusions to the fashionable habit of combing periwigs with a pocket comb in the theatre. Shadwell's *Briske* in " The Humorists " says :

" Look you, no man appears better upon a Bench in the Play house, when I stand up to expose my person between the Acts, I take out my Comb and with a *bonne mien* combe my Periwig to the tune the Fiddles play " (4to, 1671, V. i.).

l. 17. *huff*,

" to speak arrogantly or insolently ; to storm, bluster, talk big."—N.E.D.

l. 17. *dumbfound*

Dumbfounding was apparently a kind of practical joke much in vogue among Restoration playgoers. It seems to have consisted in striking a blow unexpectedly and then feigning innocence. Cf. Otway's " The Soldier's Fortune " (4to, 1681, II. i.) : " We are on his blind side ; I'll dumb found him. (*Strikes him on the shoulder*) " ; also Dryden's Prologue to " The Prophetess," l. 47 : " That witty recreation call'd dumbfounding."

l 18. *scowre*,

" to depart in haste, run away, decamp."—N.E.D.

" To scamper, to rubb, to scowre, To run away." Shadwell,
" Explanation of the Cant " prefixed to " The Squire of Alsatia,"
4to, 1688.
For another meaning of this word see note to III. iv. l. 10.

l. 21. *When our two houses did divide the Town.*
I.e. before 1682, when the old King's and Duke's companies
were united. The articles of union were signed on May 14,
1682, and the joint company started acting on November 16.
The union lasted till 1695.

l. 34. *Our Author try'd his own and cou'd not hit.*
Clearly a reference to the bad reception of "The Mulberry
Garden." ,

I. i. l. 31. *Marshal* Gloves
Marshal is an anglicized form of Maréchale, a French scent
used commonly for gloves. In Shadwell's " The Virtuoso,"
Sir Samuel Harty disguised as an Exchange woman proffers
the ladies " choice of good Gloves, Amber, Orangery, Genoa,
Romane, Frangipane, Neroly, Tuberose, Jessimine, and Marshal"
(4to, 1676, III. iii.).

l. 62. the Rose
The celebrated tavern in Russell Street, Covent Garden.
It was a favourite haunt of the Wits and is frequently mentioned
in contemporary comedies. See " Sir Charles Sedley," p. 58.

l. 74. . . . one leap out of your low Window . . .
Genest's comment is, " this has strongly the appearance of
being an allusion to the story told of young Churchill and the
Duchess." The story in question is told as follows by Wolseley
in his " Life of Marlborough " (I. 69) : " This Affair had become
known to Charles through the Duke of Buckingham, who had
quarrelled with Barbara Palmer and wished to ruin her in the
king's favour. Aware of her intimacy with Churchill, he bribed
her servant, and so contrived that the king should find the young
guardsman in her bedroom." A similar version is given in the
curious little pamphlet called " Hattegé ou les Amours du Roy de
Tamaran " (Cologne, 1676, Engl. translation : Amsterdam,
1680, 12mo.), where, according to a key given by Ch. Nodier in
his " Mélanges tirées d'une Petite Bibliothèque," the king of
Tamaran is Charles, *Hattigé* Lady Castlemaine, *Rajep* Churchill,
and *Osman* Buckingham. Neither the author of this work nor
Wolseley mention the incident of jumping out of the window.

l. 100. A Flam
A lie, or trick. Cf. Shadwell's " Bury Fair," II. i., where *Mrs.
Gertrude* denounces *Mrs. Fantast*'s compliments as " a Flam, a
meer Flam." " *Eh Mondieu !* " answers *Fantast*. . . . " Call
generous complements Flams." (4to, 1689, II. i.)

l. 100. Wheadle

A lie or cozenage; used as the proper name of a cheating gamester by Etherege in " The Comical Revenge " (4to, 1664).

l. 103. *Jamaica*

Jamaica was captured by the English naval expedition under Penn and Venables sent by Cromwell to seize Hispaniola in 1655. Charles II refused to restore it to Spain after the Restoration.

l. 108. Kidnappers

According to the N.E.D., from kid (= child) + nab or nap (= seize). Both the word and the practice which it denotes seem to have arisen in England about this time. The following quotation throws some light on *Bellamira*'s story :

" Mr. John Wilmore haveing kidnapped a boy of 13 years of age to Jamaica, a writt de homine replegiando was delivered to the sheriffs of London against him."—Luttrell's " Brief Relation," I. 183, *s.d.* May 10, 1682.

l. 123. two Whiskers !

The N.E.D. gives as a meaning of " whisking," great, excessive, " bouncing," " whopping " ; so " whiskers " here presumably means " whoppers." Hickeringill's " News from Colchester " (1673), quoted by N.E.D., has " this Whisking Lye." Professor Ernest Weekley gives me the following quotation : " A whisking lye : mendacium impudens. Littleton's Latin Dictionary, 1678."

l. 134. *Dangerfield*

Aphra Behn, in her novel " The Dumb Virgin, or the Force of Imagination," writes, " he call'd himself *Dangerfield*, which was a Name that so pleas'd me, being satisfied that it was a Counterfeit, I us'd it in a Comedy of mine." The name is not found in any of Mrs. Behn's plays, and Mr. Montague Summers, in the note on this passage in his edition of Aphra Behn's works (V. 523), conjectures that she made a present of it to Sedley. It is, however, quite as possible that Sedley took the name from the notorious Thomas Dangerfield, one of the concocters of the Popish Plot, who was tried and executed in 1685. It may be noticed that Dangerfield was actually a " Beau Garçon " and that his intrigues were well known.

l. 153. Puppy-water

A reference to the disgusting practice of using puppy's urine as a cosmetic, which seems to have been common among seventeenth-century ladies. Cf. Middleton's " A Chaste Maid in Cheapside " (4to, 1630, III. i.) :

" Now in goes the long fingers that are wash't
Some thrice a day in Urine ; my wife vses it,"

and Swift's " The Lady's Dressing Room " :

> " With Puppy-water Beauty's help,
> Distill'd from Tripsy's darling Whelp."

l. 162. As our modern Poet hath it.

The " modern Poet " is Dryden and the line is from " The
Indian Emperour " (4to, 1667), I. ii, where it is spoken by
Montezuma to *Orbellan* and *Guyomar :*

> " My Sons, let your unseemly discord cease,
> If not in friendship, live at least in peace."

l. 218. a *Cloyster*

Apparently a common threat : cf. Dryden's " Limberham "
(4to, 1680, II. i.), where *Mrs. Tricksy*, Limberham's mistress,
exclaims : " To show I can live honest, in spight of all mankind,
I'll go into a Nunnery, and that's my resolution." It may be
noticed that Dryden's own reputed mistress, Mrs. Ann Reeve,
retired from the stage and took the veil in 1675.

l. 261. I will carry them my self, . . .

The rest of this speech, though printed continuously in all
editions, is clearly an aside.

I. ii. ll. 5, 6. New *Spring Garden !*

This is the old name of Vauxhall Garden. It distinguished
it from the old Spring Garden at Charing Cross. The new
Garden was laid out soon after the Restoration. Evelyn visited
it on July 2, 1661, and found it " a pretty contrived plantation."
Pepys often went to Vauxhall and walked in the Spring Garden.
On May 28, 1667, he heard the nightingales singing there ; he
also comments on the loose company that frequented it. It is
mentioned in many comedies. Wycherley's *Hippolita*, in " The
Gentleman Dancing Master," complains that she is not allowed
" to eat a Sillybub in new Spring-Gar'n with a cousin," and *Mrs.
Frail*, in Congreve's " Love for Love," remarks that if she had
" gone to *Knights-bridge*, or to *Chelsey* or to *Spring-Garden*, . . .
with a man alone "—something might have been said.

l. 7. Colambor

According to N.E.D., which quotes this passage, a variant of
Calambour, which is a French form of Calambac, a Malay or
Javanese word for aloes or eagle-wood, greatly prized for its
scent. Madame de Sévigné mentions a rosary of Calembac in a
letter of June 8, 1680.

l. 8. Angel-water

For angelica water, " a perfumed liquid of which angelica
once formed a chief constituent ; afterwards containing ambergris,
rose, myrtle and orange-flower waters."—N.E.D., which quotes
this passage.

l. 15. the Mall

The famous walk in St. James's Park, so called from the game of Pall Mall. The original Mall was the street now called Pall Mall, which was built over under the Commonwealth. The new " Mall " was laid out by Charles II after the Restoration.

ll. 122, 123, a Parson Marry you to a great Fortune without a Licence; . . .

Sedley himself had personal experience of a " marriage " of this kind : see " Sir Charles Sedley," pp. 129, 130.

l. 137. *Knightsbridge*

Cf. Otway's " The Soldier's Fortune " (4to, 1681), III. i., where Sir *Davy Dunce* says of his wife :

" Or it may be taking the Air as far as Knightsbridge, with some smoothfac'd Rogue or another : 'tis a damn'd house that Swan, that Swan at Knights-bridge is a confounded house."

I. iii. l. 46. The Groom-Porter

An officer of the Royal Household who regulated all matters concerning gambling within the precincts of the Court. He furnished cards and dice and settled disputes arising from games of chance.

l. 74. A *Beau Garcon*

This term was used in two senses : either for an ugly, old beau or ogler, or else for a kept bully. For the first meaning cf. " *A Faithful Catalogue of Our Most Eminent Ninnies* " :

" 'Tis strange Kilgore, that refin'd Beau Garcon
Was never yet at the Bell Savage shown,
For he's a true and wonderful Baboon,"
(" Political Satires," ed. Goldsmith, 8vo, 1885, p. 14.)

Also Rochester's " On the Supposed author of a Late Poem in defence of Satyr " :

" Who needs will be an ugly Beau-*Garcon*,
Spit at, and shun'd by every Girl in Town."
(" Miscellaneous Works," 8vo, 1709, p. 97.)

For the second meaning cf. " The Rehearsal " (ed. Montague Summers, I. ii.) :

" *Bayes.* I am kept by another woman, in the City.
Smith. How kept ? for what ?
Bayes. Why for a *Beau Gerson :* I am ifackins."

l. 104. forfeited his Charter

This phrase must have had a very topical ring in 1687. After the dissolution of the Whig and exclusionist Parliament in 1681, the Government of Charles II turned its attention to attacking the municipalities, which were mostly Whig strongholds. Shaftesbury's acquittal by the London Grand Jury in November 1681 convinced the Government that they would never be able to coerce rebellious Whigs until the Corporations were remodelled. By means of writs of *Quo Warranto* all the city charters, beginning with that of the city of London, were attacked and forfeited and only restored on conditions that placed them completely in the royal power.

II. i. l. 11. Terse

Restoration slang for claret. Of uncertain origin. Perhaps from terse = clean, neat, smooth: cf. merum. Thiers, a wine-growing district in Pûy-de-Dome, has also been suggested. Cf. Shadwell, " The Humorists " (4to, 1671, IV. i.) :

" Must I stay, till by the strength of Terse Claret, you have whet yourself into courage ? "

l. 60. Does my Patron lose ? . . .

Sedley seems to be expanding Terence with the aid of a hint from Lucretius. Terence's *Gnatho* (Smoothly's prototype) merely says :

" Quidquid dicunt laudo; id rursum si negant, laudo id quoque;
Negant: nego; ait; aio; postremo imperavi egomet
Omnia adsentiri . . ."

Smoothly's description of his methods of dealing with his patron are probably suggested by the famous lines in Lucretius (IV. 1160) :

nigra melichrus est, immunda et fetida acosmos,
cæsia Palladium, nervosa et lignea dorcas,
parvula pumilio, chariton mia, tota merum sal,
magna atque immanis cataplexis plenaque honoris.

ll. 176, 177. nor any of the little Tinsel, short Liv'd Beauties of the Town, . . .

Very happily adapted from Terence's

haud similis virgost virginum nostrarum, quas matres student,
demissis umeris esse, vincto pectore, ut gracilae sient.

l. 192. *Hockamore*

See note to " The Mulberry Garden," IV. i. l. 149.

II. ii. l. 93. Juniper Water, for good Humor.

" A Cordial drink made from or flavoured with juniper."— N.E.D., which quotes the following passage from a letter of Sir W. Temple to Godolphin written in 1666 : " A little Bottle of Juniper Water which is the common Cordial in that Country."

III. i. l. 68. *Bartholomew-Fair ?*

The ancient fair held on St. Bartholomew's Day (August 22) at Smithfield, lasting for fourteen days. Originally it was a Cloth Fair, but after the reign of Elizabeth it was chiefly a place of amusement. Ben Jonson's famous comedy (first acted 1614) gives a vivid picture of the Fair in James I's reign. Pepys saw Lady Castlemaine there on August 30, 1667.

l. 75. Cony !

Literally a rabbit ; often used as a term of endearment for a woman. Cf. Beaumont and Fletcher, " Knight of the Burning Pestle," Prologue :

Wife. Husband, Husband.

Cit. What sayst thou, Conie ?

l. 93. Song.

The following version of this Song appears anonymously on p. 308 of Vol. VI of " Wit and Mirth," London, 1720 (see Bibliography, No. 39 *b*) :—

> When first I lay'd Siege to my *Chloris*,
> When first I lay'd Siege to my *Chloris* ;
> Cannon Oaths I brought down,
> To batter the Town,
> And boom'd her with amorous Stories.
>
> Billet deux like small shot did so ply her,
> Billet deux like small shot did so ply her ;
> And sometimes a Song,
> Went whistling along,
> Yet still I was never the nigher.
>
> At length she sent Word by a Trumpet,
> At length she sent Word by a Trumpet,
> That if I lik'd the Life,
> She would be my Wife,
> But she would be no Man's Strumpet.
>
> I told her that Mars would ne'er Marry,
> I told her that Mars would ne'er Marry ;
> I swore by my Scars,
> Got in Combates and Wars,
> That I'd rather dig Stones in a Quarry.
>
> At length she granted the Favour,
> At length she granted the Favour ;
> With ? out [sic] the dull Curse,
> For better for worse,
> And saved the Parson the Labour.

This version is preceded by the following setting, to which no composer's name is attached :—

l. 158. *Ethiopia*

Strictly Abyssinia, but used loosely in seventeenth-century English to denote any of the more remote parts of Africa.

l. 162. a Warden Roasted in the Embers.

A warden pie was a pie made of warden pears, baked or stewed without a crust and coloured with saffron, which gave it a yellow appearance. Cf. " A Winter's Tale," IV. iii. : " I must haue Saffron to colour the Warden Pies."

III. ii. 1. 83. *Jane Shore.*

Edward IV's mistress. She did not " Dye in a Ditch " as the popular legend had it, and the name Shoreditch existed long before her time. She is said to have strewn flowers at Henry VII's funeral, and she knew Sir Thomas More in her extreme old age.

The Duchess of Cleveland (the alleged " original " of Bellamira) was compared to her more than once. In 1682 a bitter lampoon was published entitled " A Dialogue between the D[utchess] of C[leveland] and the D[utchess] of P[ortsmouth] at their meeting in Paris with the Ghost of Jane Shore."

III. iii. 1. 70. Ecclaircissement.

One of the fashionable French words which came in after the Restoration. It is in the list that *Philotis* reads to her Frenchified mistress *Melantha* in Dryden's " Marriage-à-la-mode " (4to, 1673), III. i. :

" *Embarasse, Double entendre, Equivoque, Esclaircissement, Suittè, Beveue, Facòn, Panchant, Coup d'etourdy* and *Ridicule.*"

l. 102. *Mirabilis ?*

A fashionable cordial. Cf. Aphra Behn's " Sir Patient Fancy " (Works, ed. Montague Summers, IV. 4).

" But, Oh I'm sick at Heart, Maundy fetch me a bottle of Mirabilis in the Closet."

l. 157. *Epsome* nor *Tunbridge* Waters.

Epsom and Tunbridge were both fashionable health resorts noted for the supposed healing powers of their waters and the free and easy manners of the company that frequented them. The story of Wycherley's meeting with the Countess of Drogheda, his future wife, at Tunbridge Wells as told by Dennis is a good illustration of this passage :

" He went down to *Tunbridge* to take either the Benefit of the Waters or the Diversions of the Place, when walking one Day upon the Wells Walk with his Freend Mr *Fairbeard* of *Grey's Inn*, just as he came up to the Bookseller's, my Lady *Drogheda*, a young Widow, rich, noble, and beautiful, came to the Bookseller and enquir'd for *the Plain Dealer. Madam*, says Mr *Fairbeard, there he is for you*, pushing Mr *Wycherley* towards her. . . . In short Mr. Wycherley walk'd with her upon the Walks, waited upon her home, visited her daily at her Lodgings, while she staid at Tunbridge."

("Letters, Familiar, Moral and Critical," 8vo, 1721, p. 222.)

III. iv. l. 10. scour'd

To scour was to make a disturbance in the streets, fight with passers-by, beat the watch, etc. The Scowrers was the name given to a sect of hooligans who played these pranks and who resembled the later fraternity of Mohocks. Shadwell's comedy, " The Scowrers " (4to, 1691), gives a vivid picture of these ruffians.

l. 67. *Pretty Padder.*

Padder = thief, from pad, to rob on the highway, originally to tread or tramp. Cf. Dryden, " Limberham," Epilogue :

> " Lord with what Rampant Gadders
> Our Counters will be throned and Roads with Padders."

III. v. l. 59. thy Discourse has Fingers in it.

I can find no parallel to this phrase.

l. 72. Asinego

An anglicized form of Spanish *asnico*, a little ass, hence a fool or dolt. The word is fairly common in seventeenth-century English and is found in Shakespeare :

> " An Assinego may tutor thee."
> Troilus and Cressida, II. i.

IV. i. l. 53. the Siege of *Dunkirk.*

Dangerfield had presumably served with the English Royalist contingent in Flanders which assisted the Spaniards against the French and Cromwellians. Dunkirk was invested by Turenne on May 15/25, 1658. At the battle of the Dunes on June 4/14 the French gained a complete victory over the Spaniards. In this battle the English Royalists fighting for Spain met the Commonwealth troops, whom Cromwell had sent to help the French, hand to hand. The former, although they fought bravely, were completely worsted. Dunkirk surrendered ten days after the battle. (See " Royalist and Cromwellian Armies in France," by Sir C. H. Firth, Journal of the Royal Historical Society, New Series, Vol. XVII.)

IV. ii. l. 63. Back-Gammon.

This game was known since the Middle Ages, but was always called " tables " till the seventeenth century. The earliest quotation for the word " Back gammon " given by the N.E.D. is from Howell's Letters, *c.* 1645.

l. 63. a Tout at Tricktrack.

Tricktrack or Trictrac was an old variety of back-gammon. It survived till the nineteenth century, and is mentioned by Lamb in a letter to Dorothy Wordsworth (1819).

A Tout is " a term for a specially successful result in certain games."—N.E.D., which quotes the passage.

IV. iii. l. 46. an *Algerine.*

I.e. an Algerian vessel. Algiers had long been one of the chief nests of Moorish pirates.

l. 46. An Eunuch after the *Turkish* manner.
I.e. the operation was complete.

IV. iv. l. 18. Such as we us'd to Muster in Flanders.
Another reference to Dangerfield's service with the Royalist forces in Flanders before the Restoration. Charles was allowed by Spain to raise first four regiments and afterwards six. The total force never numbered more than 2000 to 3000 men. Sir C. H. Firth remarks that " as each of the regiments ought to have numbered 1000 to 1200 men apiece, it is evident that their ranks were never more than half full." (" Royalist and Cromwellian Armies in Flanders," Journal of the Royal Historical Society, New Series, Vol. XVII. p. 69.)

ll. 51, 52. there is a Justice, swear your loss before him . . .
Mr. G. Thorn Drury gives me the following note on the legal aspect of this passage :
" By the Statute of Winchester—13 Edward I, ann. 1285—the Hundred was, upon failure to apprehend the offenders, made liable for robberies committed within its boundaries. Although no mention is made in the Statute of any time, it was judicially decided in the reign of Elizabeth that the robbery, to render the Hundred liable, ought to be committed in the day-time, but this was not to be interpreted so strictly as to exclude the whole period between sunset and sundown, for if there was at the material time sufficient light to discern and distinguish a man's countenance the victim was not deprived of his remedy against the Hundred. This Statute and others relating to the same matter were repealed in 1827. It may be of interest to add that people travelling on a Sunday were not protected, for it was said that one ought not to travel on that day. A worthy citizen in the reign of Charles II succeeded in his claim, because though he was robbed on a Sunday, he proved that he was going to church at the time."

IV. v. ll. 31, 32. Wither'd, Worn-out, Weather-beaten, Weasil-faced.
A clever rendering of Terence's

Hic est vietus, veternosus, senex, colore mustelino.
(" Eunuchus," l. 689.)

l. 112. Stone-horse.
See " The Mulberry Garden," I. ii. 27 and note.

IV. vi. ll. 8, 9. Mum and Wormwood.
Mum was a kind of beer originally brewed in Brunswick and very popular in England in the seventeenth and eighteenth centuries. Cf. Prologue to " The Knight of the Burning Pestle," in " Covent Garden Drollery " (8vo, 1671, p. 79) :

In *Burgundy* and *Mant*, the great ones rayle
But their blind sides are found in Mum and Ale.

l. 9. Wormwood.
Wormwood wine was apparently a kind of bitters made of

wormwood. Johnson in his Dictionary cites "*Floyer on the Humours*":

"Pituitous Cacochymia must be corrected by bitters, as *wormwood* wine."

l. 10. Amber-greece
"A wax-like substance of marbled ashy colour, found floating in tropical seas, and as a morbid secretion in the intestines of the sperm-whale. It is odoriferous and used in perfumery and formerly in cookery."—N.E.D. quotes this passage.

Cf. Milton, "Paradise Regain'd," II. 341, where the meats of the feast with which Satan tempts Christ are described as

"In pastry built, or from the spit or boil'd
Gris-amber-steam'd."

ll. 16, 17. Fennel Water
"A spiritous liquor prepared from fennel seed."—N.E.D.

l. 52. *Pontack*
Pontack's was a famous ordinary in Abchurch Street, named after its proprietor : see note to Poem No. LIII. Here the word seems to be used to mean wine from Pontack's.

l. 54. *Her Breasts of Delight.*
This is part of a song sung by the squire Clodpate in Shadwell's "Epsom Wells," IV. i.

Clodpate's song runs as follows :

Her Lips are two Brimmers of Claret,
Where first I began to miscarry ;
Her Breasts of Delight
Are two Bottles of White,
And her Eyes are two Cups of Canary.

It will be remembered that Sedley is said to have had a hand in "Epsom Wells."

l. 71. *Halcyon*
I.e. the kingfisher, traditionally supposed to be harbinger of calm weather.

IV. viii. l. 5. slit her Nose.
This was a favourite method of revenge. Sir John Coventry's nose was split by bravoes in the hire of the Court because he made a sarcastic allusion to the king's mistresses in the House of Commons.

l. 5. Trant'vne.
Not in the N.E.D. Professor Weekley conjectures that it is a metaphor from a card-game, "trente et un," and compares German "kaput machen" and French "faire caput."

l. 17. *Monteculi.*
This is Raymond, Count of Montecuculli (1608–1681), a famous Italian general in the Austrian service. He was one of

the foremost strategists of the age, and left valuable military memoirs which were published in two folio volumes by Ugo Foscolo at Milan in 1807.

V. i. l. 37. leap the half Almond

" Almond " is here a form of " almain," which originally meant " German," and later was used to denote a kind of dance music and the dance which accompanied it. The " almain " apparently involved a high jump. Cf. Chapman's Alphonsus : " An Almain and an upspring that is all." Also Ben Jonson, " The Devil is an Ass," I. i. : " And late his Almain leap into the Custard " (N.E.D., which quotes this passage).

l. 38. Thou ma'st well be active, . . . thy Bones have as much Quick-silver in 'em . . .

Congreve seems to have imitated this passage in " The Old Batchelour," I. i., where Hartwell says to Sharper : " Good Mr. Young-fellow, your mistaken ; as able as your self, and as nimble too, tho' I mayn't have as much Mercury in my Limbs " (4to, 1693).

l. 73. At once I hate her, and I love her too.

Clearly a reminiscence of the famous lines of Catullus (Carmen LXXXV) :

> Odi et amo. Quare id faciam, fortasse requiris.
> Nescio, sed fieri sentio et excrucior.

l. 81. a Gib'd Cat.

I.e. a tom-cat : cf. Shakespeare, " Henry IV," Pt. I, II. i. 82, where Falstaff exclaims : " I am as Melancholy as a Gyb-Cat, or a lugg'd Beare."

The word Gib was an abbreviation of Gilbert or Tibert, the name of the cat in the mediæval beast epic. The form Gibbed or Gib'd is common in the seventeenth century, and according to the N.E.D. is due to a mistaken derivation from an imaginary verb " gib," to geld.

l. 84. Calech.

One of the many anglicized forms of the French *calèche*, a kind of light carriage which became fashionable in England in the reign of Charles II. Cf. Dryden's " Marriage-à-la-Mode " (4to, 1673, III. i.) :

> " I have been at your Lodgings, in my new *Galeche*."

l. 129. Rascal Deer.

The youngest or leanest deer of the herd : cf. " As You Like It," III. iii. :

> " The noblest Deere hath them (horns) as huge as the Rascale."

ll. 139–150. Cf. Shadwell's " A True Widow " (which that author acknowledged to have been revised by Sedley) :

> *Bellamour.* Why thou art fit to be hung up at *Barber-*

Surgeon's Hall for a Skeleton ; a Woman had as good lye with a Faggot.

Selfish. Thou art envious, the Ladies are of another mind ; I am sure you are above Whore-master's weight, and a Woman had as good lye with a pound of Candles. (4to, 1679, I. i.)

l. 130. Common shore of Physick.

The common shore according to N.E.D. was originally " the no man's land by the waterside, where filth was allowed to be deposited for the tide to wash away," but it was commonly used as equivalent to the " common sewer," and this seems to be the meaning here.

l. 144. Bear-Garden.

The Bear Garden on Bankside, Southwark, was a royal garden for the exhibition of bear and bull-baiting until the reign of William III, when it was removed to Hockley-in-the-Hole. It was closed by Col. Pride in 1655, but reopened after the Restoration.

l. 147. thou walking Skelleton that may'st be read upon alive.

The reference is undoubtedly to the lectures on skeletons or " anatomies " given to medical students, " read upon " being here the equivalent of " lectured on." Mr. P. Simpson gives me the following close parallel in Ben Jonson's " Ode to James Earle of Desmond " (Underwoods, fol., 1640, II. 194) :

> O vertues fall,
> When her dead essence (like the Anatomie
> in Surgeons hall)
> Is but a Statists theame, to read Phlebotomie.

l. 540, 541. As I was going to draw, I heard a voice

Obviously a reminiscence of Falstaff's famous excuse in " Henry IV," Pt. I, II. iv. :

" I knew ye as well as he that made ye. Why heare ye my Masters, was it for me to kill the Heire apparant ? . . . beware Instinct, the Lion will not touch the true Prince : Instinct is a great matter."

l. 541. dead doing.

An obsolete adjective meaning murderous. Cf. Spenser, " Faerie Queen," II. iii. 8, " Hold your dead-doing hand." The latest example quoted by N.E.D. is from Wesley.

AN ESSAY ON ENTERTAINMENTS

This essay is based on a fragment of the section of the Saturæ Menippeæ of M. T. Varro entitled " Nescis Quid Vesper Serus Vehat." It is described by Aulus Gellius in his Thirteenth Book, where he quotes a portion of it. Sedley may have read it in the complete edition of the extant Works of Varro published at Dordrecht, 8vo, 1619, and reprinted in 1621. The following is the text given on p. 125 of the Sixth Part of the Dordrecht edition :

Nescis Qvid Vesper
Servs Vehat

Dicit autem convivarum numerŭ, incipere oportere à gratiarum numero, & progredi ad Musarum, id est proficisci à tribus, & consistere in novem : ut cùm paucissimi convivæ sunt, non pauciores sint quàm tres, cùm plurimi, non plures quàm novem. Nam multos esse non convenit, quòd turba plerumque est turbulenta, . . .
ut Romæ quidem constat, sed & Athenis.   *Desunt*
Nusquam autem plures cubabant.   *quædam.*

Ipsum deinde convivium constat, inquit ex rebus quatuor, & tum denique omnibus suis numeris absolutum est, si belli homunculi collecti sunt, si lectus locus, si tempus lectum, si apparatus non neglectus. Nec loquaces autem, inquit, convivas, nec multos legere oportet, quia eloquentia, in foro & apud subsellia : silentium verò non in convivio, sed in cubiculo esse debet. Sermones igitur id temporis habendos censet, non super rebus anxiis et tortuosis, sed jucundos & invitabiles, & cum quadam illecebra & voluptate utiles ; ex quibus ingenium nostrum venustius fiat & amoenius.

Quod profecto inquit eveniet, si de id genus rebus ad communem vitæ usum pertinentibus confabulemur, de quibus in foro atque in negotijs agendis loqui non est otium. Dominum autem, inquit convivij esse oportet, non tam lautum, quàm sine sordibus.—A. Gell. *lib.* 13. *Cap.* 11.

In convivio legi nec omnia debent, & ea potissimum que sunt βιωφελῆ, & delectant potius, ut id quoque videatur non superfuisse. *Ibidem. Verba post delectant desunt in multis codicibus.*

Bellaria, ea maximè sunt mellita, quae mellita non sunt : πέμμασιν enim cum πέψει societas infida. *Ibidem.*

EXPLANATORY NOTES TO DOUBTFUL WORKS

THE GRUMBLER

I. vi. l. 59. *Quinquina,*
    The older form of " quinine," being the Spanish version of the Indian name for the tree from whose bark quinine is extracted.

I. vii. l. 46. *John-a-Nokes . . . Tom-a-Styles,*
    Fictitious names for parties in a legal action.

I. ix. l. 12. *Arriaga.*
    There were several eminent Spaniards of this name, notably

Pablo José de Arriaga (1562–1622) and Roderigo de Arriaga (1592–1667). As the former was a famous educationist and founded schools in Peru, it is probably to him that Mamurra refers.

II. xii. l. 3. Crack

"A woman of broken reputation, a wench, a prostitute."— N.E.D., which incorrectly cites this passage as referring to a man. The French is " gueuse."

II. xvii. l. 22. Bourree

A famous French dance popular in the sixteenth and seventeenth centuries.

It came originally from the Auvergne and the Berri, and is said to have been introduced to the French Court by Marie de Medicis (Grove's " Dancing," ed. 1895, p. 271). According to Grove it was " a careless dance."

l. 73. Minuet

The Minuet or Menuet is said to have been so called because of its short steps. It was the most popular Court dance in France and England in the eighteenth century.

l. 74. Gavotte

This was originally a peasant dance of Dauphiné. It was introduced at Court in the sixteenth century, but was never popular and became a stage dance (Grove, p. 264).

l. 76. Passvy

An anglicized form of Passe-pied, a kind of " branle " danced by the Breton peasants.

l. 78, 79. Trocanny, Tricotez, Rigadon

The French is " tracanas, tricotez, rigaudon." I can find no details of dances called " tracanas " or " tricotez." Littré gives " tracaner, passer au tracanoir, dévider " (tracanoir = " engin de moulin pour dévider la soie ") ; and as a meaning of " tricoter," " dancer, baller, tripudier, sauter."

l. 79. Rigadon

In the French " Rigaudon," a Provençal dance described in Rameau's " Le Maître à Danser " (Paris, 8vo, 1725) : " le pas dans sa construction est très singulier, il se fait à la même place sans avancer ni reculer, ou aller de côté ; & si les jambes font plusieurs movements differens, il est fort gay dans sa manière " (p. 159).

l. 83. Courante, the Bocane, the Sarabande

The Courante (Italian " Corrente " or " *coranto* "), a favourite Court dance of the sixteenth and seventeenth centuries.

The Sarabande (originally Zarabanda) is a famous dance of Arabic-Spanish origin.

The Bocane (French " Bocanne ") was a type of Courante :

" les autres Courantes figurées de ce tems là comme la Dauphine, la Duchesse, & la Bocane " (Rameau, p. 113).

III. vii. l. 16. *Flanders, . . . Piedmont, . . . Germany*
The scenes of Louis XIV's principal wars.

l. 24. *Madagascar*
In the latter part of the seventeenth century the French attempted to establish military posts on the east coast of Madagascar, and for some time held the extreme south-east point of the island.

l. 56. Shopp'd up
To " shop " meant to shut up, to imprison (N.E.D., which quotes this passage with the incorrect reference " III. i.").

III. ix. Stage Direction. a Halberd
This weapon denoted the rank of sergeant. Cf. Fielding's " Tom Jones " (1749), VII. xi. : " he . . . had . . . so well ingratiated himself with his officers, that he had promoted himself to a halbert."

III. xi. l. 12. *Monomotapa*
The name given in old maps to an extensive region in South-east Africa. The Monomatapa was actually a Bantu monarch.

DOUBTFUL POEMS AND TRANSLATIONS

XCIV, XCV.
These poems are reprinted from K (II. 32, 33), where they are attributed to Sedley by the annotators of Sir C. H. Firth's and Mr. Thorn Drury's copies.

XCVI. Upon the slighting of his Friends Love.
This poem is described in the Contents of Stephen's Miscellany Poems as follows : " *Upon the slighting of his Friends Love.* by Mr. C. S. *of* Wad. Coll."
The text is followed by the initials C. S. See Preface, Vol. I., p. xv.

CII. The Royal Knotter.
Cf. with No. XXXVI and note.

The Pastorals of Virgil

CXVI. The Third Pastoral.
ll. 144, 145. *Ticko . . . Maurus !*
The Latin here reads the names of Virgil's two notorious contemporaries, Bavius and Maevius. The translator has substituted nicknames for two poetasters of his own day.
Maurus is probably Sir Richard Blackmore, the well-known rhymester and deadly foe of the Wits (see note to Poem LIV). He was attacked under the name of *Maurus* by Dryden, in

the lines "To John Driden" of Chesterton in the "Fables," and again in the Prologue to the "Secular Masque."

I am unable to identify "*Ticko*." If it stands for Thomas Tickell, the poet (1686–1740), the translation cannot be by Sedley, for Tickell was a boy when Sedley died.

CXVII. THE FOURTH PASTORAL.

l. 56. The Latin proves that the reading of B3 is correct:

nec nautica pinus
mutabit *merces*.

CXVII. THE FIFTH PASTORAL.

l. 27. Swallow

The Latin is "saliunca" which means "wild or celtic nard." "Swallow" may possibly stand for "swallowwort," a name given both to a herb called "vincetoxicum officinale" and to the greater celandine (N.E.D., which, however, gives no parallel to the use of "swallow" for "swallowwort").

l. 115. Lyctius *Aegon*

The translator has merely copied the Latin epithet, which means "Cretan" from Lyctos, a town near Mt. Dicte.

CXIX. THE SIXTH PASTORAL.

l. 98. This the *Grynæan* Grove⟨'⟩s arise shall tell,

The old texts read "Groves," which makes nonsense. If we take "Grove's" as possessive, we can suppose "arise" to be a substantive. Cf. Sir Thomas Browne, Ps. Ep. 226, "At the arise of the Pleiades." The Latin is "His tibi Grynei nemoris dicatur origo."

CXX. THE SEVENTH PASTORAL.

l. 64. Fuz,

"An obsolete form of furze" (N.E.D.). The Latin is "ruscus," which means broom.

CXXVI. To *Phillis* WHO SLIGHTED HIM.

l. 30. LONG shall my Doctor be.

This is obviously a reference to Mr. Long, proprietor of the Rose Tavern, a favourite haunt of Sedley and his friends (see "Sir Charles Sedley," p. 58). It is a clear proof that the poem, whether it is Sedley's or not, was written in the reign of Charles II.

TEXTUAL NOTES

TEXTUAL NOTES

BELLAMIRA

Dramatis Personæ (B5 reads *MEN* before *Merryman*, and *WOMEN* before *Bellamira*.

I.   i. l. 142.   have her (Q have, her   (B3, etc. have her

      l. 163.   Peace.⟨"⟩ (Q, etc. Peace.

      l. 194.   you⟨:⟩   *Isabella* (Q   you   *Isabella ;*   (B3   you, *Isabella* (B4, B5 you ; Isabella,

      l. 227, 228.   shou'd, where shou'd I have such another (B3, etc. shou'd I have such another

      l. 261.   ⟨(*Aside*)⟩ (Q etc. omit.

I.   ii. l. 78.   me⟨,⟩   But   (Q me But   (B3, etc. me.   But

I.   iii. l. 68.   *Dangerfield*⟨,⟩   (Q *Dangerfield*   (B3, etc. *Dangerfield,*

II.   i. l. 108.   here⟨—⟩ my   (Q, etc. here my

      l. 150.   'em⟨.⟩   (Q em   (B3, etc. 'em :

      l. 176.   the little Tinsel,   (B4, B5 the tinsel,

      l. 219.   care for you, nor me, nor any man.   (B4, B5 care for you, nor any man.

      l. 251.   went⟨.⟩   (Q went   (B3, etc. went.

      l. 290.   breath.   (B4, B5 breathe.

      l. 337.   let⟨'⟩s   (Q le'ts   (B3, etc. let's

II.   ii. before l. 1.   *Stage Direction*, Enter Bellamira, ⟨*and*⟩ Isabella (Q, etc. Enter Bellamira, Isabella, *and* Thisbe.

     after l. 46.   *Stage Direction*   (Q, B3 *Enter* Thisbe   (B4, B5 omit

      l. 93.   to use   (Q to to use   (B3, etc. to use

III.   i. l. 22.   dangers⟨.⟩   (Q dangers,   (B3, etc. dangers.

      l. 86.   Wit⟨.⟩   (Q Wit   (B3, etc. Wit.

      l. 95.   fi⟨r'⟩d   (Q, B3 find   (B4, B5 fir'd

      l. 98.   *Whizzing*   (Q *Whizizng*   (B3, etc. *Whizzing*

l. 121. Loves what (Q Loves, what (B3, etc. Loves what
l. 179. ⟨o⟩f (Q ef (B3, etc. of
l. 190. ca⟨n⟩st (Q cast (B3, etc. canst
l. 192. Dunghil⟨.⟩ (Q Dunghil (B3, etc. Dunghil.
III. ii. l. 3. ⟨Lion.⟩ (Q, B3 *Pisq.* throughout (B4, B5 *Lion.*
l. 31. Q reads *Pisq.* before Pray leave me (B3, etc. after "me" and before "If I have"
l. 57. within⟨?⟩ (Q within. (B3, etc. within?
l. 69. not⟨.⟩ (Q not: (B3, etc. not.
III. iii. l. 30. you⟨r⟩ (Q you (B3, etc. your
l. 93. Fellows⟨.⟩ (Q Fellows (B3, etc. Fellows.
l. 188. have (B4, B5 hate
III. iv. l. 19. time⟨,⟩ (Q time (B3, etc. Time,
l. 40. well⟨.⟩ (Q well, (B3, etc. well.
III. v. l. 83. then⟨?⟩ (Q then, (B3, etc. then?
IV. i. l. 20. ⟨(*aside*)⟩ (Q, etc. read after "away."
l. 32. terribly, (B4, B5 terrible
IV. ii. l. 73. home! (B3, etc. home?
IV. iii. l. 63. mine ⟨there⟩ never (Q mine never (B3, etc. mine there never
IV. iv. l. 19. that ⟨in⟩ *English?* (Q that *English.* (B3, etc. that in *English.*
l. 36. wou'd ⟨not⟩ tell (Q wou'd tell (B3, etc. wou'd not tell
IV. v. l. 97. Sir you mistake, (B3, etc. You'll be mistaken;
l. 132. Damn him Rogue, (B3, etc. Damn him a Rogue,
IV. vi. l. 26. Feast, (B4, B5 feasts
l. 29. saw Play (B3, etc. saw a Play
l. 39. the Bottles are upon the Table (B4, B5 Bottles are upon table
l. 71. *Halcyon* (Q *Halcyon,* (B3, etc. *Halcyon*
l. 79. ⟨(*Aside*)⟩ *How shall we* etc. (Q [*Hows hall we* etc. (B3 (*How shall we* etc. (B4, B5 How shall we get rid of him? [*aside*
l. 91. possibl⟨y⟩ (Q possible (B3, etc. possibly
l. 112. to be rid (B4, B5 to get rid
l. 113. him. ⟨(*to Bellamira*)⟩ (Q him. [*He is gone* (B3 him. *He is gone* (B4, B5 him. He's gone.
after l. 113. *Stage Direction* ⟨Re-e⟩nter etc. (All texts *Enter Bellamira.*
IV. vii. l. 56. *Eust.* ⟨(*Aside*)⟩ (Q omits (*Aside*) (B3, etc. place it after ravish'd.
l. 78. ⟨(Aside)⟩ (All texts place this after "*Lionel.*"
IV. viii. l. 6. the Trant'vne. (B4, B5 a Trant'vne
V. i. l. 17. ⟨(*Aside*)⟩ (All texts place this after "at."
l. 32. No, before (B3, etc. Not before
l. 46. ten as (Q ten of as (B3, etc. ten as

l. 261.   Friend⟨?⟩   (Q Friend   (B3, etc. Friend;
l. 328.   so⟨:⟩   (Q so ?   (B3, etc. so :
l. 384.   instantly⟨,⟩   (Q instantly   (B3, etc. instantly,
l. 441.   hope ⟨I⟩ see,   (Q hope see,   (B3, etc. hope I see,
l. 564.   Isabella⟨,⟩   (Q *Isabella*   (B3, etc. *Isabella*,

TEXTUAL NOTES TO DOUBTFUL WORKS

THE GRUMBLER

After Dramatis Personæ   (B4, B5 MEN
After *Lolive* etc.   (B4 B5, WOMEN
Mon. *Grichard*,   (B4, B5 Grichard,
After *Mondore*, etc.   (B4, B5 Brillon, youngest Son to Grichard.
                         Mamurra, Tutor to Brillon.
                         Fadel.
                         Lolive, Footman to Grichard.
After *Hortensia*,   (B4, B5 Daughter to Grichard.
After *Catau*,   (B4, B5 Maid to Hortensia.
The House of Monsieur *Grichard*.   (B4, B5 The House of Grichard.
  I.   i. before l. 1.   Stage Direction :   (B4, B5 omit *the Grumbler's
                           Eldest Son and Daughter.*
  I.   ii. before l. 1.   SCENE II   (B4, B5 omit this and all sub-
                           sequent scene divisions in the Act.
before l. 1.   Stage Direction :   *To them,*   (B4, B5 *Enter*
  I.   iii. before l. 1.   Stage Direction :   *To them,*   (B4, B5 *Enter*
  I.   iv. before l. 16.   [*A knocking.*]   (B4, B5 [*Knocking.*
  I.   v. before l. 1.   Stage Direction :   *To them,*   (B4, B5 *Enter.*
        l.   5.   you⟨r⟩   (B3 you   (B4, B5 your
  I.   vi. before l. 1.   Stage Direction : Grichard *the Grumbler.*   (B4,
                           B5 Grichard the Grumbler and Lolive
        l.   54.   Wage⟨s⟩   (B3 Wager   (B4, B5 Wages
  I. viii. before l. 1.   Stage   Direction :   *Enter to them,* Brillon,
                           Grichard's *son, and* Catau.   (B4, B5 *Enter* Brillon
                           and Catau.
  I.   ix. before l. 1.   Stage Direction :   *to them,*   (B4, B5 omit.
 II.   i. before l. 1.   *Lolive Solus.*   (B4, B5 *Enter Lolive*
 II.   ii. before l. 1.   SCENE II   (B4, B5 omit this and all subsequent
                           scene divisions in the Act.
 II.   iv. l.   5.   light   (B4, B5 alight
 II.   v. l.   9.   look ⟨for⟩ him   (B3, etc. look him
 II. vii. before l. 1.   Stage Direction :   *to her,*   (B4, B5 omit.
 II. viii. before l. 1.   Stage Direction :   *to them.*   (B4, B5 omit.
 II.   ix. before l. 1.   Stage Direction :   *M.* Grichard . . .   (B4, B5
                           Enter Grichard . . .

after l. 38. Stage Direction: *Exeunt* etc. (B4, B5 read *Exeunt Ter. Hor.* and *Cat.*

II. xiv. before l. 1. Stage Direction: Manent, *M.* Grichard *and* Arist. (B4, B5 omit.

   before l. 1. Stage Direction: *They stand* . . . (B4, B5 (*Gri. and Ari. stand* . . .

   l. 7. ⟨go⟩ing (B3, etc. being

II. xvi. before l. 1. Stage Direction: *Enter M.* Grichard (B4, B5 *Enter* Grichard

II. xvii. before l. 1. Stage Direction: *his Boy.* (B5 *the boy.*

   after l. 38. Stage Direction: *He draws* . . . (B4, B5 *Draws* . . .

II. xix. before l. 1. Stage Direction: Manent, Aristus, Catau. (B4, B5 omit.

   ad fin. (B4, B5 [*Exeunt.*

III. i. before l. 1. Stage Direction: Lolive, Catau. (B4, B5 *Enter* Lolive *and* Catau.

III. ii. before l. 1. SCENE II (B4 and B5 omit this and all subsequent scene divisions in the Act.

   before l. 1. Stage Direction: M. *Fadel.* (B4, B5 omit M.

III. iv. l. 1. *M.* Grichard. (B4, B5 omit M.

III. vi. l. 34. Well, you won't . . . (B4, B5 You wo'nt . . .

III. vii. l. 19. 'em (B5 him

III. ix. before l. 1. Stage Direction: Lol. (B4, B5 Lolive

III. x. Chaplain ⟨. . .⟩ (B3, etc. Chaplain.

Last SCENE. Stage Direction: (B4, B5 read *Enter* Rigaut, *at the further end of the Stage* ; M St Alvar . . .

   l. 29. ⟨*Clar.*⟩ (all texts *Cat.*

   ad fin. (B4, B5 read *Exeunt omnes.*

DOUBTFUL POEMS AND TRANSLATIONS

XCVII. Upon a Gentlewoman's Refusal, etc.
   l. 3. design (B3, etc. design'd
   l. 26. gone and spent (B3, etc. quite forgot
   l. 29. atracting (B3, etc. attractive
   l. 48. both *joy* (B3, etc. rejoyce
   l. 52. at least (B3, etc. at last
   l. 55. am'rous (B3, etc. killing
   l. 61. destruction too. (B3, etc. destruction ; go

XCIX. Song. *The Doubtful Lover* Resolv'd.
   l. 15. those ⟨killing⟩ smarts, (so B3, etc. P omits killing

C. SONG. THE CAVALIER'S CATCH.
    l. 8. *James* (B3, etc. J—s
    l. 9. If that here (B3, etc. If here

CII. THE ROYAL KNOTTER.
    l. 1. ye (B4, B5 you

CIV. AGAINST HIS MISTRESS'S CRUELTY.
    V reads beneath the title, By the Same Hand
    l. 2. that (B4, B5 who
    l. 16. tis (B1, B2, B3 its (B4, B5 is

CVII. A FABLE.
    l. 4. (B4, &c. For both had different Age to different Ills,
    l. 8. (B3, &c. And said he wanted Sense as well as Hair
    l. 12. till (B3, &c. still
    l. 13. Till this poor Man, and thou, (B3, &c. Till thou, and
        this old Man,

THE PASTORALS OF VIRGIL

CXIV. THE FIRST PASTORAL.
    l. 1. *T⟨ity⟩rus* (B3, *Tytirus* (B4, B5 *Tityrus*
    l. 34. Mother Ews, (B3 Mother, Ews (B4, B5 Mother Ewes
    l. 101. wond'ring (B4, B5 wand'ring

CXV. THE SECOND PASTORAL.
    l. 20. *Menal⟨c⟩as* (B3 Menaleas (B4, B5 Menalcas
    l. 85. *J⟨ola⟩s* (B3, etc. *Jalus*

CXVI. THE THIRD PASTORAL.
    l. 29. *L⟨y⟩cisca* (B3, etc. *Lacisca*
    l. 68. *Alcim⟨e⟩don* (B3, etc. *Alcimidon*
    l. 88. *Pal⟨æ⟩mon* (B3 *Palemon* (B4, B5 *Palæmon*

CXVII. THE FOURTH PASTORAL.
    l. 50. *T⟨iphy⟩s* (B3, etc. *Typhis*
    l. 56. Wares (B4, B5 Wars
    l. 85. his (B4, B5 is

CXVIII. THE FIFTH PASTORAL.
    l. 116. *Alph⟨e⟩sibæus* (B3, etc. *Alphisiboeus* so throughout

CXIX. THE SIXTH PASTORAL.
    l. 17. *M⟨n⟩asylus* (B3, etc. *Masylus*
    l. 72. Plough⟨.⟩ (B3 Plough: (B4, B5 Plough
    l. 96. Grove⟨'⟩s (B3, etc. Groves,
    l. 100. *S⟨c⟩ylla* (B3, etc. *Sylla*
    l. 106. *T⟨e⟩reus* (B3, etc. *Tireus*

CXXI. THE EIGHTH PASTORAL.
 l. 4. sto⟨p⟩p'd (B3 stoop'd (B4, B5 stop'd
 l. 33. Shepherds' (B3, etc. shepherds
 l. 68. ⟨Rh⟩*odope* (B3, etc. *Eodope*

CXXII. THE NINTH PASTORAL.
 l. 15. M⟨e⟩*nalcas* (B3 *Minalcas* (B4, B5 *Menalcas*
 l. 40. th⟨o'⟩ (B3, etc. the
 l. 96. ⟨m⟩ay (B3, etc. way

CXXIII. THE TENTH PASTORAL.
 l. 99. *Thrac*⟨*i*⟩*a* (B3, etc. *Thracea*

A BIBLIOGRAPHY OF WORKS BY OR ASCRIBED TO SIR CHARLES SEDLEY

BIBLIOGRAPHY

1. *Earle of Pembroke's Speech*, 1648.   Single sheet.
   TheEarle of / Pembroke's / Speech / in theHouse of / Peeres, / Upon debate of the *Cities* Petition for a / Personall Treaty to be had with His / Majesty in London. / And also upon debate of those Reasons / given by their Lordships unto the / Commons for not sending the / three Propositions before a Treaty. / Printed the yeare 1648.
   Single sheet.   Broadside.
   An old Cavalier satire wrongly attributed to Sedley by the compiler of the 1722 edition of his works; see Preface, Vol. I, pp. xx, xxiii.
   (Br. Mus. E. 453. (30).)

2. *Last Will and Testament*, 1651.   Single sheet.
   The / Last Will and Testament / of the Earl of Pembroke.
   Single sheet.   Broadside.
   Like the foregoing, wrongly attributed to Sedley by the editor of the 1722 edition; see Preface, Vol. I, pp. xx, xxiii. MS. note in the Br. Mus. copy runs : " This was written by S. Butler, the Author of Hudibras."
   (Br. Mus. 1890. e. 4 (40).)

3. *Pompey the Great*, 1664.   4to.
   Pompey / the / Great / A Tragedy. / As it was Acted by the Servants of His / Royal Highness the Duke of York. / *Translated out of French by Certain* / Persons of Honour. / —*Qui se Lectori credere malunt / Quam spectatoris fastidia ferre superbi : Namque Equitis quoque jam migravit ab aure Voluptas / Omnis, ad incertos oculos, & gaudia Vana.* / Horat. / London, / Printed for *Henry Herringman*, and are to be Sold / at his Shop at the Sign of the Anchor in the Lower / Walk of the *New Exchange.* / 1664.
   Title + One leaf with prologue + B–H3 v. the Play + H4 Epilogue at the House + H4 v.   Epilogue to the King at *St. James's* + I1 (unsigned) Epilogue to the Duchess at St. *James's* + I2, I3, I4 blank leaves :—*in fours*.
   Translation of " La Mort de Pompée " of P. Corneille by the " confederate translators," viz. Waller, Buckhurst, Sedley, Godolphin, Filmer.   First Act by Waller, last by Buckhurst. The Act by Sedley (II, III or IV), his first published work.
   (Br. Mus. 643. d. 50.)

4*a*. *Mulberry Garden*, 1668, Q1.

The / Mulberry Garden, / A / Comedy / As it is Acted by / His Majesties Servants / At the / Theatre-Royal / Written by the Honourable / Sir Charles Sidley / London / Printed for *H. Herringman* at the Sign of the *Blew Anchor* in the / Lower Walk of the *New Exchange.* 1668.

? A1 blank missing + Title + A3, Dedicatory Epistle to the Dutchesse of Richmond and Lenox + A4 Dramatis Personæ + A4 v. Prologue + B–L2 the Play + L2 v. Epilogue :— *in fours.*

(Br. Mus. 841. c. 1.)

4*b*. *The Mulberry Garden*, 1675, Q2.

The / Mulberry-Garden, / A / Comedy. / As it is Acted by / His Majesties' Servants / At The / Theatre-Royal. / Written by the Honourable / Sir Charles Sidley. / London, / Printed for *H. Herringman,* at the Sign of the *Blew Anchor* in the / Lower Walk of the *New Exchange.* 1675.

A1 (unsigned) blank before title + Title + A3 Dedication to The Dutchesse of Richmond and Lenox + A4 Dramatis Personæ + A4 v. Prologue + B–L2 the Play + L2 v. Epilogue :—*in fours.*

(Br. Mus. 841. c. 4 (3).)

A page for page reprint of Q1.

4*c*. *The Mulberry Garden*, 1688, Q3.

I have never seen a copy of this edition. There is no example in the British Museum, Bodleian or Cambridge University Libraries, nor in the Dyce Collection, South Kensington, nor in Mr. Thorn Drury's Collection. I am assured of its existence by the Rev. Montague Summers and Prof. Allardyce Nicoll.

5. *Windsor Drollery*, 1671, 12*mo.*

Windsor-Drollery / An exact Collection / of the Newest / Songs, Poems and Catches, Now In Use Both in City and Count / rey. Collected by a Person of Quality. / London ; / Printed for J. M. And are to be sold / by the Booksellers of *London* and / *Westminster,* 1671.

? Frontispiece missing + Title + 6 leaves unsigned + H2–O8 Poems (half-title New / Songs A la mode / Both / *Amorous and Jovial* / by the Wits of this Age—Head title, *The Academy of Complements with many New Additions*) + O9–O12 Table (page numbers in the Table are all incorrect) :—*in twelves.*

Contains, p. 326, the Song in the Mulberry Garden, "Ah Cloris that I now could sit " ; p. 325, " Tell me prethee faithless swain," ascribed to Sedley in B3 (No. CXII of this edition) (I. 3, a slightly different version) ; also p. 4, a poem beginning

" Bright *Celia* know, 'twas not thine eyes
Alone that did me first surprise,"
which resembles Poem No. V of this edition.
(Bodl. Douce, D. 20.)

6. *Oxford Drollery*, 1671.
Oxford Drollery; / Being New / Poems, / and / Songs. / The first Part, composed by W. H. / The Second and third Parts being, upon several / occasions, made by the most Eminent and / Ingenious Wits of the said University. / And Collected by the same / Author. / *The like never before published.* / Oxford, / Printed for F. C. and are to be sold by *Thomas Palmer* / at the Sign of the *Crown* in *Westminster* / Hall, 1671.
Title + unsigned leaf with lines To The Reader by W. Hickes on recto, and advt. of books sold by Thomas Palmer on verso + A–L6 Poems :—*in eights.*
p. 94, " Prethee tell me faithless Swain," No. CXII of this edition.
(Bodl. Malone, 384.)

7. *New Academy of Complements*, 1671, 12*mo.*
The New Academy of Complements / erected / For Ladies, Gentlewomen, Court / -iers, Gentlemen, Scholars, Souldiers, / Citizens, Countrey men and all persons of what degree soever, of both Sexes, Stored with variety of Courtly and Civil Complements, Eloquent Let / -ters of Love and Friendship. / with an Exact Collection of the Newest and Choicest / Songs a la Mode, / Both Amorous and Jovial. / Compiled / by L. B. Sir C. S. Sir W. D. and others, / the Most refined Wits of this age,/ London. / Printed for Tho. Rooks at the Ink Bottle In Thread-needle Street.   1671 / Price 1s 6d.
(Br. Mus. copy) ? Frontispiece missing + B2–E7 v. " Complements," Letters, etc. in prose + E8–P4 v. Songs (G9–H2 missing) + P5 " posies." + P6 Table of letters + P7–P9 v. + ? (leaves missing) Table of Songs :—*in twelves.*
Contains the following poems by or ascribed to Sedley (no authors' names are given here, but these poems are attributed to Sedley in later publications) :
p. 85. " As in those Nations where they yet adore."
p. 221. " Ah, Cloris, that I now could sit " (Song in Mulberry Garden).
p. 122. " Phillis, though your powerful charms," (version of " Though, *Phillis*, your prevailing charms." See Table, pp. 240, 241.
(Br. Mus. 1067. e. 29.)

8. *Westminster Drollery, the Second Part*, 1672, 8*vo.*
Westminster Drollery, / The Second Part, / being / a Compleat

Collection of all / the Newest and Choicest Songs / and Poems at Court and / both the Theatres. / By the Author of the First Part, / Never Printed before. / (Publisher's Device) / London, / Printed for William Gilbert at the Half-Moon in / St. Paul's Churchyard, & *Tho. Saxbridge* at the / three Flower de Luces in Little Britain, 1672.

Title + A2 Verses " to his honoured Freind, the Author of this Book, " signed Ric. Mangie," B1–K2 v. Poems :—*in eights.*

p. 114. " Get you gone, you will undo me." See note to Poem No. XVII.

(Br. Mus. 11621, a. 45.)

9*a*. *Kemp's Collection*, 1672, 8*vo.*

A / Collection / of / Poems, / Written upon several / Occasions, By several Persons. / *Never before in Print.* / London, / Printed for *Hobart Kemp*, at the Sign of the Ship in / the Upper Walk of the *New Exchange*, 1672.

Title + A2–A4 The Table + B–F3 Poems Part I + Aa–Ee4 Poems Part II :—*in eights.*

See the account of this book in my Preface, Vol. I, p. x. For poems ascribed to Sedley see Table, pp. 240, 241.

In the Catalogue of the Gaisford sale (1890) the date of the Gaisford copy (Lot 1447) was wrongly given as 1671. This was merely due to the badly printed " 2 " on the title-page.

(Br. Mus. C. 57. k. 20 (not annotated).)

(Annotated copies in the possession of Sir C. H. Firth and Messrs G. Thorn Drury and H. F. B. Brett Smith. Mr. Brett Smith's copy is that which was formerly in the Gaisford Collection.)

9*b*. *Collins's Collection*, 1673, 8*vo.*

A Collection / of Poems / Written upon several / occasions / By several / Persons. / *With many Additions, never before in Print.* / London. Printed for *Tho. Collins* and *John Ford* in *Fleet- /Street*, and *Will Cademan* at the Pope's Head *New- / Exchange Strand.* 1673.

Title + A3, A4 Table of Contents + B–N4 Poems :— *in eights.*

A second edition of Kemp's Collection with additions. Contains the same poems by or ascribed to Sedley : see Table, pp. 240, 241.

(Br. Mus. 11631. aa. 9.)

9*c*. *Saunder's Collection*, 1693, 8*vo.*

A / Collection / of / Poems / *By Several Hands.* / Most of them Written by Per- / sons of Eminent Quality. / *But who did ever in French Authors see / The Comprehensive* English *Energy ? / The weighty Bullion of one Sterling Line, / Drawn to* French *Wire would through | whole pages shine. |* Lord *Roscommon*'s Essay on Translated Verse. | London, | Printed by *T. Warren,* for *Francis Saunders,* | at the *Blue-Anchor* in the Lower- | Walk of the *New Exchange,* 1693.

Title + A3–A5 The Publisher to the Reader + A6–A8 the Contents + B1 The Preface to the Art of Poetry (by Roscommon) + B2–T3 the Poems + T3 v.–T4 Catalogue of Books, Printed and Sold for F. Saunders :—*in eights.*

The third edition of Kemp's Collection, considerably enlarged and altered. Names of authors of most of the poems are given in the Table. For Poems by or ascribed to Sedley see Table, pp. 240, 241.

Term Catalogues *s.d.* May, 1694. (Term Catalogues, ed. Arber, II. 501.)

(Br. Mus. 1077, l. 5.)

9d. *The Temple of Death,* 1695, 8vo.

The | Temple of Death, | A | Poem ; Written by the Marquess of | *Normanby.* | *Horace* of the Art of Poetry, | Made English by the Earl of *Roscommon.* | The | Duel of the Stags, | By the Honourable Sir *Robert Howard.* | Together | with several other Excellent Poems by the | Earls of *Rochester* and *Orrery,* Sir *Charles* | *Sedley,* Sir George Etheridge, the Honourable | Mr. *Montague,* Mr. *Granvill,* Mr. *Dryden,* | Mr. *Chetwood,* and Mr. *Tate.* | To which is added several Poems of the Honourable | Madam *Wharton.* | The Second Edition Corrected. | London | Printed by *Tho. Warren* for *Francis Saunders* at the *Blue* | *Anchor* in the Lower Walk of the *New Exchange.* | MDCXCV.

Title + A3–A5 The Publisher to the Reader + A6–A8 The Contents + B1 The Preface to the Art of Poetry + B2–T3 Poems + T3 v. T4 A Catalogue of Books Printed . . . for F. Saunders :—*in eights.*

A corrected reprint of the foregoing with new title-page.

(Br. Mus. 116, 44. bbb. 13.)

9e. *Brown's Collection,* 1701, *8vo.*

A | Collection of Poems : | viz. | The Temple of Death : | By the Marquis of Normanby. | An Epistle to the Earl of Dorset : | By *Charles Montague,* Lord Halifax. | The Duel of the Stags : | By Sir Robert Howard. | With several Original Poems, | never before Printed, | By |

The E. of *Roscommon.*	Sir *George Etherege.*
The E. of *Rochester.*	Mr *Granville.*
The E. of *Orrery.*	Mr *Stepney.*
Sir *Charles Sedley.*	Mr *Dryden,* &c.

London. Printed for Daniel Brown, at the *Black | Swan* and *Bible* without *Temple* Bar ; And Benjamin | Tooke at the *Middle-Temple-Gate* in *Fleet Street,* 1701.

TABLE OF POEMS ASCRIBED TO SEDLEY IN KEMP'S (K), COLLINS'S (C), AND SAUNDERS'S (S) COLLECTIONS, SHOWING ASCRIPTIONS IN MESSRS. THORN DRURY'S (K1), BRETT SMITH'S (K2), AND SIR C. H. FIRTH'S (K3) COPIES OF KEMP'S COLLECTION.

Ascription in Table of S.	Ascription in K1.	Ascription in K2.	Ascription in K3.	First Line of Poem.	Page in K.	Page in C.	Page in S.	Page in A (Ayloffe's ed.) of 1702.	Page in B3 (ed. of 1722).
Sir Charles Sedley	Sr Charles Sidley	Sr C. Sidley	C: S:	You tell me, *Celia*, you approve,	Pt. I 17	16	83	27	I. 52
,,	Sr C. S.	Sr C. S.	,,	*Thirsis*, I wish as well as you,	19	18	85	28	I. 53
,,	,,	,,	,,	*Princes* make Laws by which their Subjects live,	20	19	86	36	I. 55
,,	,,	C. S.	,,	*Cloris*, I justly am betray'd	21	21	88	64	I. 64
,,	,,	,,	,,	*Madam*, tho' meaner Beauties might,	23	22	90	[not included: on p. 59, a poem slightly resembling it]	I. 5
No ascription in Table	Capt. Aston	Cap: Aston	Capt. Aston	*Cloris*, you live ador'd by all,	25	24	92	19	I. 46
A Person of Honour	Lod Buckhurst	Lo: Buckhurst	L: B:	Once more Love's mighty Charms are broke,	27	27	115	[not included]	I. 9
The same Author	Ld Buckhurst	,,	Lo: B:	Though, *Phillis*, your prevailing charms	28	28	116	[not included]	I. 9
Sir Charles Sedley	Sr C. S.	C. S.	C: S:	Intreaty shall not serve, nor violence,	29	29	117	[not included]	I. 11
,,	,,	[no ascription]	,,	As in those Nations where they yet adore	43	42	142	51	I. 62
,,	,,	—	,,	Ah, Pardon, Madam if I ever thought	44	43	144	52	I. 51
,,	,,	—	,,	Fear not, my Dear, a Flame will never die,	46	44	146	24	I. 51
,,	,,		,,	Thanks, fair *Urania*, to your scorn,	47	46	148	69	I. 69
,,	,,		,,	*Strephon*! O *Strephon*! once the jolliest Lad	46	44	146	24	I. 51

Author	Ascription		Attr.	First line					
Sir George Etherege	[no ascription]	—	C: S:	If I my *Celia* cou'd perswade	55	59	177	[not included]	I. 11
The same Author	—	—	,,	It is not, *Celia*, in our power	56			[not included]	I. 54
A Person of Honour *	Ld Buckhurst	—	Lo: B:	Tell me no more you love; in vain,	57			[not included]	I. 45
				Many have been the vain attempts of Wit	61			[not included]	I. 54
Sir Charles Sedley	Sr C. S.		C: S:	Fair *Amarillis*, on the Stage whil'st you	Pt. II 1	67	187	30	I. 52
,,	,,		,,	Love, when 'tis true, needs not the aid			189	17	I. 48
,,	,,		,,	Fair *Octavia*, you are much to blame,	3	71	201	25	I. 48
The same Author	,,		,,	*Phillis* this mighty zeal asswage,	5	73	203	34	I. 6
Sir Charles Sedley	,,		,,	When *Aurelia* first became	7	74	205	22	I. 56
The same Author	,,		,,	*Cloris*, I cannot say your eyes	9	76	212	15	I. 58
,,	,,		,,	*Aurelia*, art thou mad	12	77	214	54	I. 60
			,,	Love still has something of the Sea,	14	79	216	46	I. 57
[Not included]			,,	*Amintas*, I am come alone,	16	82	219	40	I. 57
			,,	Get you gone, you will undo me,	24	85	—	38	I. 57
			,,	*Phillis*, you have enough enjoy'd	26	88	—	48	I. 46
		W. Smith	,,	*Madam*, for your commands to stay,	28	89	—	49	
			,,	Awake my eyes, at night my thoughts pursue	29	90	—	49	
			,,	*Phillis*, let's shun the common Fate,	30	90	—	9	
			,,	Although no Art the Fire of Love can tame,	32	92	—	[not included]	
			,,	The Painted Apples that adorn,	32	92	—	[not included]	
			,,	Not *Celia* that I juster am,	34	94	—	11	I. 49
			,,	*Thirsis* no more against my Flame advise,	36	95	—	12	I. 50
			,,	I ask not my *Celia* would love me again,	39	97	—	53	I. 65
Ld Mulgrave	Ld Mulgrave		E: M:	*Drink* about till the day find us,	41	98	—	44	I. 60
			,,	Walking among thick Shades alone,	43	99	—	56	I. 61

Title + A2–A4, The Contents + B–Z, Aa–Ff3, the Poems + Ff3 v., Ff4, Some Books . . . Printed for B. Tooke, etc. :— *in eights.*

A re-issue with many additions, of Saunders's Collection. Contains the same versions of the same poems by or ascribed to Sedley.

This collection was reprinted without alteration for the same publishers in 1702 (8vo) and 1716 (12mo), Term Catalogues *s.d.* June 1701. (Term Catalogues ed. Arber, III. 259.) (Br. Mus. 1077. l. 13.)

10. (*Shadwell*) *Epsom Wells*, 1673, 4*to.*

Epsom-Wells. / A / Comedy, / Acted at the / Duke's theatre / Written by / Tho. Shadwell / μεγάλως ἀπολιθαίνειν ἁμάρτημα εὐγενὲς. / Licensed, *Feb.* 17. 1672/3 / *Roger L'Estrange.* / London. / Printed by J. M. for *Henry Herringman* at the Sign of the *Blew Anchor* in the Lower Walk of the *New Exchange* / MDCLXXIII.

Title (Dramatis Personæ on verso) + A2, Dedication to Duke of Newcastle + A3, Prologue by Sir C. S. + A3 v. Prologue to the King and Queen + B–N, the Play + O Epilogue + O v. list of Errata :—*in fours.*

The first prologue, almost certainly by Sedley, though not included in any collected edition of his works. In the Br. Mus. copy of Shadwell's Collected Plays (1720, 8vo, Vol. II. p. 185) the initials " Sir C. S." are completed in MS. to " Sir C. Sedley."

Dryden insinuated that Sedley had a share in the authorship of the Play ; see *MacFlecknoe,* ll. 154–5.

(Br. Mus. 644. i. 24.)

11. (*Etherege*) *The Man of Mode*, 1676, 4*to.*

The / Man of Mode, / or Sʳ Fopling Flutter. / A / Comedy. / Acted at the *Duke's Theatre.* / By *George Etherege* Esq : / Licensed, / June 3 / 1676 / *Roger L'Estrange.* / London, / Printed by *J. Macock,* For *Henry Herringman,* at the Sign of / the *Blew Anchor* in the Lower Walk of the / *New Exchange,* 1676.

Title + A2, A3, Dedication to H.H. the Duchess + A3 v. A4, Prologue by Sir Car Scroope + A4 v. Dramatis Personæ + B–N, The Play + N v. the Epilogue by Mr Dryden :—*in fours.*

Etherege's well-known comedy. Song in Act V. sc. 2 (p. 86), sung by Busy, the waiting-woman (" As Amoret with Phillis sat "), is stated in a marginal note to be " by Sir C. S." See Preface, Vol. I, p. xiv.

(Br. Mus. 644. h. 35.)

12*a. Antony and Cleopatra*, 1677, Q1.

Antony / And Cleopatra / A / Tragedy. / As it is Acted at the Duke's *Theatre.* / Written by the Honourable / Sir Charles Sedley, Baronet. / Licensed *Apr.* 24. 1677. *Roger Lestrange.* /

London. / Printed for *Richard Tonson* at his Shop under / *Grayes-Inne-Gate* next *Grayes Inne Lane.* / MDCLXXVII.

Title + leaf with prologue (Dramatis Personæ with names of Actors, Errata, advt. of " The Songs in Circe " on verso) + B–I3 v. the Play + I4, Epilogue and advt. of " The Art of Making Love " + I4 v. list of books late published by R. Tonson, etc. :—*in fours.*

Incorrectly said by Sir A. W. Ward in D.N.B., *s.a.* " Sir Charles Sedley," to be identical with " Beauty the Conquerour or the Death of Marc Antony " printed in A.

Term Catalogues, *s.d.* 28 May, 1677, where the price is given as " stitcht 1s." (Arber, Term Catalogues, I. 273.). Entered in Stationers' Register, 4 May, 1677, as follows :

Master Richard Tonson	Entred . . . under the hands of Master Roger L'Estrange and Master Warden Clark a book or copy entituled *Antony* and *Cleopatra* Written by the Honoᵇˡᵉ Sʳ Charles Sidley Barᵗᵗ, a Tragoedy. (No sum stated.)

(A Transcript of the Registers of the Stationers' Company, 1640–1708, Privately Printed, 1914, III. 34.)

The British Museum contains another copy of this edition (11777 c. 93) which until 1926 was incorrectly dated 1690 in the General Catalogue.

(Br. Mus. 644. i. 1.)

12*b.* *Antony and Cleopatra,* 1696, Q2.

Antony / And Cleopatra / A / Tragedy. / As it is Acted at the Duke's Theatre. / Written by the Honourable / Sir Charles Sedley, Baronet. / London, / Printed for *R. Bentley* in *Covent Garden ; J. Tonson* in *Fleet* / *street J. Knapton* in *S. Paul's* Churchyard ; and *S. Manship* / in Cornhill. MDCXCVI.

Title-page + leaf with prologue (Dramatis Personæ on verso) + B–I3 v. the Play + I4 Epilogue (Books . . . Printed etc. for R. Bentley on verso :—*in fours.*

A page-for-page reprint of the foregoing.

(Br. Mus. 11778. g. 39.)

13. *Tunbridge Wells,* 1678, 4*to.*

Tunbridge-Wells / or a / Days Courtship / A Comedy, / As it is Acted at the / Dukes) theatre, / Written by a Person of Quality. / Licensed, *Roger Lestrange.* / London printed and are to be sold by *Henry Rog* / *-ers* at the *Crown* in *Westminster-* / *Hall,* 1678.

Engraved frontispiece facing the title + Title + Leaf with prologue (Actors' Names on verso) + B–H1 v. the Play + Leaf with Epilogue (Books printed for H. Rogers, etc. on Verso) + extra leaves :—*in fours.*

Anthony à Wood includes this play in his list of Sedley's works, adding the following note : " Sir Ch. Sedley's name is not set to it in the title, only said to be written by a person of quality and then reputed to be written by him."
(Br. Mus. 643. d. 64.)

14. *Collection of Letters*, 1681, fol.

The Second Part / of the / Collection / of / Letters / and other / Writings, / relating to / The Horrid Popish Plott : / Printed from the Originals in the Hands / of / Sir George Treby, Kt. / (Recorder of the City of London) Chairman of the Committee of *Secrecy* / of the Honourable / House of Commons. / Published by Order of that House. / London / Printed for *Samuel Heyrick* at *Grays-Inn* Gate in *Holborn, Thomas* / *Dring* at the *Harrow*, and John Wickins at the *White Hart* / in *Fleet Street.* MDCLXXXI.

Title page + B–H1, Letters + H–K1 v. Keys, etc. :—*in twos.*

Letter from Coleman to the Internuntio at Brussels translated by Sir Charles Sedley, pp. 11 and 12 (reprinted in Appendix I of " Sir Charles Sedley," pp. 310, 311).
(Br. Mus. 807. g. 4.)

15. *Wit and Drollery*, 1682, 8*vo.*

Wit / and / Drollery / Jovial Poems. / Corrected and Amended, with New / Additions. / *Ut nector Ingenium.* / *London.* / Printed for *Obadiah Blagrave*, at the *Bear* in / *St. Pauls Church-Yard*, 1682.

Title + one leaf with Preface + two leaves with list of Books sold for O. Blagrave, &c. + A–Y Poems :—*in eights.*

p. 313.   " Ah *Cloris* that I now could sit."
(Br. Mus. 1078. c. 2.)

16a. *Dryden's Miscellany*, 1684, 8*vo.*

Miscellany Poems / Containing a New / Translation / of Virgills Eclogues, Ovid's Love Elegies, / Odes of Horace and other Authors / with several Original Poems. / By the most Eminent Hands. / Et Vos, O Lauri, carpam, & Te, proxima myrte : / Sic positae quoniam suaveis miscetis odores / Virg. Ecl. 2. / London Printed for *Jacob Tonson*, at the *Judges-head* in / *Chancery-Lane* near Fleet Street, 1684.

Title + three unsigned leaves containing Table of Contents + B–Y, A–F5, Poems and Translations + F6, Catalogue of Books printed for J. Tonson, etc. :—*in eights.*

Contains three translations from Ovid's Amores by Sir Charles Sedley, viz.—

p. 116.   Book I Elegy the eighth.   *He curses a Bawd, for going about to debauch his Mistress.*   Englished By Sir Ch. Sidly.   Begins, " There is a Bawd renown'd in *Venus* Wars " (No. XCI of this edition).

p. 122. Book II Elegy the fifth. To his false Mistress. Englished by Sir Ch. Sidly. Begins, " Cupid begon who wou'd on thee rely " (No. XCII of this edition).
p. 144. Book III Elegy the fourth. To a Man that lockt up his Wife. Englished by Sir Ch. Sedley. Begins, " Vex not thyself and her vain man since all " (No. XCIII of this edition).

These translations were not reprinted in any collected edition of Sedley's works. They appear again in the second edition of this collection (8vo, 1692), but are omitted from the third (8vo, 1702), which however, contains a prologue by Sedley. (Br. Mus. 995. b. 23.)

16*b*. *Dryden's Miscellany*, 1702, 8*vo*.
Miscellany Poems : / The First Part. / Containing Variety of New Translations / of the / Ancient Poets. / Together with Several / Original Poems, / *By the Most Eminent Hands.* Publish'd by Mr. Dryden. / *Et vos*, O Lauri, carpam & T*e*, *Proxima* Myrte : / *Sic positae quoniam suaveis miscetis odores. Virg. Ecl.* 2. The Third Edition. / London, / Printed for *Jacob Tonson*, within *Grays-Inn* / *Gate* next *Grays-Inn* Lane, 1702.

Engraved Frontispiece + Title + A2–A4 v. Table + B–Z, Aa–Dd4 Poems :—*in eights.*
p. 254. A Prologue by Sir Charles Sedley beginning " Envy and Faction rule the Grumbling Age." (B3 l. 1.)

This edition of Dryden's (or Tonson's) Miscellany omits the translations of Ovid's Elegies by Sedley included in the first and second editions and inserts this prologue, which had already appeared in Higden's " The Wary Widdow " (No. 25 of this Bibliography).
(Br. Mus. 1077. l. 34.)

17. *Academy of Complements*, 1684, 12*mo*.
The / Academy / of Complements / With many New Additions / of / Songs and Catches *A la mode.* / Stored / with Variety of Complemental and / Elegant Expressions of Love and / Courtship. / Also witty and Ingenious Dialogues / and Discourses, / Amorous and Jovial : / with Significant Letters / upon Several Occasions. / Composed for the use of Ladies and / Gentlewomen / *By the most refined Wits of this Age.* / London : Printed for *P. Parker*, at the / *Leg* and *Star* in Cornhil, 1684.

Title + B–I6, " Compliments " etc. + K–R12. New Songs *A la Mode* Both Amorous and Jovial. By the Wits of this Age (drop title) :—*in twelves.*
(L3 and L4 misprinted B3 and B4.)
p. 315. " Ah *Cloris* that I now could sit."
" *Phillis* though your powerful charms."
p. 350. " Tell me prethee faithless swain."

p. 371. " *Phillis* lets shun the common fate."
No authors' names.
(Collection of G. Thorn Drury, Esq., K.C.)

18. *Stephens' Miscellany*, 1685, *8vo*.

Miscellany | Poems | and | Translations | by Oxford *Hands.* |
—*Si Quis tamen haec quoque, si Quis* | *Captus amore legat*—Virg.
Ec. | London. | Printed for *Anthony Stephens*, Book-seller near |
the *Theatre* in *Oxford*, 1685.

Title + A2, The Publisher to the Reader. + A3, A4, The
Contents + B–Z, Aa–Dd3, Poems and Translations + Dd4,
Catalogues of Books Printed for, and sold by Anthony Stephens,
etc. :—*in fours.*

Contains, p. 165, " Upon the Slighting of his Friend's Love.
by Mr. C. S. of Wadham " (title in Contents). Begins,
" Love guides my hand and shews me what to write,"
signed at the end C. S.

(Br. Mus. 11641. bbb. 38.)

19. *Bellamira*, 1687, 4to.

Bellamira, | Or The | Mistress, | A Comedy : | As it is Acted by
Their Majesties Servants. | Written by the Honourable | Sir
Charles Sedley Baronet. | Licensed, *May* 24. 1687. | *Rog.
L'Estrange.* | London : | Printed by *D. Mallet*, for *L. C.* and
Timothy Goodwin, at the | Maiden-Head over against St.
Dunstans Church | in *Fleet-Street.* 1687.

Title + A2, Preface to the Reader + A3, Prologue + A3 v.
Dramatis Personæ + A4, Advertisement of Mixt Essays, etc.
by Saint Evremont, Printed for T. Goodwin, etc. + B–I4, the
Play + I4 v. Epilogue :—*in fours.*

Term Catalogues *s.d.* June, 1687. (Term Catalogues, ed.
Arber, II, 200.)

Entered in Stationers' Register, 17 June, 1687, as follows :

[Page 248]

Tymothy Goodwin and Langley Curtis	Entered . . . booke or copy entituled *Bellamira or the Mistress* a comedy as it was acted by their Majesties Servants written by the honourable Sr Charles Sedley, Barronet, Lycenced by Sr Roger Lestrange 24 May, 1687. Entred under the hand of Master Warden Clavell.

(A Transcript of the Registers of the Stationers' Company,
III. 321.) (Br. Mus. 641. h. 34.)

20. *Theatre of Complements*, 1688, 12mo.

The Theatre of Complements : | Or, a Compleat | New
Academy. | containing, *viz.* | First, Elegant Expressions of Love |
and Friendship, with variety of Courtly and | Civil Comple-

ments in the whole Art of / Wooing ; Fitted to the Humours of / both Sexes. Secondly, Letters both moral and amo- / rous ; with their several Answers. / Thirdly, an Exact and Compleat Colle- / ction of all the Best New Songs and / Catches, used both at the Court and / Theatres : / Composed by the most Refined Wits of the Age. / Licensed Aug. 7. 1688. / *London*, Printed for *Abel Roper* at the *Bell* over against / (page clipped).

Title + B–P5, " Elegant Expressions," Poems, etc. + ? P6 Blank :—*in twelves*.

(K3 misprinted I3 ; on E6, p. 83, " Part III. An Exact Collection of all the choise new Songs by the most refin'd Wits of the Age.")

     p. 19.   " As *Amoret* with *Phillis* sat."
     p. 186.   " As in those Nations where they yet adore."
     p. 203.   " *Phillis* though your powerful charms."
     p. 220.   " Ah *Cloris* that I now could sit."
     (Collection of Mr. G. Thorn Drury.)

21. *Poetical Recreations*, 1688, 12mo.

Poetical / Recreations : / Consisting of / Original Poems, / Songs, Odes, &c. / with several / New Translations / in Two Parts. / Part I. / Occasionally Written by Mrs. Jane Barker / Part II. / By several Gentlemen of the Universities, / and Others. / ... *pulcherrima Virgo* / *Incedit magna Juvenum stipante catervâ* / *Virg.* / London, / Printed for *Benjamin Crayle*, at the *Peacock* / and *Bible*, at the West end of St. *Pauls.* / 1688.

Frontispiece (Publishers' Sign of Peacock and Bible with " Licensed and Entred according to Order ") + Title + A3, A4, The Publisher to the Reader + A5–A10, Commendatory Verses to Mrs. Jane Barker + A11, A12, Table of Poems in the First Part + A12 v. List of Errata + B–H8, Miscellanea Poems Part I (by Mrs. Barker) + Title Page of " Miscellanea or the Second Part of Poetical Recreations Compos'd by Several Authors " + Aa2–Aa4 v. Table + Bb–Tt8, The Poems + Tt8 v. Books Lately Printed for Benj. Crayle, etc. :—*in twelves*.

Contains the following poems printed as Sedley's in the editions of 1722 and its successors.

     Pt. II. p. 114.   " The Lover's Will " begins, " Let me not sigh my last, before I breathe " (actually by Donne, see Preface, Vol. I, p. xvi.).

     p. 122.   " Upon a Gentlewoman's Refusal of a love letter from one she was ingag'd to, by Sir C. S.," begins, " Not hear my *Message* but the *Bearer* shun ! " (No. XCVII of this edition).

     p. 137.   " An Ode," begins, " O Ye blest *Pow'rs*, propitious be " (here assigned to " *Mr.* R. D. of Cambridge ").

     p. 138.   " An Ode of Anacreon's Paraphras'd,"

begins, "I wonder why Dame *Nature* thus" (actually by Alexander Brome: see Preface, Vol. I, p. xvi).

p. 149. The Young Lover," begins, "Tush, never tell me I'm too" (here ascribed to "*Mr.* Wright," actually by A. Brome: see Preface, Vol. I, p. xvi).

p. 150. "Song. The Prodigal's Resolution," begins, "I am a lusty lively Lad," (No. XCVIII of this edition).

p. 151. "Song. The *Doubtful Lover* Resolv'd," begins, "Fain wou'd I *Love*, but that I fear."

p. 153. "Song. The Cavalier's Catch," begins, "Did you see this *Cup* of *Liquor*," (No. XCIX of this edition).

p. 159. "To my Much-esteemed Friend Mr. J. N. on his reading the First line of Pindar" begins, "Hold, there's enough, nay 'tis o'er mickle," (here assigned to "*Mr.* Whitehall"). See Preface, Vol. I, p. xvi.

p. 231. "Song" begins, "*Damon* to *Sylvia*, when alone" (here assigned to "Mr. Hovenden Walker"). See Preface, Vol. I, p. xvi.

p. 245. "Song," begins, "*Evadne*, I must tell you so" (No. CI of this edition).

p. 246. "The Same Inverted," begins, "*Evadne*, I must let you know" (here attributed to Mr. Walker). See Preface, Vol. I, p. xvi.

(Br. Mus. 994. g. 3.)

22a. *Reflections upon our Late and Present Proceedings*, 1689.
Reflections / upon / Our Late and Present / Proceedings / in / England. / (Publishers' Device) / *London :* Printed in the Year 1689.
A1, Title Page + A2–B4, Reflections, etc. Included in B3, B4 and B5.
(Br. Mus. T. 1675 (15).)

22b. Reflections / upon / Our Late and Present / Proceedings / in / England. / (Publisher's Device) / *Edinburgh*, Re-printed in the Year 1689.
A1, Title Page + A2–A4 v. Reflections, etc.
Reprint of the above.
This tract is reprinted in the Somers Collection of Tracts ed. by Sir Walter Scott. London, 1813, 4to. Vol. X, p. 178, and also in B3, B4 and B5.
(Br. Mus. 8138. bb. 20.)

23. *Speech*, 1691.
The / Speech of Sir Charles Sidley / in the House of Commons / (the Speech follows here) / London. Printed for L.C. near Fleet-bridge, 1691.
Single Sheet. Broadside.
This Speech is reprinted in all the collected editions of Sedley's Works and also in The Somers Tracts, ed. Sir Walter Scott, 1813, 4to, Vol. X. p. 331.
(Br. Mus. 816. m. 3. 98.)

24. *The Gentleman's Journal*, 1691/2–1694, 4to.

24*a.* The / Gentleman's Journal : / or, the Monthly Miscellany. / By Way of / Letter / to a / Gentleman in the Country. / Consisting of / *News, History, Philosophy, Poetry, Music, Translations,* &c. / March 1691–2 / *Multa Poetarum veniat Manus, auxilio quae / Sit mihi- / satis est Equitem mihi plaudere.* Hor. / Licensed, *March* 9th, 1691. R. *Midgley.* / London : Printed for *Rich. Parker* ; And are to be sold by *Rich. Baldwin.* / near the *Oxford-Arms* in *Warwick Lane.* 1692.
Title (contents on verso) + A2, A3, Dedication to Rt. Hon. William Earl of Devonshire + A4–E, text :—*in fours.*
p. 8. Sedley's Song—" *Phillis, then say that all my vows.*"
This version has an extra stanza which appears in B3 (I. 4) but not in A (p. 106).

24*b.* The Gentleman's Journal : / or the Monthly Miscellany. / . . . May 1692. . . .
Title (Contents on Verso) + B–E, Text :—*in fours.*
p. 1. Sedley's " Anniversary Ode, sung before her Majesty," beginning, " *Love's Goddess sure was blind this Day.*"

24*c.* The Gentleman's Journal : / or the Monthly Miscellany. / . . . August 1692. / . . .
Title (Contents on verso) + A2–F, text :—*in fours.*
p. 14. Sedley's " Nuptial Song " beginning, " *See Hymen comes, how his Torch blazes.*"

24*d.* The Gentleman's Journal : / or the Monthly Miscellany. / . . . October 1692. /
Title (Contents on verso) + B–F, text :—*in fours.*
p. 1. Sedley's translation of Martial, Bk. II. Ep. 72, beginning, " *O Times ! O Manners ! Cicero cry'd out.*"
p. 15. Sedley's lines " To a Devout young Lady," beginning, " *Phillis, this mighty zeal asswage,*"

24*e.* The / Gentleman's Journal : / or the / Monthly / Miscellany. / . . . November 1692. / . . .
Title (Contents on verso) + B–F, text :—*in fours.*
p. 1. Sedley's epigram, beginning, " *How shall we please this Age ? if in a Song.*

24*f*.   The / Gentleman's Journal : / or the New Monthly Miscellany /
. . . January 1692–3. / . . .
    Title (Contents on verso) + A2, Dedication to Rt. Hon.
Charles Montague *s.d.* Peter Motteux + A2–E2, F–F4, text :—
in fours.
       p. 21.   Sedley's Epigram "On a Cock at Rochester,"
beginning, " *Thou cursed Cock, with thy perpetual noise.*"

24*g*.   The Gentleman's Journal : / Or the New Monthly Mis-
cellany. / . . . February 1692–3. / . . .
    Title (Contents on verso) + G–K, F–F4, text :—*in fours.*
       p. 61.   Sedley's Prologue to "The Wary Widdow," beginning,
" *Envy and Faction rule the Grumbling Age.*"

24*h*.   The / Gentleman's Journal : / Or the Monthly Miscellany. /
. . . August, 1693. / . . .
    Title (Contents on verso) + Oo–Qq, Ss–s, (repeated)–Ss4,
text :—*in fours.*
       p. 258.   Lines " To the Old Beaux " beginning, " *Scrape no
more your harmless chins* " here ascribed to " A Person of
Quality."

24*i*.   The / Gentleman's Journal : / Or the Monthly Miscellany. /
. . . September, 1693 . . .
    Title (Contents on verso) + Tt–Zz, text :—*in fours.*
       p. 297.   Sedley's translation of Martial, Bk. II. Ep. 41,
beginning " *Ovid, who bid the ladies laugh.*"

24*j*.   The / Gentleman's Journal : / Or the Monthly / Miscellany. /
. . . November, 1693. / . . .
    Title (Contents on verso) + Ff–Kk, text :—*in fours.*
       pp. 365–6.   Sedley's epigram " To Cloe " beginning,
" *Leave off thy Paint, Perfumes and Youthful Dress.*"

24*k*.   The / Gentleman's Journal : / Or the Monthly / Miscellany. /
. . . January and February, 1694. / . . .
    Title (Contents on verso) + leaf with dedication to Rt. Hon.
Charles, Earl of Shrewsbury + B–E, text :—*in fours.*
       p. 12.   Sedley's translation of Martial, Bk. II. Ep. 12,
beginning, " Tho thou dost Cashou breathe, and
foreign Gums."

24*l*.   The / Gentleman's Journal :—/ Or the Monthly Miscellany
. . . August and September, 1694.
    Title (Contents on verso) + Cc–Mm4, text :—*in fours.*
       p. 233.   " Phillis *Knotting ; a Song* by *Sir* Ch. Sedley,
beginning, ' Hears not my *Phillis* how the Birds.' "

25.   (*Higden*) *The Wary Widdow*, 1693, 4to.
    The / Wary / Widdow : / or Sir Noisy Parrat, / A Comedy. /
As it is Acted at the Theatre Royal. / By their Majesties
Servants. / Written by *Henry Higden* Esq. / *Lectori Credere*

mallem / *Quam spectatoris fastidia ferre Superbi.* / London, / Printed for *Abell Roper*, at the *Mitre* near *Temple-Bar* / and *Tho. Raining*, Bookseller in *Doncaster.* / M. DC. XCIII.

Title (Dramatis Personæ on verso) + A2, Dedication to the Earl of Dorset + A3, A4, Preface + 2 leaves inserted (first signed " a "), complimentary verses by Caryl Worsley and others + verso of second inserted leaf, the Prologue by Sir Charles Sydley + B–H2 v. the Play + H3, H4, Songs + H4 v. Epilogue spoken by Mrs. Lassells :—*in fours.*

The Prologue is ascribed here to Sedley and reprinted as his in B3 and its successors.

(Br. Mus. 644. h. 41.)

26. (*D'Urfey*) *The Intrigues at Versailles*, 1697, 4to.

The / Intrigues / At / Versailles : / or / A Jilt in all Humours / A / Comedy / acted by / His / Majesty's Servants, / at the / Theatre in *Lincoln-Inn-Fields.* / Written by Mr. D'Urfey. / *Wit will be wit tho' slighted by the Clown* / *As Roses sweet tho' Asses tread 'em down.* / London, / Printed for *F. Saunders* in the *New Exchange*, P. *Buck* in *Fleet Street*, / *R. Parker* at the *Royal Exchange*, and H. Newman in the Poult- / ry. 1697.

Title + A2–A3 v. Dedication to Sir Charles Sedley, and . . . his son + A4, Prologue + A4 v. Dramatis Personæ and advertizement of books " Lately Publisht " + B–I1 v. The Play + I2, I2 v. The Epilogue :—*in fours.*

Contains in the Epistle Dedicatory Sedley's Poem " The Young *Lady's* Advice to the Old *Beaux* " beginning, " Scrape, scrape no more your Bearded chins."

(Br. Mus. 644. h. 24.)

27. *Poems on Affairs of State*, 1698, 8vo.

Poems / on / Affairs of State : / from / Oliver Cromwell, / To this Present time. / Written by the / greatest Wits of the Age, *Viz.*, /

Lord Rochester,	*Mr. Dryden,*
Lord *D—t,*	*Mr. Prior,*
Lord *C—ts,*	*Charles Blount, Esq.,*
Duke of *Buckingham,*	*Mr. Wicherley,*
Dr. K.	Mr. Shadwell,
Dr. *Wild,*	*Mr. Tho. Brown,*
Sir Charles S—dly,	*Capt. Ayloffe,*
Sir Fleetwood S—d	*Mr H—bt,*

Part III / With other Miscellany Poems ; / And a new Session of the present / *Poets.* The whole never before / Printed. / Printed in the Year 1698.

A1 blank leaf before title + A2, Title + A3–A5, Contents (verso of A5 blank) + A6–A8, To all the Lovers of Wit and Poetry + B (p. 1), B8 leaves, C4 leaves, D–X8 (p. 312), Miscellany Poems (head title) :—*in eights.*

(p. 204 misprinted 304, p. 284 misprinted 684; pagination otherwise regular.)

Contains on p. 161 " Prologue to the Stroulers by Sir Ch— Sidley."

28. *Commendatory Verses,* 1700, fol.

Commendatory Verses, / on the / Author of The Two Arthurs, / and the / Satyr against Wit ; / By some of his particular Friends. / *Insanit* Scaevola *factus Eques.* / *Innocuos permitte Sales ; Cur* ludere *nobis* / *Non liceat, licuit si* jugulare *tibi?* / Mart. / [Publisher's Device] / London : / Printed in the Year MDCC.

Title + A2, Epistle Dedicatory, sd. O.S. + B–H2, Poems :— *in twos.*

Lines beginning, " A Grave Physician, us'd to write for Fees," in p. 2, assigned to Sedley in a pencil note in Br. Mus. copy and also included with slight variations in all collected editions.

(Br. Mus. 163. n. 12.)

29. *Gildon's New Miscellany,* 1701, 8vo.

A / New / Miscellany / of / Original Poems, / on several Occasions / Written by the /

E *of* D	*Mr* Granvill,
Sir Charles Sidley	*Mr* Dryden,
Sir Fleetw. Shepheard	*Mr* Stepney.
Mr Wolsely,	Mr Rowe.

And several other Eminent Hands, / Never before Printed. / London, Printed for *Peter Buck* at / the Sign of the *Temple* in *Fleet-Street George Strahan* at the *Golden-Ball,* over against the *Royal-Exchange* in *Cornhil.* 1701.

Title + A2–A5, Dedication to the Hon. Benedict Leonard Calvert Esq. *signed* Charles Gildon + A6–A8, The Contents + A8 v. Errata + B–Z3, the Poems + Z4, Books Printed and Sold by Geo. Strahan, etc. :—*in eights.*

Some copies lack Charles Gildon's signature to the Dedication. Contains the following poems ascribed to " Sir Charles Sedley " in the Table :

p. 88. A Song on the King's Birthday, begins, " Behold the Happy Day again."

p. 90. A Translation from Horace, Ode 8, 1. 2, begins, " Did any Punishment attend."

Also (no author's name in Table) two poems, which had already appeared in Kemp's, Collins's and Saunders's Collections and which are ascribed to Sedley in the Table of the last.

To Caelia, against Honour, begins, " You tell me *Caelia* you approve," p. 258 (incorrectly in Table, p. 262).

The answer begins, " Thirsis I wish as well as you," p. 260.

(Br. Mus. 1077. l. 12.)

30. *Miscellaneous Works*, 1702, 8vo.
The / Miscellaneous Works / Of the Honourable / *Sir* Charles Sedley, Bar^t containing /

Satyrs,	Translations,
Epigrams,	Essays, and
Court-Chara-	Speeches in Par-
cters,	liament.

Collected into one Volume. / To which is added, / The Death of *Marc Antony* : / A Tragedy never before Printed. / *Published from the Original Manuscripts by Capt.* Ayloffe. / London : / Printed, and sold by *J. Nutt,* near Stationers / Hall. 1702.
Half-title " The Works of Sir *Charles Sedley,* Bart." + Title + A3–A8, Preface to the Reader signed W. Ayloffe + B–P3, Poems and Verse Translations + Title of " Speeches in the House of Commons, Letters and Essays " (there are actually no letters in text) + P4–Q8, Speeches and Essay on Entertainments + Title of Beauty the Conquerour or the Death of Marc Antony etc. Never before Printed. Printed etc. for J. Nutt . . . London 1702. + Verso of Title Dramatis Personæ + Aa2–Dd8 v. Beauty the Conquerour :—*in eights.*
(Collection of the Editor : no copy in Br. Mus. or Bodleian.)

31*a*. *The Happy Pair*, 1702, F.1.
The / Happy Pair : / or, a / Poem / on Matrimony. / By the Honourable / Sir Charles Sidley, Baronet. / London : / Printed for *John Nutt,* near *Stationers-Hall,* / MDCCII.
Title + A2–D2 v. the Poem + extra blank leaves :—*in twos.*
(Br. Mus. 1347. m. 30.)

31*b*. *The Happy Pair*, 1705, F.2.
I have never seen a copy of this book. Mr. Thorn Drury gives me the following note : " Title as in F1 to ' Baronet.' Then, ' The Second Edition corrected. London, printed for John Chantry without Temple-bar, and sold by Benj. Brag in Avemary Lane, 1705. Price 6d.' [7th Oct., 1704. N. L.] fol. 6 leaves." " N. L." stands for Narcissus Luttrell, who noted the date of publication on his copy.

32. (*Buckingham*) *Miscellaneous Works*, 1704, 8vo.
Miscellaneous Works, / Written by His Grace, / George, Late. Duke of Buckingham. / *Collected in One Volume from the Original Papers.* / Containing /

Poems on several Subjects.	And the Farce Upon *Seg-*
Epistles.	*moor* Fight.
Characters.	With Letters, by and to the
Pindarics.	Duke of *Buckingham,* by
The Militant Couple, a Dialogue.	Persons of Quality.

Also *State Poems* on the Late Times, by

Mr *Dryden,*	Earl of *D—*
Sir *George Etherege,*	Mr. *Congreve,*

Sir *Fleetwood Sheppard,*	Mr. *Otway,*
Mr. Butler, Author of *Hu-*	Mr. *Brown,*
dibras,	Capt. *Ayloffe,* &c.

Never Before Printed. With the late Duke of *Buckingham's* Speeches in the / House of Lords, upon Conference with the *Commons* / To which is added, / *A Collection of Choice Remarkable Speeches, that were spoken in* / *both Houses of Parliament, by several Noblemen, and Commoners* / *in relation to the Government and Liberty of the Subject.* / In the Reigns of

K. Charles I	*K. Charles II.*
The Usurpation of the *Rump,*	and
and *Oliver Cromwell.*	*K. William III. &c.*

London : Printed for and Sold by *J. Nutt* / near *Stationers-hall,* 1704.

Frontispiece + Title + A2–A5 v. The Preface + A6–A8, The Contents + B1–O3, A Collection of State Poems and Satyrs etc. + New title-page, etc. + Aa1–Mm8 v. Speeches in the House of Lords, etc., etc. :—*in eights.*

p. 86. The Royal Knotter, by Sir Charles Sedley.
p. 117. *Advice to Lovers,* by Sir Charles Sedley.
p. 118. The Petition by the same Hand.
(Br. Mus. 1085. k. 28.)

33. *Poems on Affairs of State,* 1704, 8vo.
Poems / on / Affairs of State, / From 1640. to this present / Year 1704. / *Written by the Greatest Wits of the Age,* / Viz.

The late Duke of *Bucking-*	Col *M—d—t,*
ham,	Mr *St. J—ns,*
Duke of *D—re,*	Mr *Hambden,*
Late E. of *Rochester*	Sir *Fleet-Shepherd,*
Earl of *D—t,*	Mr *Dryden*
Lord *J—rys,*	Mr *St—y*
Lord *Hal—x,*	Mr *Pr—r*
Andrew Marvel, Esq. ;	Dr *G—th,* &c. /

Most of which were never before publish'd. / Vol. III. / Printed in the Year 1704.

Title + A2–A6, The Index + A6 v. Errata + B–Z, Aa–Hh2 v. The Poems :—*in eights.*

On p. 438 occurs a very garbled form of Sedley's Song, " Not *Celia* that I juster am " (here " Not, *Celia,* that I am more just,"). See note to Poem No. III.

34. *The Diverting Post,* 1704.
The Diverting Post, / For the Entertainment / of / Town and Country / Vol. I. For the Year 1705. / . . . *Dulces ante omnia Musae,* / *Omne tulit punctum qui miscuit Utile dulci :* / London. / Printed for H. Playford. And sold for him by *John Nutt,* near

Stationer's Hall and at most Booksellers Shops in *London* and *Westminster*, 1706. Price stitched 3s. / Where the First packet of Diverting Posts, for January, is to be had for 6d each Month, or Subscribe at 3s the Year, and to any Person or Coffee House the 7 sub Gratis, and what County in *England*, They which take Seven, / or a greater Number, shall have them sent every Month to them without any Charge.

34*a*. *The Diverting Post*, Numb. 4.
> From *Saturday* Nov. 11. to *Saturday* Nov. 18. 1704. (Half-title)
> Single Sheet printed on both sides.
> On verso, " 'Thirsis *to* Celia '' beginning, '' Tell me no more you love; in vain.''
> This is reprinted from Kemp's Collection, p. 57, Pt. I (see Table, pp. 240, 241), where it is ascribed to Sedley by the annotator of Sir C. H. Firth's copy.
> Also '' Celia's *Answer*,'' beginning, '' *Thirsis* I wish as well as you,'' an exact reprint of Sedley's '' Her Answer '' (No. XII of this edition).

34*b*. *The Diverting Post*. / From *Saturday*. June 13 to *Saturday* Jan. 20. 1704.
> Single Sheet printed on both sides.
> On recto, lines '' By Sir Charles *Sidley*, Written Extempore,' beginning, '' The Noble Man, why he's a thing.''
> These lines are not printed elsewhere.

35. *Poems Relating to State Affairs*, 1705, 8vo.
> A New / Collection / of / Poems / Relating to / State Affairs, / from Oliver Cromwel / To this present Time : / By the Greatest / Wits of the Age : / Wherein, not only those that are Contain'd in / the Three Volumes already Published are / incerted, but also large Additions of chiefest / Note, never before Published. / The whole from their respective Originals, / without Castration. / London, / Printed in the Year, MDCCV.
> Title + Aa2, A3 recto, The Preface + A4–A8, The Contents + B–Z, Aa–Pp, Poems on State Affairs :—*in eights*.
> p. 264. *On the* Infanta *of* Portugal, begins, '' How Cruel was *Alonzo's* Fate,'' a version of Sedley's poem '' On Don Alonzo, who was cut in pieces for making Love to the Infanta of Portugal,'' printed in Ayloffe's ed., p. 104. (No. XLVIII in this edition : see note, Vol. I. p. 284.)
> p. 381. *A Fable*, beginning, '' In *Aesop's* Tales an honest Wretch we find,'' printed as Sedley's in Briscoe's ed. of 1722 (III. 4, 5) and its successors.
> (Collection of the Editor.)

36. *The Poetical Works*, 1707, 8vo.
> The / Poetical Works / of the Honourable / Sir *Charles Sedley* Baronet, / and his Speeches in Parliament, / With / *Large*

Additions never before made Publick. | Published from the Original MS. by Capt. Ayloffe, | a near Relation of the Authors. | With a New Miscelany of Poems by several | of the most *Eminent Hands.* | And a Compleat Collection of all the Remarkable | Speeches in both *Houses of Parliament :* Discovering the Principles | of all *Parties* and *Factions ;* the Conduct of our *Chief Ministers,* the Management of Publick Affairs, and the | Maxims of the Government, from the year 1641 to the | Happy Union of *Great Britain :* By several Lords and Commoners. |

Viz.

The Duke of *Albemarle,*	*Algernon Sidney,* Esq.
Earl of *Clarendon,*	Mr *Waller,*
Earl of *Bristol,*	Sir *Francis Seymour,*
Lord *Wharton,*	Mr *Pym,*
Earl of *Pembrook,*	*Richard Cromwell,*
Lord *Hollis,*	Mr *Strode,*
Lord *Brook,*	Sir *William Parkins,*
Earl of *Argile,*	Sir *William Scroggs,*
Lord *Melvil,*	Sir J— P—
Lord *Haversham,*	And several other Lords and
Lord *Belhaven,* &c.	Commoners.

London, Printed for Sam. Briscoe, and Sold by *B. Bragg,* | at the *Raven* in Pater-noster-Row, 1707.

Title + A2–A4 v. Preface to the Reader + A5–A8, The Contents + B–O8 v. Poems by Sedley and others + P1.–P8 v. Sedley's Speeches + New Title Page (A Compleat Collection of all the Remarkable Speeches in Both Houses of Parliament . . . By several Lords and Commoners . . .) + Aa2–Mm4, Speeches by various hands + Mm4 v. New Books . . . Printed for Sam. Briscoe . . . :—*in eights.*

This is the first of Briscoe's editions. Ayloffe had nothing to do with it, having died in 1706. See Preface, Vol. I, pp. xix, xx. It is entered in Term Catalogues, *s.d.* May and June, 1708. (Term Catalogues, ed. Arber, III. 599.) (Br. Mus. 11623. e. 11.)

37. *The Poetical Works,* 1710, 8vo.

The | Poetical Works | Of the Honourable | Sir Charles Sedley Bar. | and his | Speeches in Parliament, | with | *Large* Additions never *before made* Publick. Published from the original MS. by *Capt. Ayloffe.* | To which is perfixed, | The Earl of Rochester's *Mountebank Speech,* on *Tower-Hill.* | With a New *Miscelany* of Poems by several of the | most *Eminent Hands.* | As also a Compleat Collection of all the Remarkable | Speeches in both *Houses of Parliament :* From the Year | 1641, to the Happy Union of *Great Britain.* | By several Lords and Commoners, | Viz. |

The Duke of *Albemarle*, Lord *Belhaven* &c.
Earl of Clarendon, *Algernoon* S*idney*, Esq. ;
Earl of *Bristol*, Mr. *Waller*,
Lord *Wharton*, Sir Francis *Seymor*,
Earl of *Pembrook*, Mr *Pym*,
Lord *Hollis*, *Richard Cromwell*,
Lord *Brook*, Mr *Strode*,
Earl of *Essex*, Sir *William Parkins*,
Earl of *Argyle*, Sir *William Scroggs*,
Lord *Melvil*, Sir *J— P—*,
Lord *Haversham*,

The Second Edition / To which is Added, / The State of a *Secretaries* Place, and the Dangers Incident / to it. *Writen* by Robert Cecil *Earl of* Salisbury. / Never Printed before. / *London*, Printed for *Sam. Briscoe*, and Sold by *James Woodward* in St. *Christophers Church-yard*, near the *Royal Exchange*, and *John Morphew* near Stationers-Hall, 1710.

(Collection of Mr. G. Thorn Drury.)

Title + A2–A4 v. Preface to the Reader, + A5–A8 v. Contents–d1 (unsigned), d2, d3 (unsigned), d4 (unsigned), The Earl of Rochester's Mountebank Speech + B1–L1 v. Poems by Sedley and Others + P1–P8 v. Sedley's Speeches and Essay on Entertainments + Aa–Nn v. A Compleat Collection of Speeches, etc. (not by Sedley), + Nn v. Advt. of Books Just Published for Sam. Briscoe :—*in eights.*

This edition was advertised in the " Tatler " for January 10–12, 1709, as " Just Published The 2d Edition of the Poetical Works of the Honourable Sir Charles Sedley " (full title follows).

(No copy in Br. Mus. or Bodleian.)

38. (*Buckingham*) *Works*, 1715, 8vo (Second Volume).
The Dramatick / Works / Of his Grace / George Villiers, / Late Duke of Buckingham. / Vol. II. / Viz.

A Key to the Rehearsal : Or / a critical View of the Au-/ thors exposed in that Play. / The Rehearsal : A Comedy / Acted at the *Theatre Royal*, / By her Majesty's Servants. / The Chances : A Comedy.	Acted by Her Majesty's Ser / vants, at the *Theatre-Royal*. / A Conference on the Doc- / trine of *Transubstantion*, / between the *Duke* and an / *Irish Priest.*

With His / Miscellaneous Poems, / Essays and Letters. / *Adorn'd with Cuts.* / London : Printed for *Sam. Briscoe. Rich. Wellington*, / *George Strahan, Ralph Smith* and *Jonas Brown*, 1715.

Title + A2, A3, Contents + engraved frontispiece + title page of Key to the Rehearsal + A2–A7, The Publisher to the

Reader + A8 Plays named in the Key + B–Z, Aa–Bb6 v.
Text :—*in eights.*
pp. 307–314. A Speech in Parliament by Sir Charles
Sedley, On the Bill for disbanding the Army, Anno 1699.
(Br. Mus. 12271. c. 33.)‧

39*a*. *Wit and Mirth*, 1719, Vol. V. 12mo.
Wit and Mirth : / or / Pills / to Purge / *Melancholy* ; / being / a
Collection of the best Merry Ballads / and Songs, / Old and
New. / Fitted to all Humours, having each their proper tune for
either Voice, or Instrument : / Most of the Songs being new
Set. / Vol. V. / (Device of Shakespeare's Head) / London /
Printed by W. Pearson, for J. Tonson, at Shakespear's Head,
over-against / *Catherine Street* in the Strand, 1719.
Title + A2–A4 Alphabetical Table + B–Q8 Poems :—*in
Twelves.*
Sedley's Song " Hears not my Phillis now the Birds " is
printed on pp. 148–9, with a musical setting by Henry Purcell.
It is here called " The Knotting song." *The Words by Sir
Charles* Sidney (*sic*).
(Br. Mus. G. 18347.)

39*b*. *Wit and Mirth*, 1719, Vol. II. 12mo.
Title as foregoing except Vol. VI for Vol. V. Title + A3–A6,
Alphabetical Table + B–R6 v. Poems :—in *Twelves.*
p. 308. Sedley's Song from Bellamira III. i. (slightly
different version) beginning here : " When first I lay'd
Siege to my *Chloris*," see note to Song in Bellamira
III. i.

40. *The Works*, 1722, 2 vols. in 12mo.
The / Works / of the Honourable Sir / Charles Sedley, Bar^t /
In Two Volumes. / Containing his / *Poems, Plays*, &c. / with
/ Memoirs of the Author's Life, / by an Eminent Hand. / and /
His Picture curiously engrav'd from / an Original Painting. /
Sedley *has that prevailing gentle Art / That can with a
resistless Charm impart / The Loosest Wishes to the Chastest
Heart ; / Raise such a Conflict, kindle such a Fire, / Betwixt
declining* Virtue and Desire, / *Till the poor vanquish'd Maid
dissolves away / In Dreams all Night, in Sighs and Tears all
Day.* / Rochester. / London, / Printed for S. Briscoe, at the
Belle-Savage on / *Ludgate-hill*, and sold by *T. Bickerton* in
Pater-noster / Row. MDCCXXII.
Vol. I :
Frontispiece (Portrait of Sir Charles Sedley engraved by
Van der Gucht) + Title as above + second title indicating
contents + A2–A6, Dedication to the Duke of Chandos, signed
Sam. Briscoe + A2–A6, Some Account of the Life of Sir

Charles Sedley + a–a5, Contents of the First Volume + B–K2, Poems and Translations + K3, Title-page of Antony and Cleopatra, a Tragedy printed in the year 1617 [*sic*] + K4 Prologue–K4 v. " Persons " (Dramatis Personæ) with names of actors as in 4tos + K5–Q2, Antony and Cleopatra + Q2 v. Epilogue + R–R6 and two other leaves (first signed R +), Reflections upon, our Late Proceedings in England (Prose) + S–T1 v. Sir Charles Sedley's Speeches + T1 v.–T2 v. An Essay on Entertainments + T2 v.–U4 the Earl of Pembroke's Speech, etc. + U4–U6, The Last Will and Testament of the Earl of Pembroke + U6, U6 v. Codicil + X1 (unsigned) Title-page of the Oration of Cicero for M. Marcellus Done into English by Sir Charles Sidley, London. Printed in the year 1719 + X2–Y6, the Oration (concludes with " The End of the First Volume ") + New Title (signed X), " The Pastorals of Virgil by Sir Charles Sidley Bart. London, Printed in the year 1719 " + X2, X2 v. Preface + X3–Z, Aa–Bb5, The Pastorals, + Bb6, Bb6 v. New Books printed for Sam. Briscoe etc. :—*in twelves.*

Vol. II :

Title of the Second Volume + A2–A5, Ayloffe's Preface as in 1702 edition + A5 v. A6, the Contents + A–B Poems +Aa Title " The Mulberry Garden a Comedy, London, Printed in the year 1722 " + Aa2, Aa2 v. Dedication to the Dutchess of Richmond and Lenox—Aa3, " Dramatis Person " + Aa3 v. Prologue + Aa4, Bb–Hh1 v. The Mulberry Garden + Hh2, Epilogue + Hh3, Title-page of Bellamira or the Mistris +Hh4, Prologue + Hh4 v. Dramatis Personæ + Hh5–Qq1 v. Bella-mira : Or the Mistris + Qq2, the Epiloque + Title of the Grumbler a Comedy, London printed in the Year 1719 (Dramatis Personæ on verso) + A2–A4 v. Rr–Xx4, the Grumbler + Xx5–Yy2 v. Venus or Adonis or the Amour of Venus (a poem) + Yy3, Title-page of the Tyrant King of Crete a Tragedy, London Printed in the Year 1722 + Yy3 v. " Drammatis Personæ " + Yy4–Zz, Aaa–Ddd, The Tyrant King of Crete :—*in twelves.*

For an account of this book see Vol. I, pp. xx–xxv. It contains much that was never previously assigned to Sedley and is the origin of all subsequent editions of the eighteenth century. (Br. Mus. 644. a. 33.)

41. *The Works*, 1776, 2 vols. in 8vo.

The / Works / Of the Honourable / Sir Charles Sedley, Bart. / In Prose and Verse. / in Two Volumes. / Containing / The Translations of Virgil's Pastorals, the / Battle and Government of Bees, &c. / with his / Speeches, Political Pieces, Songs and Plays, / The greatest Part never printed before, *viz.*

The Happy Pair,	Bellamira, or, the Mistress,
Antony and Cleopatra, a	a Comedy.
Tragedy,	The Grumbler, a Comedy.
The Mulberry Garden, a	The Tyrant King of Crete,
Comedy,	a Tragedy.
Venus and Adonis,	

With / Memoirs of the Author's Life, / Written by an Eminent Hand. / Vol. I. / London : / Printed for T. Davies, Russell Street, Covent Garden. / MDCCLXXVI.

Vol. I.   Title + A2–A5, Briscoe's Dedication + A6–A9, Life of Sedley as in 1722 ed. + A10–A12 Contents + B–P12 text (P12 v. blank) :—*in eights.*

Vol. II.   Title + A2–A5 Ayloffe's Preface as in 1722 ed. + A6, Contents + B–P1 text (P1 v. blank) :—*in eights.*

(Br. Mus. 12268. aaaa. 6.)

42. *The Works,* 1778, 2 vols. in 12mo.

The / Works / of the Honourable / Sir Charles Sedley, Bart. / In Prose and Verse. / in Two Volumes. / containing / The Translations of Virgil's Pastorals, the / Battle and Government of Bees, &c. / with his / Speeches, Political Pieces, / Poems, Songs, and Plays, / the greatest Part never printed before, *viz.*

The Happy Pair	Bellamira, or, the Mistress,
Antony and Cleopatra, a	a Comedy.
Tragedy	The Grumbler, a Comedy.
The Mulberry Garden, a	The Tyrant King of Crete,
Comedy.	a Tragedy.
Venus and Adonis.	

With / Memoirs of the Author's Life, / Written by an Eminent Hand. / Vol. I. / London. / Printed for J. Ireland, No. 95, the Corner / of Beaufort Buildings, Strand. / MDCCLXXVIII.

Vol. I.   Title + A2–A5, Briscoe's Dedication + A6–A9, Life of Sedley as in 1722 ed. + A10–A12, Contents of First Volume + B–P Text :—*in twelves.*

Vol. II.   Title + A2–A5 v. Preface to the Reader by W. Ayloffe + A6. The Contents of the Second Volume + B–P1, text + P1 v.–P2, Advt. of Books published for T. Davies :—*in twelves.*

(Bodl. Douce S. 742.)

43. *Musa Proterva,* 1889, 8vo.

MUSA PROTERVA : / Love-Poems of the / Restoration. / edited by A. H. Bullen. / LONDON : / Privately Printed. / 1889.

2 Title pages + pp v.–x. v. Preface + pp. 1–128 Poems :—*in eights.*

Contains the following poems by Sedley :—

p. 66.   Ah, Chloris, that I now could sit.

p. 68.　Phillis, men say that all my vows.
　　69.　Aurelia, art thou mad.
　　70.　Celinda, think not by disdain.
　　71.　Phillis, let's shun the common fate.
　　72.　Chloris, I cannot say your eyes.
　　73.　Not, Celia, that I juster am.
　　74.　Phillis, this early zeal assuage.
　　75.　Love still has something of the sea.
　　76.　Amintas, I am come alone.
　　79.　Smooth was the water, calm the air.
　　80.　Phillis is my only joy.
　　81.　Damon, if thou wilt believe me.
　　82.　Young Corydon and Phillis.
　　84.　When first I made love to my Chloris.
　　85.　Love when 'tis true needs not the aid.

44.　*Lyrics* (*Suckling, Sedley, and Rochester*), 1906.
　　　The Pembroke Booklets / (First Series) / IV / Sir John Suckling / Ballads and other Poems / Sir Charles Sedley / Lyrics / John Wilmot / (Earl of Rochester) / Poems and Songs / (Device) / J. R. Tutin / Hull / 1906 / Large Paper Edition Limited to 250 copies.
　　　Frontispiece (Portrait of Suckling) + Title (quotations on verso) + pp. 3, 4, Contents + pp. 5–10, Preface (signed William G. Hutchinson) + pp. 11–41, Lyrics by Suckling + pp. 42–49, Lyrics by Sedley + pp. 50–64, Lyrics by Rochester.
　　　Contains eight lyrics from one of the eighteenth-century editions of the Works, viz.—
　　　　Phillis, this early zeal assuage.
　　　　I am a lusty lively lad.
　　　　Tush ! never tell me I'm too young.
　　　　Ah Cloris ! that I now could sit.
　　　　Love still has something of the Sea.
　　　　Fair Aminta, art thou mad.
　　　　Scrape no more your harmless Chins.
　　　　Not, Celia, that I juster am.
　　　Texts are those of the 1722 edition of the Works.

FIRST LINE INDEX TO POEMS